The EVERYTHING®
Learning Latin Book

Dear Reader:

Over the past twenty-six years I've studied and taught from many Latin books. I don't like any of them very much. Here is the book *I* wish existed when I was first learning Latin. The traditional approach lulls students into a sense of false security. Simpler things come first, then gradually grow more complex. Unfortunately, those complexities are more common, and when they suddenly appear, they don't fit the simplicity you had been trained to expect.

This book breaks from tradition. Since what you learn first sticks with you the best and becomes a template for the rest, the order of presentation has been changed so you get the most often seen grammar and vocabulary first, then move toward the finer, less common stuff. In other words, this book is based on frequency. Still, there are some common points that must be postponed because they rely on other knowledge.

If you're like me, you get a sort of endorphin rush from exercising your brain with something new and challenging. Latin is challenging because it's so *different*, not because it's hard. Read on with an open mind and you'll see.

Welcome to the EVERYTHING® Series!

These handy, accessible books give you all you need to tackle a difficult project, gain a new hobby, comprehend a fascinating topic, prepare for an exam, or even brush up on something you learned back in school but have since forgotten.

You can choose to read an *Everything*® book from cover to cover or just pick out the information you want from our four useful boxes: e-questions, e-facts, e-alerts, and e-ssentials.

We give you everything you need to know on the subject, but throw in a lot of fun stuff along the way, too.

We now have more than 400 *Everything*® books in print, spanning such wide-ranging categories as weddings, pregnancy, cooking, music instruction, foreign language, crafts, pets, New Age, and so much more. When you're done reading them all, you can finally say you know *Everything*®!

QUESTIONS?
Answers to common questions

FACTS
Important snippets of information

ALERTS!
Urgent warnings

ESSENTIALS

Quick handy tips

PUBLISHER Karen Cooper

DIRECTOR OF ACQUISITIONS AND INNOVATION Paula Munier

MANAGING EDITOR, EVERYTHING SERIES Lisa Laing

COPY CHIEF Casey Ebert

ACQUISITIONS EDITOR Lisa Laing

DEVELOPMENT EDITOR Elizabeth Kassab

EDITORIAL ASSISTANT Hillary Thompson

Visit the entire Everything® series at *www.everything.com*

THE

EVERYTHING®

LEARNING LATIN BOOK

Read and write this classical language
and apply it to modern English
grammar, usage, and vocabulary

Richard E. Prior, Ph.D.

Adams Media Corporation
Avon, Massachusetts

For Scott and the Boys

An Everything® Series Book.
Everything® and everything.com® are registered trademarks of F+W Media, Inc.

Published by Adams Media, a division of F+W Media, Inc.
57 Littlefield Street, Avon, MA 02322 U.S.A.
www.adamsmedia.com

ISBN 10: 1-58062-881-8
ISBN 13: 978-1-58062-881-5
Printed in the United States of America.

10 9

Library of Congress Cataloging-in-Publication Data
Prior, Richard E.
The everything learning Latin book / Richard E. Prior.
p.   cm.
ISBN 1-58062-881-8
1. Latin language—Self-instruction. I. Title. II. Series:
Everything series.
PA2094.5 .P75 2003
478.2'421—dc21
2002153898

This publication is designed to provide accurate and authoritative information
with regard to the subject matter covered. It is sold with the understanding
that the publisher is not engaged in rendering legal, accounting, or other professional advice. If legal advice or other expert assistance is required, the services of a competent professional person should be sought.
  —From a *Declaration of Principles* jointly adopted by a Committee of the
American Bar Association and a Committee of Publishers and Associations

Many of the designations used by manufacturers and sellers to distinguish
their products are claimed as trademarks. Where those designations appear in
this book and Adams Media was aware of a trademark claim, the designations
have been printed with initial capital letters.

This book is available at quantity discounts for bulk purchases.
For information, call 1-800-289-0963.

Contents

Acknowledgments / ix
Top Ten Reasons to Learn Latin / x
Introduction / xi

The Key to Understanding Latin / 1
The Significance of Syntax **2** • How Latin Syntax Works **2** • Learning Endings **4** • Learning Vocabulary **6** • Parts of Speech **6** • Vocabulary-Building Strategies **7**

Helps and Hindrances / 9
Derivatives **10** • The Roman Invasion(s) **10** • A Very Different World **12** • The Roman Alphabet **14** • Vowels **16** • Consonants **16** • Accent **17**

The Importance of Verbs / 19
Studying Latin Verbs **20** • The Anatomy of a Latin Verb **20** • What Is Verbal Aspect? **23** • The Continuous Aspect (a.k.a. the Present System) **24** • The Completed Aspect (a.k.a. the Perfect System) **25** • The Aorist Aspect **25** • Parts and Labor **26**

The Imperfect and Perfect Tenses / 31
Dissecting a Latin Verb **32** • The Imperfect Tense **36** • The Perfect Tense **38** • The Irregular Verb *Sum* **41**

5 Knowing Nouns / 43

The Anatomy of a Latin Noun 44 • Latin's Case System 46 • The Declensions 47 • Principal Parts for Nouns 51 • Subjects and Objects 54 • The Nominative Case 55 • The Accusative Case 57

6 Using Adjectives / 59

Adjective/Noun Agreement 60 • The "Parts" of an Adjective 63 • First/Second Declension Adjectives 63 • Third Declension Adjectives 66 • Substantives 71

7 Making Comparisons / 73

Forming Comparisons with Adjectives 74 • The Superlative Degree 76 • Irregular Comparison 78 • Forming Adverbs 79 • Comparison of Adverbs 81

8 Prepositions and the Ablative Case / 85

Prepositional Phrases 86 • The Ablative Case 88 • The Instrumental Ablative 91 • Talking about Time 96 • Talking about Places 97 • Special Places 98

9 Genitive Case and Dative Case / 103

What Is the Genitive? 104 • Genitive Case Forms 104 • Third Declension i-Stem Nouns 105 • The Uses of the Genitive Case 107 • The Dative Case 110 • The Uses of the Dative Case 111 • The Word "And" 114

10 Grammatical Mood / 117

What Is Grammatical Mood? 118 • The Imperfect Subjunctive 119 • The Pluperfect Subjunctive 120 • Showing Purpose 122 • Showing a Result 123 • Cum Clauses 124

11

Time and Tense / 129

The Present Indicative 130 • Using the Present Indicative 131 • Forming the Future Indicative 132 • Using the Future Indicative 134 • The Pluperfect and Future Perfect Indicative 135 • Using These Two Tenses 136

12

Vocabulary Building / 143

The Essential Verb "to Be" 144 • The Small but Useful Verb "Go" 147 • The Verb "to Bring" 148 • Willing or Not 149 • Infinitives 152 • Vocabulary Building 152

13

Pronouns / 159

Personal Pronouns 160 • Demonstrative Adjectives 161 • Demonstratives as Pronouns 165 • Reflexive Pronouns 166 • Intensive Adjectives and Pronouns 168 • Relative Pronouns 170 • Special Declension Adjectives 174 • Numbers 175

14

Grammatical Voice / 179

What Is Grammatical Voice? 180 • Understanding Passive Voice 181 • Ablative of Agent 189 • The Middle Voice 189

15

Participles / 195

Introducing Participles 196 • Using Participial Phrases 200 • Gerunds 205 • Gerundives 206 • The Supine Form 208

16

Asking Questions / 213

True or False? 214 • What Are They Asking? 215 • Indefinite Adjectives and Pronouns 218 • The Present and Perfect Subjunctive 219 • Conditions 221

17

Infinitives / 227
The Form of Infinitives **228** • The Subjective Infinitive **229** • The Objective Infinitive **231** • Indirect Discourse **232**

18

Getting Attention and Giving Commands / 239
Interjections **240** • The Vocative Case **240** • Giving Commands **241** • The Hortatory and Jussive Subjunctives **245** • Clauses after Verbs of Fearing **246** • Wishing in the Subjunctive **247** • The Potential Subjunctive **247** • The Deliberative Subjunctive **248**

19

Reading Latin / 251
The Reading Process **252** • In the Beginning **253** • Understanding Taxis **256** • Reading Caesar **257** • Tradition **258**

20

Quae cum ita sint . . . / 259
A Foundation for the Romance Languages **260** • A Deeper Understanding of English **261** • Latin and the Law **262** • Uses in Medicine **262** • Learning History **263** • Influences on the Church **264** • Maintaining Proficiency **264**

Appendix A • Latin-English Vocabulary / **268**

Appendix B • Latin Literature / **283**

Appendix C • Answer Key to Exercises / **286**

Index / 299

Acknowledgments

My thanks to Hugh, my bud, for insights;
Franklin, my grand, for strength and inspiration;
Tarquin, Numa, and Sherman, my boys, for unconditional love;
and Scott, my always, for life.

Top Ten Reasons
to Learn Latin

1. Unlock the meanings behind the common Latin phrases you hear and use every day, such as ad hoc, mea culpa, and ad nauseam.

2. Develop an excellent basis from which to learn Spanish, Italian, French, and other languages.

3. Build your English vocabulary by learning Latin roots.

4. Strengthen your reading and comprehension skills.

5. Improve your English grammar and usage.

6. Understand medical, mathematical, legal, and scientific terminology.

7. Read the ancient texts of Cicero, Vergil, and Horace.

8. Enhance your understanding of the Romans and their influence on the modern world.

9. Boost standardized tests scores.

10. Write with greater clarity and efficiency.

Introduction

▶ LATIN HAS ACQUIRED A REPUTATION for being a useless and lethal pursuit, a bitter medicine cruelly administered by strict schoolmarms old enough to be native speakers themselves. Perhaps you've heard this little schoolboy chant: "Latin is a dead language, that is plain to see. First it killed the Romans, and now it's killing me." In truth, Latin is more akin to the luscious grape cluster hanging just out of the fox's reach in Aesop's fable. Rather than apply any effort to obtain the prize, he skulked off muttering how sour they probably were. If only he had tried hard enough to taste even a single grape!

As off the mark as that little ditty is, it does bring up some important points. First, what does "dead" mean when applied to a language? Language is a living thing. It grows and changes day by day, imperceptibly, just as an infant grows to adulthood. There was never any calendar date marked when the folks in Rome stopped speaking Latin and started speaking Italian! The confusion may lie in the names we give languages. *Ure Faeder the eart in heofenum* is the beginning of the Lord's Prayer in English as English was spoken fifteen hundred years ago. English isn't a dead language, but it isn't spoken like that anymore, so we call that kind of English *Old English*. Likewise, the language of Caesar could be called Old Italian. (Or Italian Modern Latin!) Studying Latin, then, is studying the snapshot of a whiz kid who is now grown-up.

The story of ancient Rome represents about 25 percent of all recorded history. If ancient Rome and her language are dead, tenacious ghosts remain. Nearly a billion people today speak Modern Latin (i.e. [*id est*—that is], French, Spanish, Portuguese, et al. [*et alia*—and the others]). If you look out your window and see bricks, concrete, or a paved road; if you turn on the news or pick up a newspaper and see any reference to law or government; you're looking at Rome's ghost. In fact, if you speak English, you're perpetuating Rome's linguistic legacy. Thanks to the forced importation of Norman French into England in 1066, over 60 percent of English vocabulary is derived from Latin, not to mention the fact that centuries ago the Latin language was considered so perfect that many fussy grammar rules (e.g. [*exemplī gratiā*—for the sake of example], not ending sentences with a preposition, avoiding double negatives, not splitting infinitives, etc. [*et cetera*—and the others]) were imposed on English.

The second point that that ridiculous schoolboy rhyme evokes involves Latin's deadly effect on students. All too often people approach foreign languages as if they were simple questions of word substitution. This tack only leads to frustration, disaster, and sour grapes. Language may seem to be nothing more than words, just so many beads on a string, but it has a crucial component called syntax. Syntax is how words show their relationship to one another. How can you tell what or who is performing the action of the verb? How do you know whether the action of the verb is over, in progress, or hasn't happened yet? If Tim makes a reference to "Melanie's cat," how can you tell whether Melanie owns the cat, the cat owns Melanie, or Melanie is just the name of the cat? The key is syntax, and the syntax of Latin is the adventure of this book. It's a very different critter from the system English uses, so set aside your notion of how language works and prepare to see the world through new eyes— Roman eyes! Ⓔ

Chapter 1

The Key to Understanding Latin

You're all set for some hot coffee, but one sip makes you spit and declare that it's horrible coffee . . . even though you know it's tea. Studying Latin is a lot like that. If you insist that Latin is a substitution code for English, you'll only get more and more ready to spit. There are some crucial differences in the way English and Latin operate as languages.

The Significance of Syntax

The most striking difference between English and Latin lies in syntax—the way words show their relationship to each other in a sentence. A word sitting by itself has a meaning, but that's all. When it's in a string with other words, though, it has to have a way to show how it interacts with the other words around it. Exactly how that relationship is shown doesn't matter. What matters is that all the speakers of the language agree on the rules.

When you speak or write English, words just seem to come out and fall into place in a way that makes sense. In fact, the key to English syntax really is "place"! Consider these two sentences:

Money the gave Jeff me when at were yesterday party the we.
Jeff gave me the money yesterday when we were at the party.

Take a closer look at those examples. Who did something? What did he do it to? Who benefited from his action? Where did it happen? Now for the big question: How do you know any of these things? Both sentences contain the same words; the only difference is word order. Languages that rely on word order to make sense are called analytical.

Using word order to show the relationship between words is an arbitrary way to do it. It's just what English speakers all agree to do. Take a look at the concept of this sentence: Mark loves the dog. Does Mark come first in time? Does the dog? They are all there; they all "happen" simultaneously. Since they are all there together at the same time, there is no real reason for Mark to have to come first in the sentence. The only reason he comes first is because the rules of English dictate that if he is the one with the affection, he has to come before the verb in the sentence. Swap the word order—the dog loves Mark—and the meaning changes dramatically.

How Latin Syntax Works

Latin's m.o. (*modus operandī*—way of operating) is based on quite a different system of rules. Let's visit Mark and his best friend again, but this time in Latin.

Marcus canem amat. (Mark loves his dog.)
Canem Marcus amat. (Mark loves his dog.)
Amat canem Marcus. (Mark loves his dog.)
Marcus amat canem. (Mark loves his dog.)
Canem amat Marcus. (Mark loves his dog.)
Amat Marcus canem. (Mark loves his dog.)

How can all six mean the same thing?!

Here's another example. See if you can figure out what tiny change in the Latin made such a big change in the meaning.

Marcum canis amat. (The dog loves Mark.)
Canis Marcum amat. (The dog loves Mark.)
Amat canis Marcum. (The dog loves Mark.)
Marcum amat canis. (The dog loves Mark.)
Canis amat Marcum. (The dog loves Mark.)
Amat Marcum canis. (The dog loves Mark.)

In the English version you know who's doing what to whom based on which noun comes before or after the verb. The doer comes first, then the action, then the do-ee. In the Latin version, what comes first really doesn't matter. The position may change, but as long as the endings don't, the meaning remains the same. Inflected languages like Latin use word endings as flags to show who's doing what to whom.

Although word order is not crucial to Latin syntax, it does suggest a bit of nuance. A grammatical subject has immediate association with a verb. A topic, however, comes as if an answer to a question—the most important bit. *Marcum canis amat* would stress whom the dog loves. *Canis Marcum amat*, on the other hand, tells who loves Mark. Different order, same endings, different emphasis.

Learning Endings

Since Latin depends on endings for words to show their relationships to one another in a sentence, two things should be immediately clear. First, knowledge of English grammar is extremely important. There will be plenty of review along the way, so even if you are learning it for the first time, there is no need to worry.

Second, since there are many ways words can show their relationship to one another to make up a sentence, there will be a lot of endings. A *whole* lot. But again, not to worry! As you move through this book you'll encounter sets of endings bit by bit. While it may seem a little rough going at first, you'll be getting a feel for them and recognizing their patterns in no time.

Your best approach to learning endings is to take each set as they come, chapter by chapter; learn to recognize or even memorize them; and practice working with them in the exercises provided in each chapter. The more practice you get, the better your chances of internalizing them and making them virtually instinctual. Since the entire Latin language operates on a system of inflections (i.e., endings), these inflections cannot be dismissed as insignificant pains in the neck. They are the keys to understanding!

By now you may be wondering if you are up to the challenge of learning endings so well that they become second nature to you. Rest assured that you can. In fact, you already do use endings without thinking about it. Here is a little experiment that will highlight the existence (and importance!) of word forms in English. Read this little sentence out loud and listen closely:

Me sended he Seth checks for we these morning.

Unless you're Tarzan, this sentence doesn't sound quite right. What makes it sound off kilter is that the forms are either incorrect or not there. Here is the same sentence with the endings adjusted to conform to the rules of English grammar:

I sent him Seth's check for us this morning.

Can you hear the difference? If you compare the two sentences, you will see that each contains the same words in the same order. The only thing that varies between them is word form. For example, "I" and "me" both refer to the same person. They aren't two different words; they are two different forms of the *same* word.

Now that you can see how English has different forms and endings much like Latin does, how do you know which is correct? Read those two examples again and consider how you know which is the better sentence. When you read them, you didn't stop at each word to scrutinize and analyze and recite grammar rules. You just knew, didn't you? The second attempt sounded right. The first one just sounded flat out stupid. That is your "monitor" kicking in. Your monitor is your internalization of the way a language works, and that happens only with exposure to that language.

All babies acquire language the same way. Just repetition of sounds at first, then simple words, then two-, then three-word sentences, then generalization of the rules and forms ("Her goed to the store," then eventually, "she went"). Exposure and practice are the only ways to develop this internal sense.

FACT

Inflected languages have a habit of slowly changing to analytical ones, then back again. A couple of thousand years ago (i.e., about the same time Latin was spoken), ancient English was also highly inflected. Over time it lost most of its endings and had to add helping words and count on word order for syntax. Now, in modern English, some of those helping words are becoming new endings. For example, look at the way the word "would" contracts to form "I'd," "you'd," "she'd," and so on.

Earlier in this chapter you saw an example illustrating endings in Latin swapping to turn the meaning of a sentence on its head. The subject of the sentence (the doer of the action) was written *Marcus* or *canis*, and the direct object (the receiver of the action) changed to *Marcum* or *canem*. In the sentence earlier, the noun "Seth" became "Seth's" in order to show possession. The English ending "–s" also appears in the word "check" to distinguish between singular and plural. The pronouns "I," "he," and "we" are only used as subjects. To make them objects, you have to change them to "me," "him," and "us," respectively. Not even adjectives escape inflection: "this/these." Verbs take endings as well, as in "send" becoming past tense by changing the final *d* to *t* (not adding "–ed" like most English verbs).

Latin may have a lot of endings, but at least word order isn't much of a concern. English is a bear—it relies on both! If you can handle English, Latin will be a piece of cake.

Learning Vocabulary

The most obvious difference between languages is words. As you have seen, the really big difference between languages is syntax, which is not so obvious. You can look up words in the dictionary, but without knowledge of the way a language uses those words to create sentences, they're just words. The goal of this book is to teach you how Latin works. Once you know that, you'll be able to do something with the words you look up.

Latin's vocabulary isn't very large, only around 10,000 words. That may seem like a lot, but compared to English's quarter million (give or take), it's nothing. On top of that is the fact that a great many of those words are the results of mixing and matching bases, prefixes, and suffixes. Master the elements and you're home free.

Parts of Speech

You are probably familiar with the parts of speech from your school days or watching the *School House Rock* lessons that used to be tucked in among Saturday morning cartoons.

- **Nouns:** person, place, thing, or idea (e.g., "buddy," "basement," "potato," "honesty")
- **Pronouns:** words that stands in for a noun (e.g., "she," "who," "those")

- **Verbs:** actions or states of being (e.g., "love," "hang," "go," "dream")
- **Adjectives:** qualities of nouns (e.g., "greedy," "colorful," "slick")
- **Adverbs:** qualifiers for verbs (e.g., "beautifully," "there," "fast," "yesterday")
- **Prepositions:** words that identify a relationship (e.g., "in," "about," "of")
- **Conjunctions:** words that join like things (e.g., "and," "because," "although")
- **Interjections:** exclamatory words (e.g., "Wow!" "Ouch!" "Yuck!")

As you will soon see, some parts of speech in Latin have "parts." English words do, too. For example, if you were learning English as a foreign language, the only way you'd know that the plural of "child" is "children," or the past tense of "put" is "put," is by learning those bits as you learn the words.

The little Latin-English dictionary in Appendix A contains the most common words in Latin literature. If you learn these, you will have 80 percent of all you need. They really are the essentials! It is still recommended that you use a Latin dictionary. There are many on the market, ranging from pocket size to monster size. Stick to the more modest size and you'll do fine.

Vocabulary-Building Strategies

There are a few good, time-tested ways to learn vocabulary. Different students have different learning styles, so try a few different approaches to see what works best for you.

- **Straight memorization:** The old-fashioned method is just plain rote memorization. It's dull at best, tedious at worst, not to mention the fact that the words gained tend to be so isolated that they can be unintelligible when they appear in sentences.

- **Flash cards:** Modern life is a game of hurry up and wait. Here's something to do during those waits. Draw and quarter some 3" × 5" index cards. On each little card write Latin on one side and English on the other. (Use pencil; ink bleeds through and makes it easier to cheat!) Keep a little stack in your pocket, and pull them out to quiz yourself many times a day. Make your self-inflicted pop quizzes quick and keep them to no more than a few minutes. Remember to go back and review the old ones now and then.

- **Steno pad:** Steno pads are great because they're ruled right down the middle. On the left side write Latin, on the right, English. Compile your list only from exercises. (It helps to remember things in context.) Take a 3" × 5" index card, and, starting at the top of a pad page, quiz yourself. Whatever you don't remember goes on the next line on the card. When the card is full, stop and keep the card in your pocket for the day. If you make it down a whole pad page correctly, put a tick at the top of that page. Five ticks up top and that page is a goner. Move on to the next.

- **Look it up:** As you do exercises or read, look up every word you can't remember either in the back of this book or in a dictionary. The more important words will keep reappearing. The less important words won't. Eventually you won't have to look up those high-frequency words anymore.

FACT

Several studies on language learning have found that while the brain enjoys the stimulation of learning new things, it can also get saturated. This is especially true with studying vocabulary. To keep from spinning your wheels, keep your sessions working with this book limited to about half an hour. Several short sessions stick better than a few long ones.

Chapter 2

Helps and Hindrances

Learning anything new has easy parts, challenging parts, and just plain hopelessly boring parts. Learning endings, for example, is basically straight memorization. There are some patterns among the endings that help, and they will be pointed out as they come, but on the whole, it's pure drudgery. On the vocabulary side, however, there are some things that can grease the skids for you.

Derivatives

You will find it a blessing that what makes Latin useful to know also makes it easy to learn. Around 60 percent of English vocabulary comes from Latin. English words that come from Latin words are called derivatives. Some of these derivatives are of the disestablishmentarianism variety, but there are also many very common ones, such as the word "common," from the Latin word *communis*, which means—you guessed it—"common." The majority, however, are simply five-dollar words for things we already have English words for. Earlier you probably weren't surprised to see that the Latin word *canis* means "dog." You know what a canine is! That being the case, it probably wouldn't surprise you to learn that the Latin word for cat is *felis*.

FACT

Latin and English are distant cousins. Probably around five thousand years ago, a group of people we call the Indo-Europeans began migrating from the area in southern Russia near the Black Sea. As they moved into Europe, they broke off into groups and the language grew and changed in different ways. Latin is a member of the Italic branch; English is from the Germanic one.

The Roman Invasion(s)

Before you started reading this chapter, you may have thought that Latin existed in English only in phrases like *carpe diem* and *habeas corpus*. There are many little phrases and abbreviations like that, but Latin's contribution to our language is far more than legal terms and mottos. In fact, Latin crashed on the shores of England in three successive waves.

Roman Britain

The Romans were in Britain for a few centuries, but not too many Latin words survived into English from that time. Julius Caesar made a couple of visits there in 55 and 54 B.C.E., but it wasn't until Claudius annexed it as a province in the 40s C.E. that there was a constant Roman presence. Latin was a very foreign language to them. Much of the contact between the two peoples came at Roman military camps (*castra*) and plantations (*villae*). Locals came to trade so frequently with these newcomers that towns grew up beside the Roman establishments. These settlements by locals often distinguished themselves by having names ending in *–chester* or *–ville*. One of the best things the Romans brought to Britain was a fermented grape juice they called *vinum* (WEE-noom). Since when the Romans talked the ends of words kept changing, the Brits just called it *wine*. Latin words coming into English at this time were usually only heard and not written, so they often went through some strange shifts in pronunciation and spelling.

FACT

The people of Britain at that time spoke various Celtic languages. During the Roman years, no form of English was spoken in Britain. The Anglo-Saxons began taking over the island as the Romans were pulling out late in the fifth century.

The Norman Invasion

In 1066, William the Conqueror of Normandy invaded England. The result was an aristocracy, who spoke a form of very late Latin/ early French, ruling natives who spoke English. In order for the two to communicate, the peasants had to pick up a whole lot of French words. The English language virtually doubled its vocabulary, but with two class levels. What the commoners called a *cow*, the aristocracy called a *boeuf*. Since the upper classes never dealt with steak on the hoof, only cow on the plate, the barnyard animal stayed a "cow" while the meat became "beef." Latin words that came into English in this wave had already aged a bit and arrived slightly Frenchified. For example, the Modern English word "receipt" came from the Norman French *receite*, which came from the Latin *recepta*—something you get back.

From the Renaissance to Today

Starting around the year 1300, new thoughts, new art, and new sciences needed new words. At that time Latin was the universal language in Europe among scholars and writers. It had become the old standby. Whether you were in Italy, Germany, Spain, France, or England, Latin was always Latin. When new words needed to be created, people could turn to Latin (and sometimes Greek) to make new ones up that everyone, regardless of their everyday language, could understand. We still go back to Latin to get bases, suffixes, and prefixes to create words for things that never existed before. Take "television" for example. The *tele–* part is from Greek, meaning "far," while the *–vision* part is from Latin, meaning "seeing." People are still dipping back into Latin to make new words even as you read this!

ALERT!

English derivatives from Latin are often very handy in learning Latin vocabulary, but don't rely on them exclusively. There are words whose meanings have shifted a little, with the result that they don't look like what they have come to mean. For example, the English word "invention" was made from the Latin *inventiō*, which is related to the Latin verb *inveniō*. *Inveniō* looks like it means "come in," but it really means "find" or "come upon."

A Very Different World

The ancient Roman world and our modern world are very different indeed. The Romans had words for things, actions, institutions, and customs that existed and were important to them back then. Our society is different, so we, too, have peculiar words. What's Latin for "keyboard"? Keyboards didn't exist back then—of course the Romans had no word for them!

The Romans also saw their world differently. A good example of this phenomenon can be found in something as simple as words for color. (Think of everyday color words, not the strange made-up terms you can find when looking at samples at the paint store.) You may take color for granted, but look around the room and imagine what it would look like without Red Dye No. 87! The Romans did have dyes, of course, but they were all organic. Our loud synthetic colors tend to overwhelm those more natural tones. Without the distraction of neon yellow, Roman eyes could see distinctions between shades and found them important enough to have specific words for them. For example, Latin has two everyday words for "white": *candidus* (bright, shiny white) and *albus* (dull, flat white).

There is something else you should be aware of for learning Latin vocabulary. When you look words up in the dictionary, the meanings given really aren't this *or* that, they're this *and* that. Here is another color example that will demonstrate. Consider the Latin word *caeruleus*. If you look it up in the dictionary you will see it means "blue, green, gray." Though it may seem that the Romans were all colorblind, the fact is that we don't have a regular word for that color. *Caeruleus* is really something akin to the color of the sea. We are accustomed to thinking that the ocean is blue, but look again. It's more gray than it is blue, but it's too green to be gray, and it's too blue to be green . . . actually, it's all of them at the same time. It's *caeruleus*!

The English-to-Latin translation exercises in each chapter are the most challenging. They are useful because they force you to apply everything you have learned. Do not, however, judge your progress by how well you do on them. Always remember that your ultimate goal is to be able to read, not speak or write. You should focus your energy on being able to *recognize* endings, grammar, and vocabulary.

There are no exact one-to-one equivalents between English and Latin words. Languages draw arbitrary lines and have words that reflect how their speakers see the world. As you learn your Latin vocabulary, you will notice that almost all Latin words have a range of possibilities to pick from for translation. As with *caeruleus*, a Latin word really means the intersection of *all* the possibilities you find in the dictionary. In order to translate Latin into English, you have to pick one possibility, but any single one you pick is wrong since there are no one-to-one equivalents. If that's true, translations are nothing more than interpretations of the original. By learning Latin you are letting the Romans speak directly to you for themselves.

Unlike English, Latin is perfectly phonetic—everything is spelled exactly as it is pronounced; there are no silent letters. Every letter has one sound value. Learning Latin pronunciation is important to help you learn and appreciate Latin as a language. Try *not* to pronounce Latin words using English rules. Latin rules are easier anyway!

The Roman Alphabet

Speakers of modern languages tend to pronounce Latin words using the rules for pronunciation for their own language. By studying how sounds change over time and examining ways other ancient languages with different alphabets wrote Latin words, scholars have deduced how Classical Latin (i.e., the Latin of Caesar's time) probably sounded.

The biggest difference between our alphabet and the Roman one is that, for the Romans, each letter represented only one sound, making Latin a truly phonetic language. Apart from that, there aren't many differences between the two. In fact, our alphabet is properly called the *Roman* alphabet! When the Romans borrowed it from their neighbors to the north, the Etruscans, they adapted it to suit the sound system of Latin. The Etruscans had done the same thing when they got it from the Greeks, who got it from the Phoenicians, who had adopted it from their neighbors, the Egyptians. Quite a pedigree!

QUESTION?

What is "Church Latin"?
Church Latin is the Latin that has been used by the Roman Catholic Church for centuries. It's really just a later form of Latin whose pronunciation is more like Italian. The most notable difference comes with the letters *g* and *c*. When followed by the vowels *e* or *i*, *g* is soft (like in English "general"), and a *c* has a *ch* sound (as in "cheese").

Table 2-1   The Roman Alphabet

Roman Letter	English Sound	Latin Example	Pronunciation
a	M*a*	*animal*	AH-nee-mahl
b	*b*ig	*bibo*	BEE-bo
c	*c*ake	*cecidit*	kay-KEE-diht
d	*d*og	*dona*	DOE-nah
e	fianc*é*	*edimus*	AY-dee-moos
f	*f*ood	*facile*	FAH-kee-lay
g	*g*et	*gerere*	GAY-ray-ray
h	*h*ound	*hora*	HO-rah
i	mach*i*ne	*ii*	EE-ee
k	*k*ibble	*kalendae*	kah-LAYN-di
l	*l*ab	*lavitur*	LAH-wee-toor
m	*m*inute	*monitus*	MO-nee-toos
n	*n*orth	*nihil*	NEE-heel
o	n*o*te	*opera*	O-pay-rah
p	*p*ail	*poposcit*	po-POS-keet
q	*q*uake	*quid*	KWEED
r	*r*ide	*robur*	RO-boor
s	*s*alad	*discamus*	dees-KAH-moos
t	*t*one	*tutus*	TOO-toos
u	t*u*be	*ululare*	oo-loo-LAH-ray
v	*w*ine	*video*	WEE-day-o
x	e*x*it	*exit*	AYX-eet
y	t*oo*th	*zephyrus*	zay-FOO-roos
z	*z*ip	*zona*	ZO-nah

You may have noticed a couple letters missing, namely *j* and *w*. *J* was added to distinguish between Latin's vowel *i* and the consonant *i*. The letter *w* was added to do the same thing for Latin's consonant *u*.

Vowels

The vowels in Latin are the same as in English (*a, e, i, o, u*), but their pronunciation is a bit different. If you say the sentence "Ma made these old boots," then repeat it saying only the vowels, you will be able to remember how Latin vowels sound. (*Y* occurs only in words borrowed from Greek, to represent the Greek letter upsilon. Don't worry about it.) The Romans didn't use any accent marks, little dots, or squiggles. Actually, they didn't even use punctuation! We modern students of Latin, however, use a long mark called a macron over vowels to show that they are long. The only difference between a long and a short vowel in Latin is that you hold a long vowel twice as long as you do a short one.

Latin also has a few diphthongs. Diphthongs are two vowels that sit right next to each other and are pronounced so quickly that they blend into a single, new sound.

Table 2-2	Latin Vowel Combinations			
Roman Letter	English Sound	Latin Example	Phonetic Spelling	
ae	*ai*sle	*aedificium*	i	i-dee-FEE-kee-oom
au	n*ow*	*audire*	ow	ow-DEE-ray
eu	T*ue*sday	*heu*	ue	HUE
oe	b*oy*	*foedus*	oy	FOY-doos

Consonants

Native speakers of English often have a hard time believing that Latin is phonetic. What you write is what you say, nothing more, nothing less, and every letter has only one value. When you see a double letter, you say each of them separately, so *vacuum* ("an empty thing") is pronounced WAH-koo-oom, and *mitteris* ("you will be sent") is meet-TAY-rees.

Here is a list of a few consonants and consonant combinations to watch out for.

- *C* is always hard, as in English "cake."
- *G* is always hard, as in English "get."

- *I* can be a consonant as well as a vowel, just as the letter *y* in English can, and makes the same sound as in English "yes."
- *GN* sounds more like the *ng* in English "sing."
- *BS* sounds more like *ps*.
- *CH* sounds pretty much like a plain *c* with a whisp of air after it, as in English "deckhand." It never makes the English "ch" sound like in "church."
- *TH* just sounds like a *t* followed by an *h*, as in the English word "hothouse." It never makes the English *th* sound like in "think."
- *PH* sounds like a *p* followed by an *h*, as in the English phrase "up hill." It's not exactly an *f* sound, but it's pretty close.

Accent

The rules for accent in Latin are really easy. Every Latin word has as many syllables as it has vowels and diphthongs. The last syllable of a word is called the ultima, the next to the last one is the penult, and the one before that (the third from the end) is the antepenult. The rule is that if the penult is long, it gets the stress. If it's short, then the antepenult does, so the word *hominēs* ("people") would be pronounced *HOminēs,* but *hominēsque* ("and people") would be *homiNESque.*

Now that you've had a little linguistic theory, some study tips, and a bit of history, you are ready to embark on your journey into the ancient world. Language is a reflection of culture, and no culture has had more influence on us today than that of the Romans. *Valē!* ("Hang in there!"). Ⓔ

Chapter 3

The Importance of Verbs

Verbs show actions or states of being and form the core of a complete sentence. All other words in a sentence serve to modify the core (i.e., the verb) in some way, either directly or indirectly. Verbs are the center of attention! Because of their importance, they are a very good place for us to start.

Studying Latin Verbs

Latin's verb system is just that, a system. It has many components that are sometimes quite confusing. Imagine having a huge pile of jigsaw puzzle pieces in a heap before you. Where do you begin? Not by picking up random pieces, assuming that they will immediately snap together. You start by becoming familiar with the picture on the box that shows what the finished image will look like.

In essence, this chapter is the picture on the box. The picture is not the puzzle itself, nor is it something you should feel compelled to commit to memory. The picture is merely a guide. As you pick up the pieces of the Latin verb system, keep coming back to this chapter and reviewing the big picture. Let this first part of the chapter wash over you and do not worry if it doesn't make much sense at first. It will soon.

ALERT!

Pace yourself! Don't let yourself become overwhelmed. Too much information too quickly leads to intellectual indigestion. If you study out loud and use the exercises as tools (not as tests), you'll learn better and faster. Break your study sessions up into chunks of time no longer than half an hour each. It is also best to go over what you have done in your previous session before moving on to something new. You can never have enough review!

The Anatomy of a Latin Verb

English verbs are pretty wimpy. They have only three forms that don't require helpers. For example, you can say "I drink." If the subject is "he," "she," or "it," the verb takes an *s* to become "drinks." There is also the past-tense form "drank," which never takes the *s*. (Of course, the forms "drinking" and "drunk" exist as well, but they are really verbal adjectives, so for now we'll set them aside.)

Latin verbs, unlike English ones, are bulging with distinct forms! In the last chapter you were introduced to how Latin relies on endings to show who does what to whom. Verbs are in the inflection business as well, and they have endings for things you might never have thought a verb could have an ending for. Latin verbs have inflections to encode information for five characteristics:

Person

As a grammatical term, "person" refers to the relationship between the subject of a verb and the speaker. There are three persons in Latin, with the unoriginal names "first," "second," and "third." The first person is the speaker ("I" or "we"). The second person is the one or ones being spoken *to* ("you"). Finally, the third person is what or who is being spoken *about* ("he," "she," "it," or "they").

Number

Number is a fairly straightforward grammatical concept: A verb is either singular or plural.

FACT

In archaic Latin, and the ancient forms of all Indo-European languages, there was a third number called the dual. It denoted two of something. However useful it might have been, it disappeared.

Tense

The term "tense" is not quite as straightforward. It refers to when an action took place (we'll call this a time reference) and its duration (also known as aspect). Latin has six tenses. The present, imperfect, and future show action in progress (aspect) in the present, past, or future (time reference). The perfect, pluperfect, and future perfect show action completed (aspect) in the present, past, and future (time reference).

Mood

Grammatical mood is difficult to explain. It refers to the way a speaker *treats* an action. Latin has three moods. The indicative mood treats the action as a fact. (I am opening the window.) The subjunctive mood treats an action as an idea. (I might open a window.) Finally, there is the imperative mood, which treats an action as a command. (Open the window!) In Indo-European, there was also an optative mood that treated an action as a desire. (I'd like to open the window.) In Classical Latin, which is what you are studying now, the optative has merged with the subjunctive so that the subjunctive mood actually does the work of both.

Voice

Voice is the fifth characteristic of Latin verbs. It refers to a subject's relationship to a verb as performer or receiver of an action. In active voice, the subject of the verb performs the action. (He broke the glass.) In passive voice, the subject receives the action. (The glass was broken.) Passive voice is handy when you don't know—or don't want to admit—who did something. (Mistakes were made.) There is a third voice called the middle, in which a subject performs an action in such a way that the doer is affected for better or worse by the outcome. It's unlike anything in English, so there are no examples that do it justice. "I bathed the dogs" would be active voice. "The dogs were bathed" would be passive. Middle voice would say, "I bathed the dogs" (because I can't stand having stinky dogs hanging around the house, or something like that understood).

ALERT!

Don't be surprised when you see a little Latin phrase explode into a mile-long sentence in English! With all its compact verb forms, you will find that Latin is a very economical language. English often uses many words to express an idea that Latin can say with just one. The English verb in the example above—"were being called"—translates into Latin as *vocābantur*.

Let's pull all these characteristics together now by describing the verb in this sentence: "They were being called to duty."

Person: third person (somebody other than you or me)
Number: plural (more than one)
Tense: imperfect (action in progress in the past)
Mood: indicative (action treated as fact)
Voice: passive (subject received the action)

What Is Verbal Aspect?

In the preceding section you were introduced to the five characteristics of individual verbs. Each category probably made sense to you on its own, but the idea of Latin having six verb tenses may have been a little puzzling. Six does, after all, seem a bit many. If you take the idea of verb tense as a reference to time, it is. Present, past, future. What else can there be? To answer that question, you need to know about something called verbal aspect.

FACT

In Proto-Indo-European, Latin's grandmother language, there were nine different unique tense forms, one for each aspect and time frame. Greek, Latin's sister, dropped them to seven; Latin condensed them to six; and distant cousin English distilled them to just one, making up for the rest with helping verbs and participles.

Simply put, verbal aspect refers to the way a speaker views an action. In other words, is the action treated as something in progress and unfolding before your eyes, like the way a film unfolds before its audience? Or is the speaker referring to something that is all done? Another possibility is that the speaker is discussing an action in a more casual, general way, without specifying process or completion.

Take a look at **TABLE 3-1** below. The rows give time reference points for an action; the columns show the viewpoint (i.e., aspect).

Table 3-1	Action and Aspects		
Time/Aspect	Continuous (Present System)	Completed (Perfect System)	Aorist
Now	Present Tense *currit* he is running	Perfect Tense *cucurrit* he has run	Present Tense *currit* he runs
Earlier	Imperfect Tense *currēbat* he was running	Pluperfect Tense *cucurrerat* he had run	Perfect Tense *cucurrit* he ran
Later	Future Tense *curret* he will be running	Future Perfect Tense *cucurrerit* he will have run	Future Tense *curret* he will run

The Continuous Aspect (a.k.a. the Present System)

The first aspect column in **TABLE 3-1** shows the continuous aspect—the one that views an action as something in progress. If the action is in the middle of happening right now, Latin uses the present tense. To do this in English, we have to use a pronoun, followed by a form of the verb "to be," plus the "–ing" form of the verb. In Latin, the verb *currit* means, and would be translated as its English equivalent, "he is running."

Likewise, if the action were seen as in progress at an earlier time, Latin would use the imperfect tense *currēbat*. Notice how English simply bumps its present tense "is" to the past tense "was." Finally, if the action is viewed as being in the middle of happening later on, Latin uses its future tense, *curret*, and English continues its pattern, shifting to the future of its verb "to be."

The Completed Aspect (a.k.a. the Perfect System)

The second column in **TABLE 3-1** switches from seeing something in progress to something as completed (hence the name!). The real tricky part in understanding this aspect lies in its point of reference. While "he has run" describes an action that took place in the past, as you can see on the chart, it falls into the "now" time frame. Why? Because the completed aspect emphasizes *the point of completion*, not the time of the actual act. In the phrase "he has run," you are really saying that, as of right now, he isn't running anymore. He *is* finished! English shows this aspect by using present, past, and future forms of its verb "to have" with the past participle. (We'll come back to participles soon.) If you take a closer look at the Latin words, you'll notice that the biggest and most consistent change between aspects appears in the base of the verb: from *curr–* to *cucurr–*.

The Aorist Aspect

You can see that in the last column of the chart there are no new tense forms for Latin. For some unknown reason, the Romans abandoned the aorist forms and chose to recycle forms for other tenses instead. The use of the aspect, however, remained. In a nutshell, the aorist aspect puts action, well, in a nutshell. The English "he runs" doesn't say that the action is happening as we speak, nor does it say that it is freshly finished. It merely (and rather vaguely) states that it is known to happen. The English "he does run" is also aorist, just a more emphatic form.

ALERT!

The words "present" and "perfect" in the terms "present system" and "perfect system" can be misleading. The systems (i.e., aspects) are differentiated by their verb stems. The systems themselves get their names from the first tenses formed at the top line of the table.

Parts and Labor

The concepts you have learned so far in this chapter have shown you the multitude of things that are encoded in a Latin verb. Keeping those things in mind, it's time to leave the realm of theory and take a peek into the world of practice. Since Latin verbs are constructed of bits and pieces, it will be helpful for you to learn about the raw materials you will have to work with before learning how to build them.

Principal Parts

Native speakers of English, not to mention those learning English as a second language, have drilled into their heads what are called principal parts of verbs: "go, went, gone"; "sing, sang, sung"; and the notorious "lie, lay, lain" versus "lay, laid, laid." Those sequences represent the present tense, past tense, and past participle forms of a verb.

Participles are adjectives made from verbs. English has two participles. There is a present participle that contains the continuous aspect idea (e.g., "breaking"), and a past participle for the completed aspect (e.g., "broken"). Read these three short sentences and this will be easy to see: The cup is red. The cup is breaking. The cup is broken.

Latin has its own system of principal parts. In Latin, though, there are four, and they follow a somewhat different pattern than the principal parts of an English verb do. Their reason for existence, however, is the same. Once you understand what the principal parts are, you will have all the basic information you will need about a verb to put it into any person, number, tense, mood, or voice.

Let's use the principal parts of the Latin verb for "give, gave, given" as an example to explore what these parts are all about.

dō, dare, dedī, datum

1. *dō* ("I give") is the first person singular, present, indicative, active. It tells you whether or not a verb is an *–iō* verb. (More on this very soon!)

2. *dare* ("to give") is the present infinitive active. It provides the present stem and shows to which conjugation a verb belongs. (This comment will make sense soon, too.)
3. *dedī* ("I gave") is the first person singular, perfect, indicative, active. It provides the stem for perfect system forms.
4. *datum* ("given") is the "supine." It has special uses, which we will talk about in detail later. It also supplies the base for certain participial forms.

The principal parts of a verb provide you with all the information you need to construct or recognize each and every possible form of a verb. The first two parts provide "need to know" information for making present system forms, and the last two have information for the perfect system. In the next chapter you will be working with tenses formed from the second and third parts. The first and fourth principal parts will each have their own chapters later.

ALERT!

When you learn verbs in your vocabulary, it's a good idea to learn all four principal parts, even if you don't know what they are all used for yet. If you don't, when the time comes for you to learn what those mysterious principal parts are used for, you'll have to go back and relearn all your vocabulary.

Even though you won't be working with the first principle part fully at the moment, it still has an important role for you. First of all, it is the only way to tell whether a verb is an "*–iō* verb." Also, Latin dictionaries list verbs by their first principle part, so you have to know them in order to look a verb up in the dictionary, or at least be able to predict how a verb's principal parts might go. (There is a rhythm to them and you will catch on to it over time.) Since a Latin verb can appear in as many as almost three hundred different forms, a dictionary that had separate listings for *every* form of *every* verb would be enormous!

The Conjugations

If a well-shuffled deck of cards were handed to you and you were asked to sort them into a few groups based on common characteristics, what would you do? Odds are you would go by suit, putting the spades in one pile, the hearts in another, and so on. Scholars have done the same thing with Latin verbs. All verbs are divided into groups called conjugations.

Not counting a few odd verbs—the jokers in the deck—that are called the irregulars, there are four of these conjugations. They are distinguished by their second principle part (the infinitive) and have the uninspired names "first," "second," "third," and "fourth."

- All verbs with *–āre* for their infinitive ending are "first conjugation": *putō, putāre, putāvī, putātum.*
- All verbs with *–ēre* for their infinitive ending are "second conjugation": *video, vidēre, vīdī, vīsum.*
- All verbs with *–ere* for their infinitive ending are "third conjugation": *dīcō, dīcere, dīxī, dictum.*
- All verbs with *–īre* for their infinitive ending are "fourth conjugation": *veniō, venīre, vēnī, vēntum.*

There is another group of verbs called third conjugation *–iō* verbs (e.g., *faciō, facere, fēcī, factum*). Their infinitive ends in *–ere*, so by the rules, they are third conjugation. Their first principle part, however, ends in *–iō* like fourth conjugation, and almost all their forms look the same as those of fourth conjugation verbs.

ALERT!

Second and third conjugation verbs are tricky to recognize at first glance—they each have an –e– in their infinitive. For second conjugation verbs, the –ē– is long (notice the macron). For third conjugation, the –e– is short. This may seem like a trivial detail right now, but you will see soon that it is actually quite huge!

Knowing to which conjugation a verb belongs is very important for recognizing and forming the present system tenses. How a verb forms its present and future tenses depends on its conjugation. Of the three tenses in the present system, the imperfect tense is the least affected by the differences among the conjugations. You will learn the imperfect tense formally in Chapter 4. The present and future tenses will be introduced in a later chapter.

ALERT!

The word "conjugation" can be confusing. Sometimes it refers to a classification, as we've been using it here. It can also refer to a chart that shows all the forms of a verb in a certain tense. To "conjugate" means to make a chart like that.

You will be glad to know that all the perfect system tenses behave themselves: All their forms are made the same way regardless of conjugation. Not even the irregular verbs stray from this rule!

Chapter 4

The Imperfect and Perfect Tenses

This chapter introduces you to the two most common verb tenses in Latin, which are called the imperfect and perfect. They are past tenses that look at action two different ways. The imperfect tense sees an action in the middle of happening; the perfect tense sees it as done and over. They are a good place to begin.

Dissecting a Latin Verb

In the previous chapter you got an overview of Latin's entire verb system, including the characteristics of verbs (person, number, tense, mood, voice), the concept of verbal aspect (continuous or completed), the way verbs are classified into conjugations (first through fourth), and how each verb has a set of principal parts that provides raw materials for constructing any form you might require or encounter. Before we begin building imperfect and perfect tense forms, let's tear a verb apart to see where all those elements you just read about appear.

Most English verb forms must be cobbled together by lining up several words; for example, "they used to be told." Latin verbs, on the other hand, manage to convey the same information, but in a compact manner that requires only one word. For instance, the Latin version of the example used previously would be *dīcēbantur*. The word *dīcēbantur* can be cut up into three sections: a verb stem, a tense indicator, and a personal ending.

Verb Stems

The verb stem is the basic foundation onto which you attach the tense indicator. The stem carries the meaning of a verb, of course, but it also tells you which aspect you are working with. The stem used to show a verb in the continuous aspect (i.e., present system) is made from the second principle part (i.e., the infinitive) minus the infinitive ending (e.g., *–āre, –ēre,* etc.) or at least the final *–re*. The continuous aspect stem for the verb *dīcō, dīcere, dīxī, dictum* ("to say, tell"), then, would be *dīcē–*. If you want the stem for the completed aspect (i.e., perfect system) of this same verb, then you would need to jump to the third principal part and drop the final *–ī*. For the verb *dīcō* it would be *dīx–*. It still means the same thing. Only the aspect has changed.

Tense Indicators

The traditional term "tense indicator" is somewhat misleading. It is true that it does indicate tense, but it also indicates mood (indicative, subjunctive, or imperative). The tense indicator shows up either as an extra syllable added to the verb stem, or, in present system tenses, as a slight change in the vowel at the end of the verb stem. For the verb that we have been using as an example, the tense indicator is *–ba–*, which tells you that the tense is imperfect and the mood is indicative.

Personal Endings

Now that you know where verb stems come from and what tense indicators are, it is time to finish our verb off with an ending. Perhaps the most important of all the elements of a Latin verb are the personal endings. If you recall the five characteristics of verbs discussed in Chapter 3 (person, number, tense, mood, and voice), you might think that personal endings have to do with "person." You are correct, but they also tell you number (singular or plural) and voice (active or passive). In the case of our example verb *dīcēbantur*, the personal ending *–ntur* says that the verb is third person, plural, and in the passive voice. Personal endings are real workhorses!

Active and passive voice each have their own set of personal endings. You will learn about passive voice in a later chapter. For the time being, we will work only with active voice. Here is what active personal endings look like:

Table 4-1 Personal Endings for Active Voice		
Person	**Singular**	**Plural**
First	*–m*	*–mus*
Second	*–s*	*–tis*
Third	*–t*	*–nt*

Another way to look at personal endings is to think that they do the same work pronouns do in English, so you could "translate" the above chart like this:

Table 4-2 Meanings for Personal Endings		
Person	**Singular**	**Plural**
First	*I*	*we*
Second	*you*	*you*
Third	*he, she, it*	*they*

The imperfect tense, for example, is built by taking the present stem of a verb, adding the tense indicator for the imperfect tense, then tacking on a personal ending. If you dissect the third person plural of the verb *dabant*, for instance, you can see how the verb is assembled:

da + *ba* + *nt*
give + were ___ing + they

The Latin verb is a neat little package that reads in the opposite direction from English: It gives the meaning, then indicates the tense, then says who was doing it. The personal ending caps the verb off with a built-in subject.

When an actual noun subject is expressed, verbs keep their personal endings, even if they are a bit redundant. *Latrābant.* ("They were barking.") *Canēs latrābant.* ("The dogs were barking.")

Here is a complete conjugation of the verb *dō* in imperfect tense:

Table 4-3
Conjugation of the Verb *dō, dare, dedi, datum* in Imperfect Tense

Person	Singular	Plural
First	*dabam* (I was giving)	*dabāmus* (we were giving)
Second	*dabās* (you were giving)	*dabātis* (you were giving)
Third	*dabat* (he/she/it was giving)	*dabant* (they were giving)

How can the personal ending *-t* mean "he" or "she" or "it"?
The third person singular ending refers only to a singular someone or something that is neither you nor I. It isn't gender specific. If the context is a paperweight, you'd probably say "it" is on the table rather than "he" or "she."

TABLE 4-4 will introduce you to some of the verbs that you will learn more about in the rest of this chapter.

Table 4-4	Vocabulary
accipiō, accipere, accēpī, acceptum	to take, receive, welcome
agō, agere, ēgī, āctum	to do
amō, amāre, amāvī, amātum	to love, like
audiō, audīre, audīvī, audītum	to hear
capiō, capere, cēpī, captum	to take, catch, grab
dīcō, dīcere, dīxī, dictum	to say, tell
dō, dare, dedī, datum	to give
faciō, facere, fēcī, factum	to make, do
habeō, habēre, habuī, habitum	to have, hold, consider
pōnō, pōnere, posuī, positum	to put, place
sum, esse, fuī, futūrus	to be
teneō, tenēre, tenuī, tentum	to hold, grasp
veniō, venīre, vēnī, vēntum	to come
videō, vidēre, vīdī, vīsum	to see

FACT

The verbs *agō* and *faciō* both mean "to do," but in different ways. *Faciō* refers to being busy and having something to show for it when you're done. *Agō* is more of a generic verb. How it is understood and translated depends on context. For example, it can mean "drive" with horses, "transact" with business, "plead" with a court case, "deal" with a situation, just to name a few possibilities.

Recognizing Conjugations

Look at each verb in the vocabulary list in **TABLE 4-4**. Indicate the conjugation (first, second, third, third –*iō*, or fourth) each verb belongs to. Check your answers in the back of the book.

The Imperfect Tense

The imperfect is the past time tense of the continuous aspect. Its emphasis is on action in progress. The tense indicator –*ba*– makes the imperfect among the easiest tenses to recognize. That's a good thing since it's among the most commonly seen! There are many ways to translate the imperfect. The important thing is that you keep in mind the basic concept behind the continuous aspect.

Forming the Imperfect Tense

Forming the imperfect is fairly simple. First you need the verb's present stem. (The present stem is the second principle part minus the final –*re*.) Next comes the imperfect tense indicator (–*ba*–). Finally there is a personal ending. Here are some examples, all in the third person plural.

Table 4-5		Imperfect Tense Forms			
Conjugation	Verb	Present Stem	Tense Indicator	Personal Ending	Result
First	*amō, amāre*	*amā*	*ba*	*nt*	*amābant*
Second	*habeō, habēre*	*habē*	*ba*	*nt*	*habēbant*
Third	*dūcō, dūcere*	*dūcē*	*ba*	*nt*	*dūcēbant*
Third –*iō*	*capiō, capere*	*capiē*	*ba*	*nt*	*capiēbant*
Fourth	*veniō, venīre*	*veniē*	*ba*	*nt*	*veniēbant*

Compare the present stems in the above table. Present stem formation is basically the infinitive (second principle part) minus the final –*re*. Third conjugation –*iō* and fourth conjugation verbs wander from that rule a little. Both their present stems end in –*iē*–. You will find that third conjugation –*iō* and fourth conjugation verb forms are almost always identical.

Using the Imperfect Tense

The imperfect tense shows an action that was in the middle of happening or happened repeatedly over a period of time in the past.

Sometimes it even shows something that was starting to happen in the past. The action may still be going on in the present, but for the imperfect tense, that doesn't matter. The imperfect tense emphasizes that something was occurring or at least used to occur.

Let's explore some possible ways to translate the verb *veniēbant* from the verb *veniō, venīre, vēnī, vēntum* ("to come").

they were coming	they came (over and over again)
they used to come	they started to come
they kept coming	they were beginning to come
they were in the habit of coming	

With that many possibilities, how are you supposed to know which is right? Well, to the Roman mind, *veniēbant* is *veniēbant*. It means all of those things at the same time. (Remember *caeruleus* in Chapter 2?) English, with its penchant for piling up words, has many ways to get this idea across; Latin has only one. So to translate the Latin, you need to rely on context. When you are reading, you will get a sense of what sounds best in a particular situation and your intuition should guide you.

Practice Conjugating the Imperfect

Conjugate each of these verbs in the imperfect tense into first person, second person, and third person singular and plural forms. Check your answers at the back of the book.

1. *pōnō, pōnere, posuī, positum* _____

2. *capiō, capere, cēpī, captum* _____

3. *amō, amāre, amāvī, amātum* _____

4. *habeō, habēre, habuī, habitum* _____

5. *audiō, audīre, audīvī, audītum* _____

The Perfect Tense

The perfect tense can show an action that was completed at the time of speaking (or writing), or it can just make a general reference to something that happened in the past. It is by far the most common of the tenses and the easiest to form.

Perfect tense formation is extremely straightforward. All verbs, regardless of conjugation (even the irregular verbs!), form perfect tense the same way. Perfect tense forms consist of the perfect stem and a personal ending. The perfect stem is the third principle part of a verb minus the final –ī. The perfect tense also has its own set of special personal endings.

Perfect Stems

Perfect stems come from the third principal part of a verb. They are variations on a verb's present stem (second principle part minus the final –re). There are four ways a perfect stem can vary from a present stem. Some verbs even use more than one of these methods to distinguish their perfect and present stems. If you know what to look for, you will easily be able to recognize perfect stems when you run across them in a sentence.

Here are the four different ways verbs alter their present stems to form perfect stems:

Syllabic Augment: the present stem gains a –v or –u at the end.
- *amō, amāre, amāvī, amātum* (to love)
- *moneō, monēre, monuī, monitum* (to warn, advise)
- *dormiō, dormīre, dormīvī, dormītum* (to sleep)

Temporal Augment: the central vowel of the present stem lengthens.
- *videō, **vidēre**, **vīdī**, **vīsum*** (to see)
- *faciō, **facere**, **fēcī**, factum* (to make)
- *agō, **agere**, **ēgī**, āctum* (to do)

Aorist: the present stem adds an *s*, or its last letter becomes an *s*.
(Note: The letter *c* or *g* followed by an *s* becomes *x*.)
- *maneō, **manēre**, **mānsī**, mānsum* (to stay)
- *plaudō, **plaudere**, **plausī**, plausum* (to clap)
- *dīcō, **dīcere**, **dīxī**, dictum* (to say)

Reduplication: the first letter or syllable of the present stem is repeated. (Note: Prefixes take the place of a reduplicated syllable.)

- *currō, currere, cucurrī, cursum* (to run)
- *recurrō, recurrere, recurrī, recursum* (to run back)
- *pellō, pellere, pepulī, pulsum* (to beat)
- *repellō, repellere, reppulī, repulsum* (to beat back)

Perfect Personal Endings

The perfect tense has its own set of special personal endings. (Don't be nervous, this is the only tense that does!) These special endings are shown in **TABLE 4-6**.

Table 4-6	Special Personal Endings for Perfect Tense	
Person	**Singular**	**Plural**
First	*–ī* (I)	*–imus* (we)
Second	*–istī* (you)	*–istis* (you)
Third	*–it* (he/she/it)	*–ērunt* (they)

Forming the Perfect Tense

A verb in perfect tense consists of a perfect stem, which you get from taking the third principle part and dropping the final *–ī*, then adding one of the special perfect personal endings. A full conjugation of the verb in perfect tense would look like **TABLE 4-7**.

Table 4-7	Perfect Tense of *dō, dare, dedī, datum*	
Person	**Singular**	**Plural**
First	*dedī* (I gave)	*dedimus* (we gave)
Second	*dedistī* (you gave)	*dedistis* (you gave)
Third	*dedit* (he/she/it gave)	*dedērunt* (they gave)

Using the Perfect Tense

The perfect tense takes on the role of two original tenses on the aspect chart (**TABLE 3-1**). As the present time completed tense, it stresses the current "doneness" of an action. As the past time aorist aspect tense, it simply refers to something that happened. Those two functions merge to create a tense that denotes a single completed act. The possible translations for the form *vēnērunt* are few:

> they came (just once)
> they did come
> they have come

The imperfect tense (continuous aspect) and the perfect tense (completed aspect) are often contrasted with one another. Here is a sentence that makes the distinction very clear: *Canēs latrābant cum advēnit.* ("The dogs were barking when he arrived.")

The barking took place over a period of time and was in progress (imperfect *latrābant*) when the arrival—a single completed act (perfect *advēnit*)—occurred.

Practice Conjugating the Perfect

Conjugate these verbs fully in the perfect tense. Check the back of the book to see how well you do.

1. *pōnō, pōnere, posuī, positum*

2. *capiō, capere, cēpī, captum*

3. *amō, amāre, amāvī, amātum*

4. *habeō, habēre, habuī, habitum*

5. *audiō, audīre, audīvī, audītum*

The Irregular Verb *Sum*

The most notoriously irregular verb in any language is the verb "to be." Just look at how unpredictable it is in English: I "am," you "are," he "is" ... with past tense forms "was" and "were," not to mention having "been" for a participle!

Latin's version of this verb with an identity crisis is *sum, esse, fuī, futūrus*. It may have weird principle parts and a strange-looking perfect stem, but it follows the rules for perfect tense conjugation.

Table 4-8   Perfect Tense of the Verb *sum* (to Be)

Person	Singular	Plural
First	*fuī* (I have been *or* was)	*fuimus* (we were)
Second	*fuistī* (you have been *or* were)	*fuistis* (you were)
Third	*fuit* (he/she/it has been *or* was)	*fuērunt* (they were)

The imperfect forms of *sum*, however, do not.

Table 4-9   Imperfect Tense of the Verb *sum* (to Be)

Person	Singular	Plural
First	*eram* (I was)	*erāmus* (we were)
Second	*erās* (you were)	*erātis* (you were)
Third	*erat* (he/she/it was)	*erant* (they were)

Latin-to-English Translations

Translate each of the following Latin words into English.

1. *accēpī* ....

2. *amābās* ....

3. *cēpit* ....

4. *dabāmus* ....

5. *dīcēbat* ....

6. *erant* ....

7. *fēcimus* ....

8. *fuērunt* ....

9. *agēbam* ....

10. *habuistis* ....

English-to-Latin Translations

1. she used to love

....

2. you (plural) have given

....

3. he was (and maybe still is)

....

4. he was (and isn't anymore)

....

5. I did

....

Chapter 5

Knowing Nouns

A noun is a person, place, thing, or idea. This may seem simple, but there is much more to nouns than that. Nouns bring the actions that verbs represent out of abstraction and into a real world. Just who was he who did that? To whom did he do it? In what place? Using what tool? Whose tool was it? The verb may be the essential core of a sentence, but nouns are what make gossip worthwhile!

The Anatomy of a Latin Noun

The two most essential parts of speech are verbs and nouns. In Chapter 3 you were presented with a map of the entire verb system: the picture on the puzzle box. Latin nouns also have a system that is unlike English and requires an overview. As you did with verbs, take your time reading about the noun system, and don't be upset if it doesn't all make sense at first. Latin wasn't built in a day! As with the overview of the verb system, return to this chapter and review it when you learn new concepts involving nouns. With every review the picture will become increasingly clear.

Noun endings are crucial in Latin. They are the only way you know how a noun functions in a sentence. They must be learned by heart. The best plan is to make yourself a chart, adding to it as you learn new sets of endings. Keep this chart out when you do your exercises and refer to it as necessary.

Nouns in Latin have a set of special characteristics just as verbs do. The list for nouns, however, is much shorter. There are three main characteristics by which nouns can be described. They are gender, number, and case.

Gender

Words in English have gender. When we speak English, we don't even think about words as having any gender at all. It is easy to think of the word "woman" as being feminine, the word "man" as masculine, and the word "book" as neuter (*neuter* is the Latin word for "neither"). The fact that these words really do have gender is revealed when we use pronouns to stand in for nouns.

We saw *Denise* at the auto parts store.
We saw *her* at the auto parts store.

She was telling *the guy* what she wanted.
She was telling *him* what she wanted.

He said he could find *the part* in the back.
He said he could find *it* in the back.

We don't even think twice about "Denise" being a "she," "the guy" being a "he," and "the part" being an "it." In saying those things, though, we're showing we know gender and use it in language.

In English things are pretty cut-and-dried. Words that refer to things that have male physical characteristics are masculine (e.g., Bob, guy, gentleman). If the physical characteristics are female (e.g., Emily, gal, lady), then the word is feminine. If neither applies, we consider it neuter and say it. (The only exception is for the word "ship." We still refer to a ship as a "she.")

FACT

Latin also has nouns that could refer to a male or a female, just as English. For example, take the words "citizen" (*civis*) or "dog" (*canis*). These words are said to have common gender. It should also be pointed out that in a mixed group—males and females— masculine is always the correct grammatical gender. A zillion women are feminine, but let one guy in and the group's gender switches to masculine.

English draws its lines for gender of nouns on purely natural criteria. In grammar, that rule for gender distinction is called natural gender. Latin also recognizes the same three genders (masculine, feminine, and neuter), and also assigns gender to nouns based on physical characteristics. In addition, Latin uses what is called grammatical gender. Grammatical gender works much like the English word "ship." There is no anatomical reason for a ship to be a "she." That's just what we say. Likewise, in Latin a table (*mēnsa*) is a "she," and so is a tree (*arbor*). Even things like trust (*fidēs*) and dirt (*humus*) are feminine. There are also objects in Latin that are grammatically masculine, like a cart (*carrus*). To the Roman mind, some nouns didn't fit either category. They were declared neuter: *tempus* ("time") for instance.

Number

As with verbs, there are two numbers: singular and plural.

Case

The concept of grammatical case is difficult to explain. To say that case refers to a system of endings for nouns that reveal a noun's function in a sentence is not especially satisfying. When English was a highly inflected language (i.e., one that relied on endings rather than word order), cases were abundant. In modern English, we are left with only one case for nouns and three for pronouns. That one surviving noun case in English is the genitive case. It refers to the ending "'s" (or "s'" in the plural) to show one noun's possession of another, as in "Donna's garden."

Latin's Case System

Latin's (and English's) case system goes back to Proto-Indo-European. There were special endings (case endings) attached to nouns to show how they functioned in a sentence. The system works the same as when we add "'s" to a word to show possession, but there were other endings to show many other functions. In the eyes of our linguistic forebears, there were eight different things a noun could do in a sentence, so there were eight different cases to show each of those eight things. (Remember, a case is just a certain group of letters at the end of a word.) Six of those things related to the verb. For example, one case showed that that noun was the subject of the verb. Other cases indicated that the action was going away from, toward, or alongside the noun. A fifth case identified a noun as the place where something happened, while a sixth case showed on whose behalf something was done. A seventh case linked two nouns together in a special relationship (like possession), and an eighth turned a noun into an exclamation (e.g., Gail!).

Latin condensed these original eight into five cases to show a noun's function in a sentence. Actually, Latin has seven cases, but you don't see one very often and the other is reserved for certain words. We will cross those bridges when we come to them.

FACT

The modern descendants of Latin are called the Romance languages: They include French, Spanish, Italian, Romanian, Portuguese, Provençal, Catalan, and many others. (They are called Romance because of their Roman origin.) In them, all the cases have merged into one and they have to rely on word order for meaning.

The Declensions

Nouns are divided into classes called declensions. The concept of noun declensions in Latin is even easier than verbs because you can divide English nouns into groups as well. Have a look at **TABLE 5-1**:

Table 5-1	**English Declensions**				
First	**Second**	**Third**	**Fourth**	**Fifth**	**Sixth**
car	church	ox	goose	deer	louse
dog	tomato	child	foot	moose	mouse

Can you see on what basis these words are divided into these declensions (i.e., groups)? Look at how each group forms its plurals. Different groups for different endings. Our first declension takes an "–s" to form its plural, and the second declension takes an "–es" to show more than one. The third declension adds "–en," but "child" is a bit of an exception because it inserts an *r* before the ending. We could call words with this variation, third declension *r*-stems. The fourth declension changes "oo" to "ee," while the fifth declension doesn't add or change anything at all. The strangest of our English declensions is the sixth. The internal "ous" becomes "ic." (Even stranger is that we don't live in a "hice"!)

Latin has five declensions, plus a handful of irregular nouns. (You will meet the irregulars along the way, one by one.) Because of all the cases involved, Latin nouns have more than just a plural to worry about. Every noun can take ten forms, one for each of the five cases, singular and plural.

Here is an overview of each of the five declensions. Remember: This is just a roundup of all the forms. Don't try to learn all of them all at once!

In the rest of this chapter, you will work with only the nominative and accusative case forms. They appear in these charts in boldface to make them easier for you to pick out. The others are presented simply so you can see the big picture.

First Declension

The gender of all first declension words is feminine unless the word refers to a male being (e.g., *nauta*, "sailor").

Table 5-2	First Declension: "wing"				
Case	Singular	Plural	Case	Singular	Plural
Nominative	**āla**	**ālae**	Accusative	**ālam**	**ālās**
Genitive	ālae	ālārum	Ablative	ālā	ālīs
Dative	ālae	ālīs			

Second Declension

Second declension words are either masculine or neuter. The first word declined in **TABLE 5-3**, *servus*, is a typical second declension masculine noun with a nominative singular ending in "–us." The next word, *puer*, takes all the same endings that *servus* does, it just doesn't have the "–us" in the nominative singular.

The third word seems to work like *puer*, but if you look closer, you will notice that after the initial form *ager*, suddenly the endings are pasted onto *agr–*. The *e* dropped out! This phenomenon is called a stem change.

There are a few second declension –er words that change their stems, but where you will see it as a normal course of events will be in third declension.

Before we move on to third declension, there is still one word to discuss: *templum. Templum* is a typical second declension neuter word. The –*um* in the nominative singular is what gives it away. Compare the endings across the whole chart and you will see that they are all the same, except in a couple of places. Neuter nouns are very easy to work with if you remember the double neuter rule:

- Nominative and accusative forms are always the same.
- Nominative plural always ends in –*a*.

Case	slave	boy	field	temple
		Singular		
Nominative	**servus**	**puer**	**ager**	**templum**
Genitive	servī	puerī	agrī	templī
Dative	servō	puerō	agrō	templō
Accusative	**servum**	**puerum**	**agrum**	**templum**
Ablative	servō	puerō	agrō	templō
		Plural		
Nominative	**servī**	**puerī**	**agrī**	**templa**
Genitive	servōrum	puerōrum	agrōrum	templōrum
Dative	servīs	puerīs	agrīs	templīs
Accusative	**servōs**	**puerōs**	**agrōs**	**templa**
Ablative	servīs	puerīs	agrīs	templīs

Table 5-3   Second Declension

Third Declension

Most Latin nouns are third declension, so it is an extremely important group. They also constitute the least friendly of the declensions. They're not hostile; they're just very particular. Here are the most important facts to keep in mind when working with them:

- Third declension has words of all genders. In **TABLE 5-4**, for example, *homō* is masculine, *māter* is feminine, and *iter* is neuter.
- There is no predictable nominative singular ending in third declension. You must learn each one as you learn your vocabulary.
- Most third declension words have stem changes. You must learn them as you learn your vocabulary as well.
- The endings always go on the modified stem.
- The endings are the same for masculine and feminine words. Neuters follow the double neuter rule.

Table 5-4	Third Declension		
Case	person	mother	route
	Singular		
Nominative	**homō**	**māter**	**iter**
Genitive	homin*is*	matr*is*	itiner*is*
Dative	homin*ī*	matr*ī*	itiner*ī*
Accusative	**homin*em***	**matr*em***	**iter**
Ablative	homin*e*	matr*e*	itiner*e*
	Plural		
Nominative	**homin*ēs***	**matr*ēs***	**itiner*a***
Genitive	homin*um*	matr*um*	itiner*um*
Dative	homin*ibus*	matr*ibus*	itiner*ibus*
Accusative	**homin*ēs***	**matr*ēs***	**itiner*a***
Ablative	homin*ibus*	matr*ibus*	itiner*ibus*

Fourth Declension

Fourth declension words are masculine. There are two common exceptions, namely *manus* ("hand") and *domus* ("house"), which are feminine. (There are also a few neuters, but they are too uncommon for you to worry about them.)

Table 5-5 Fourth Declension: "hand"		
Case	**Singular**	**Plural**
Nominative	**man***us*	**man***ūs*
Genitive	man*ūs*	man*uum*
Dative	man*uī*	man*ibus*
Accusative	**man***um*	**man***ūs*
Ablative	man*ū*	man*ibus*

Fifth Declension: Trust

Fifth declension words are all feminine with one exception—*diēs* ("day"), which is masculine. There are no neuters. Fifth declension has the smallest population of all the declensions. Ironically, the most common noun in the whole Latin language, *rēs* ("thing"), belongs to this group.

Table 5-6 Fifth Declension: "trust"		
Case	**Singular**	**Plural**
Nominative	**fid***ēs*	**fid***ēs*
Genitive	fid*eī*	fid*ērum*
Dative	fid*eī*	fid*ēbus*
Accusative	**fid***em*	**fid***ēs*
Ablative	fid*ē*	fid*ēbus*

Principle Parts for Nouns

The term "principle parts" actually refers only to verbs, but we can extend it to nouns for the moment. For verbs, you can tell which conjugation a verb is by looking at its second principle part, the infinitive. Verbs with –*āre* are first conjugation, –*ēre* are second, and so on. Latin nouns are classified into declensions based on how they form their genitive case.

The genitive case is the second one down on the charts, right after the nominative. When you look a noun up in the dictionary, or when you learn your vocabulary, you will find dictionary entries that look like this:

terra, –ae, f. (land, earth)   *tempus, temporis*, n. (time)
deus, –ī, m. (god)   *exercitus, –ūs*, m. (army)
caelum, –ī, n. (sky, heaven)   *fidēs, –eī*, f. (trust)
rēx, rēgis, m. (king)

Each entry provides you with four pieces of information, and they are all you need to be able to work with or understand that noun. First is the nominative case form. This is especially important for third declension words since there is no regular, predictable nominative ending for third declension words. The second item is the genitive singular form. The third is an abbreviation referring to the word's gender. The fourth bit of information is meaning and usage.

The second item, the genitive form, is extremely important. It tells you two crucial things. First, it says what declension the word belongs to. Their nominative forms or genders don't play a role in that decision. Here is a breakdown of how to tell them apart.

- All nouns with a genitive in *–ae* are first declension.
- All nouns with a genitive in *–ī* are second declension.
- All nouns with a genitive in *–is* are third declension.
- All nouns with a genitive in *–ūs* are fourth declension.
- All nouns with a genitive in *–eī* are fifth declension.

In addition to signaling declension, the genitive form shows you whether the word has a stem change, and if it does, what that change is.

In the list of words given above, you know *terra* is first declension because its genitive form is *–ae* (or *terrae* once you attach the ending). *Deus* is second declension and becomes *deī* when you decline it. *Caelum* is also second declension. The word *rēx* is third declension. The second form for *rēx* tells you that it is third declension because it ends in *–is,* and that *rēg–* is the stem that all the endings will go on.

Table 5-7	Vocabulary
canis, canis, c.*	dog
dea, deae, f.	goddess
deus, deī, m.	god
diēs, diēī, m.	day
dominus, dominī, m.	master
domus, domūs, f.	house
exercitus, exercitūs, m.	army
homō, hominis, m.	person, man (as opposed to an animal); people
locus, locī, m.**	place
manus, manūs, f.	hand
mulier, mulieris, f.	woman
nihil, n.***	nothing
nōn (adverb)	not
pater, patris, m.	father
rēs, reī, f.	thing, matter, affair, situation, stuff
rēx, rēgis, m.	king
servus, servī, m.	slave
tempus, temporis, n.	time
vir, virī, m.	man
vīta, vitae, f.	life

* c. is for common gender. Dogs can be masculine or feminine.
** The plural of *locus* can be masculine (*locī*) or neuter (*loca*).
*** *Nihil* also contracts to *nīl*; *nihil* is indeclinable, meaning it doesn't take any endings.

EXERCISE

Practicing Noun Declensions

For each of the nouns in the vocabulary list above, tell which declension it is, then give the accusative singular and plural forms. Check your answers in the back of the book.

Earlier in this chapter when we sorted English nouns into declensions based on their endings, it was jokingly noted that the plural of "house" is not "hice." Likewise, if the plural of "foot" is "feet," why shouldn't "deer" be the plural of "door"? It just isn't! You might have noticed a similar situation in the previous list: *deus, deī* (second declension); *tempus, temporis* (third declension—with a stem change!); and *exercitus, exercitūs* (fourth declension). For each of these words, the nominative ends in *–us,* but that information by itself doesn't tell you which declension the word belongs to. You also have to know the genitive to know that. If the genitive of *deus* is *deī,* then it's second declension and can take only second declension endings.

The word "declension" with reference to nouns works much like the word "conjugation" does with verbs. A declension can be the group a noun belongs to, but it can also refer to a chart that shows all a noun's forms. To decline a noun means to make a chart showing all the endings.

Subjects and Objects

There is an old saying that the headline "Dog Bites Man" is not news. "Man Bites Dog" *is* news. The humor in this relies on knowing who sunk teeth into whom. Or, in grammatical terms, which is the subject and which is the object. The biter is the subject of the verb. The one on the receiving end (ouch!) is the object, or, more precisely, the direct object.

English is an analytical language. It shows subjects and objects by their position in a sentence. In essence, there are slots where words can be plugged in: subject–verb–direct object. Whatever fills the first slot, be it dog or man, performs the action. Whatever fills the slot after the verb receives the action. In English, that's how news is made.

But Latin is an inflected language. Subjects and objects are determined by case endings. Nominative case endings show the subject, regardless of a noun's position in a sentence. Accusative case endings show the object.

Word order in Latin is usually subject–object–verb. But it doesn't have to be in that order. If this order changes, the emphasis shifts. *Vir canem mordet* ("man bites dog") is normal word order. It answers the question "Who bites dog?" (Man.) *Canem vir mordet* still means "man bites dog" (same case endings), but it answers the question "What does man bite?" (Dog.)

The Nominative Case

The primary use of the nominative case is to show the subject of a verb. A verb's personal ending already represents a subject ("I," "you," "he," "she," "it," etc.), so nominatives are not necessary unless more information is needed. In that situation, a word in the nominative case can pinpoint exactly who or what is performing the action. If a nominative subject is expressed, it appears *in addition to* the personal ending.

> *veniēbat* (he was coming *or* she was coming *or* it was coming)
> *rēx veniēbat* (the king was coming)

If the nominative subject is plural, the verb ending must also be plural. This is called subject/verb agreement.

> *habēbant* (they used to have)
> *virī habēbant* (the men used to have)

Table 5-8 Nominative Case Endings		
Declension	**Singular**	**Plural**
First	*–a*	*–ae*
Second	*–us/r–*	*–ī*
Third	—	*–ēs*
Fourth	*–us*	*–ūs*
Fifth	*–ēs*	*–ēs*

A sentence can be divided into two parts. There is the subject; then there is the rest of the sentence. The rest of the sentence—what is being said about the subject—is called the predicate. In the sentence "the plant on the windowsill fell over onto the floor," the subject is what is being talked about, namely, the plant on the windowsill. The predicate is what you have to say about it: it fell onto the floor.

QUESTION?

What is agreement?
Two words are said to agree when they share whatever characteristics they have in common. Nouns have gender, *number*, and case. Verbs have person, *number*, tense, mood, and voice. So subjects and verbs agree in number.

If the person or thing in the predicate is the same person or thing as the subject, then their endings (their cases) have to agree. As you know, the subject of a sentence in Latin goes in the nominative case. If you have to put a word in the nominative case in the predicate to make it agree with the subject, it is called a predicate nominative.

Gulliēmus erat rēx. (William was king.)

Gulliēmus is the subject, so he's in the nominative. *Rēx* is also in the nominative because "king" refers to the same person as "William." Another way to look at it is that the verb *erat* ("was") works like an equals sign (=). What's on one side has to be the same as what's on the other side.

ALERT!

Forms of the verb "to be" (*sum*, *esse*) usually sit in the middle or at the end of a sentence. When they appear at the very beginning of a sentence, they usually just show existence: *Virī erant Romānī.* ("The men were Romans.") *Erant virī Romānī.* ("There were Roman men.")

The Accusative Case

The basic concept of the accusative case is to set an endpoint to an action. It shows what is directly affected and where the action stops. When you hit the ball, the hitting stops when you connect with the ball. If you go to Rome, the going stops when you get to Rome.

The most common function for a word in the accusative case is called the direct object. For example, the phrase "she ate" begs the question "Ate what?" That "what" is the direct object. "She ate a salad." Ah! That's better. According to the sentence, a salad is what she ate and that's where the eating stopped. "Frank took . . ." Took what? You can't just take; you have to take *something,* be it my advice, a nap, a bullet, a snapshot, or cash from the till. That *something* is the direct object. Look again at our dog sentence—which is the direct object in each sentence?

> *Canis virum mordet.* (Dog bites man.)
> *Vir canem mordet.* (Man bites dog.)

5-9	Accusative Case Endings					
Declension	Singular	Plural		Declension	Singular	Plural
First	*–am*	*–ās*		Fourth	*–um*	*–ūs*
Second	*–um*	*–ōs*		Fifth	*–em*	*–ēs*
Third	*–em*	*–ēs*				

Lined up in a chart, accusative case forms reveal remarkably easy to learn and recognize patterns. That's a real blessing since it is among the most common cases. A verb can get by with personal endings for its subject and not need a nominative, but for a direct object, a noun in the accusative is the only game in town.

ALERT!

There are two kinds of verbs: transitive and intransitive. Transitive verbs are ones that show an action that is performed on something (e.g., "kick," "sell," "leave"). They *must* have a direct object. Intransitive verbs are ones that show a state of being or motion from place to place (e.g., "be," "sleep," "rely," "go"). They *cannot* have a direct object.

Latin-to-English Translations

Translate the following Latin sentences into English.

1. *Servum tenuit.*

2. *Dominī servōs habēbant.*

3. *Canis mulierem amābat.*

4. *Mulierēs hominēs accēpērunt.*

5. *Dominōs servī nōn amābant.*

English-to-Latin Translations

Translate each of the following sentences into Latin.

1. They were considering the situation.

2. People considered the king god.

3. The woman used to like the house.

4. You had time.

5. The man loved his dog.

Chapter 6

Using Adjectives

Now that you've met verbs and nouns, it's time to add some color to them. Adjectives are the modifiers that describe a noun, making a general reference more specific. A dog can become a brown dog, or a dark brown dog, or a tiny, dark brown dog. In this chapter you will see how adjectives work in Latin. You will find that everything you learned about nouns will be important here as well.

Adjective/Noun Agreement

When two words share form characteristics, they are said to agree. Latin nouns bear the characteristics of gender, case, and number. Latin adjectives also have gender, case, and number. Since adjectives have to agree with whatever noun they go with, they must be able to appear in any gender, any case, and any number.

Here are some sentences with the adjective *bonus* ("good") that will illustrate the principle of adjective/noun agreement.

Dominus bonus servum habēbat.
　　(The good master used to have a slave.)

Dominus servum bonum habēbat.
　　(The master used to have a good slave.)

Dominus servōs bonōs habēbat.
　　(The master used to have good slaves.)

Dominus multōs servōs bonōs habēbat.
　　(The master used to have many good slaves.)

Dea erat bona. (The goddess was good.)
Deae erant bonae. (The goddesses were good.)

Vitam bonam habuit. (He had a good life.)
Virī bonī vitās bonās habuērunt. (The good men had good lives.)

Modifiers in Latin tend to follow the words they modify. (Adjectives referring to size or quantity are the exception.) If you think about it, it makes a tad more sense than what we do in English, which is describe something before even saying what it is that's being described.

That seems simple enough, doesn't it? Let's take a closer look at the grammar of the last sentence in the example.

Virī   Nominative plural because it's the subject. (*Vir* is second declension masculine.)

bonī   Nominative plural masculine because it *agrees with* the subject.

vitās   Accusative plural because it is the direct object. (*vīta* is first declension feminine)

bonās   Accusative plural feminine because it *agrees with* the direct object.

habuērunt   Third person plural (because the subject is plural), perfect tense (because they don't have them anymore).

That still seems pretty simple. Nouns have case uses (such as nominative case to show a subject). An adjective simply duplicates (i.e., agrees in) the gender, case, and number of the noun it is modifying.

Table 6-1 Vocabulary	
alius, –a, –ud	another, other
aliī . . . aliī	some . . . others
aut, conj.	or
aut . . . aut, conj.	either . . . or
bonus, –a, –um	good
brevis, –e	short
difficilis, –e	hard, difficult
dūcō, dūcere, dūxī, ductum	to take someone someplace, lead
dulcis, –e	sweet
et, conj.	and, even, too
et . . . et, conj.	both . . . and
facilis, –e	easy
fēlix, fēlīcis	happy, lucky
fortis, –e	strong, brave

continued on following page

Table 6-1   Vocabulary—*continued*

gravis, –e	heavy, serious
iam, adv.	now, already (basic idea: *at this point in time*)
ingēns, ingentis	huge
inveniō, invenīre, invēnī, inventum	to find
longē, adv.	far
longus, –a, –um	long
magnus, –a, –um	large, great
malus, –a, –um	bad, evil
meus, –a, –um	my
mīles, mīlitis, m.	soldier
multus, –a, –um	much, many
neque (nec), conj.	and . . . not
neque . . . neque, conj.	neither . . . nor
nunc, adv.	now (basic idea: *right now as we speak*)
omnis, –e	every, all
petō, petere, petīvī, petītum	to ask, look for, attack, to go after something
quia, conj.	because
quoque, adv.	also
saepe, adv.	often
sed, conj.	but, instead, rather
semper, adv.	always
senex, senis	old
sī, conj.	if
sīc, adv.	like this, thus
suus, –a, –um	his, her, its (own)
tristis, –e	sad
tum, adv.	then
tuus, –a, –um	your (singular)
vetus, veteris	old

The "Parts" of an Adjective

In order for you to read the entries for adjectives in the dictionary, or even look them up effectively, you need to know what are the "parts" dictionaries list for adjectives. There are two groups of adjectives: first/second declension adjectives and third declension adjectives.

Dictionaries list first/second declension adjectives by giving you the nominative singular for each of the three genders. The entry for the word *bonus*, for example, is *bonus, –a, –um*. Compare this to the chart for *bonus* in **TABLE 6-2** and you will see that the dictionary entry represents the nominative singular masculine, feminine, and neuter in that order: *bonus, bona, bonum*, just like the first row of the chart.

The dictionary listings for third declension adjectives are trickier because third declension adjectives fall into three sub-groups. We will discuss them separately.

First/Second Declension Adjectives

First/second declension adjectives take all their endings from . . . you guessed it, first and second declensions. They go to first declension for their feminine forms, and second declension for their masculine and neuter forms. A full declensional chart for a first/second declension adjective looks like this:

Table 6-2   The First/Second Declension Adjective *bonus, –a, –um* (good)

Case	Masc.	Fem.	Neut.
		Singular	
Nominative	*bonus*	*bona*	*bonum*
Genitive	*bonī*	*bonae*	*bonī*
Dative	*bonō*	*bonae*	*bonō*
Accusative	*bonum*	*bonam*	*bonum*
Ablative	*bonō*	*bonā*	*bonō*

continued on following page

Table 6-2   The First/Second Declension Adjective *bonus, –a, –um* (good) —*continued*

	Plural		
Nominative	*bonī*	*bonae*	*bona*
Genitive	*bonōrum*	*bonārum*	*bonōrum*
Dative	*bonīs*	*bonīs*	*bonīs*
Accusative	*bonōs*	*bonās*	*bona*
Ablative	*bonīs*	*bonīs*	*bonīs*

ALERT!

Adjectives must agree with the nouns they modify in gender, case, and number, but not in declension!

When first/second declension adjectives are paired with first or second declension nouns, they're usually a perfect fit in that they rhyme (e.g., *vīta longa, servōs bonōs*). When first/second declension adjectives are mated with third, fourth, or fifth declension nouns, however, they usually *don't* rhyme.

Here are some examples in the nominative singular:

homō bonus (a good person)   *domus bona* (a good house)
mulier bona (a good woman)   *rēs bona* (a good thing)
tempus bonum (a good time)

When nouns appear in other cases than the nominative, their adjectives continue to agree in gender, case, and number. They also stay whatever declension they happen to be—that never changes. Here are the same noun/adjective combinations in the accusative plural:

hominēs bonōs (good people)   *domūs bonās* (good houses)
mulierēs bonās (good women)   *rēs bonās* (good things)
tempora bona (good times)

In all these examples, the adjective and its noun agree in gender, case, and number. The adjective *bonus, –a, –um* happens to be a first/second declension adjective; *rēs* happens to be a fifth declension noun. That doesn't matter. They still can and do agree in gender, case, and number, so *rēs bonās* may not look like a perfect match, but they're both feminine accusative plural, and that's all the matters.

Practice with First and Second Declension Adjectives

Translate the following adjective/noun pairs, then give their case and number. Example: *canēs malōs* bad dogs (acc. pl.)

1. *vīta longa*

2. *deās bonās*

3. *rem aliam*

4. *domūs magnās*

5. *hominēs malōs*

6. *manūs meās*

7. *pater suus*

8. *servōs altōs*

9. *tempus bonum*

10. *tempora bona*

Third Declension Adjectives

Just as first/second declension adjectives take their endings from first and second declension nouns, third declension adjectives take their endings from third declension nouns. There are a few exceptions to this, though. Here is a chart showing the endings for third declension adjectives.

Case	Masc.	Fem.	Neut.
Table 6-3	**Third Declension Adjective Endings**		
		Singular	
Nominative	*	*	*
Genitive	–*is*	–*is*	–*is*
Dative	–*ī*	–*ī*	–*ī*
Accusative	–*em*	–*em*	*
Ablative	–*ī*	–*ī*	–*ī*
		Plural	
Nominative	–*ēs*	–*ēs*	–*ia*
Genitive	–*ium*	–*ium*	–*ium*
Dative	–*ibus*	–*ibus*	–*ibus*
Accusative	–*ēs*	–*ēs*	–*ia*
Ablative	–*ibus*	–*ibus*	–*ibus*

* No predictable ending.

The differences among the forms for third declension nouns and third declension adjectives are given in bold to help you distinguish them. They largely consist of the letter *i* appearing in places you wouldn't have expected. The ablative singular is –*ī* instead of –*e*. The genitive plural is –*ium* instead of plain –*um*, and the neuter plural shows –*ia* rather than the usual simple –*a*. (Notice how the double neuter rule applies for adjectives, too!)

As you may recall, third declension nouns do not have any predictable endings for the nominative singular. You have to learn them by memorization. Third declension adjectives have the same quality—hence the asterisks in the chart above. Also like third declension nouns, third declension adjectives are predictable once you get past the nominative and know the stem change (if there is one). Unlike third declension nouns, however, third declension adjectives can be grouped into three types, which makes things a little easier. The groupings are determined by the number of different nominative singular forms (called terminations) an adjective has.

ALERT!

Remember, adjectives agree with their nouns only in gender, case, and number. Wherever third declension adjective endings vary from those of third declension nouns, that variation appears when third declension nouns and adjectives are together. "With every woman," for instance, would be *cum omnī muliere*. Both *omnī* and *muliere* happen to be third declension words, but their endings don't quite look it.

Third Declension Adjectives of Three Terminations

Third declension adjectives of three terminations have three different forms for their nominative singular—one for each gender.

Table 6-4 Third Declension Adjectives of Three Terminations: *ācer, ācris, ācre* ("sharp, fierce")			
Case	**Masc.**	**Fem.**	**Neut.**
Singular			
Nominative	*ācer*	*ācris*	*ācre*
Genitive	*ācris*	*ācris*	*ācris*
Dative	*ācrī*	*ācrī*	*ācrī*
Accusative	*ācrem*	*ācrem*	*ācre*
Ablative	*ācrī*	*ācrī*	*ācrī*
Plural			
Nominative	*ācrēs*	*ācrēs*	*ācria*
Genitive	*ācrium*	*ācrium*	*ācrium*
Dative	*ācribus*	*ācribus*	*ācribus*
Accusative	*ācrēs*	*ācrēs*	*ācria*
Ablative	*ācribus*	*ācribus*	*ācribus*

In the dictionary listing *ācer, ācris, ācre* ("sharp, fierce"), the first form, *ācer*, is the masculine nominative singular, the second is the feminine, and the last one is neuter. Based on this adjective classification system, you could say that all first/second declension adjectives are adjectives of three terminations, since they all have three nominative singular forms (*–us, –a, –um*), a different one for the masculine, feminine, and neuter.

Third Declension Adjectives of Two Terminations

Take a look at the declension below for the adjective *omnis, omne* ("every," "all"). You will notice that in the nominative singular, the masculine and feminine forms are identical and only the neuter is different. Third declension adjectives with only two different nominative singular endings are called third declension adjectives of two terminations. Their listing in the dictionary looks like this: *omnis, –e*.

Case	Masc.	Fem.	Neut.
Table 6-5 Third Declension Adjectives of Two Terminations: omnis, –e ("every," "all")			
Singular			
Nominative	*omnis*	*omnis*	*omne*
Genitive	*omnis*	*omnis*	*omnis*
Dative	*omnī*	*omnī*	*omnī*
Accusative	*omnem*	*omnem*	*omne*
Ablative	*omnī*	*omnī*	*omnī*
Plural			
Nominative	*omnēs*	*omnēs*	*omnia*
Genitive	*omnium*	*omnium*	*omnium*
Dative	*omnibus*	*omnibus*	*omnibus*
Accusative	*omnēs*	*omnēs*	*omnia*
Ablative	*omnibus*	*omnibus*	*omnibus*

The first word in the dictionary listing, *omnis,* is the same for the masculine and feminine nominative singular. The *–e* part means that its neuter nominative singular is *omne*. Virtually all third declension adjectives of two terminations follow the pattern –*is*, –*e* in their dictionary listing.

Third Declension Adjectives of One Termination

Third declension adjectives of one termination have only one form for the nominative singular. The same form works for all three genders. The tricky part comes in the dictionary listing for them. Since third declension adjectives of one termination almost always have stem changes when they appear in any case other than the nominative singular, a dictionary can't just give you the nominative singular as it does for all other kinds of adjectives. If it did, there would be no way for you to know that the adjective *ingēns* ("huge"), for example, changes to *ingent*– when you start putting endings on it. To get around this problem, a dictionary gives you the genitive singular form, which illustrates the stem change. Therefore, the listing for *ingēns* is: *ingēns, ingentis*.

Table 6-6 Third Declension Adjectives of One Termination: *ingēns, ingentis* ("huge")			
Case	**Masc.**	**Fem.**	**Neut.**
Singular			
Nominative	*ingēns*	*ingēns*	*ingēns*
Genitive	*ingentis*	*ingentis*	*ingentis*
Dative	*ingentī*	*ingentī*	*ingentī*
Accusative	*ingentem*	*ingentem*	*ingente*
Ablative	*ingentī*	*ingentī*	*ingentī*
Plural			
Nominative	*ingentēs*	*ingentēs*	*ingentia*
Genitive	*ingentium*	*ingentium*	*ingentium*
Dative	*ingentibus*	*ingentibus*	*ingentibus*
Accusative	*ingentēs*	*ingentēs*	*ingentia*
Ablative	*ingentibus*	*ingentibus*	*ingentibus*

The first form of the dictionary listing is the nominative singular for the masculine, feminine, and neuter genders. The second form is the genitive. The sole purpose of the second word in the entry is to inform you of the stem change. With this information, you know that *ingentem montem* ("huge mountain") is the accusative singular from the nominative *ingēns mōns*.

Practice with Third Declension Adjectives

Translate the following adjective/noun pairs then give their case and number. Example: *omnēs mulierēs* all women (acc. pl. or nom. pl.)

1. *nihil facile*

2. *mulierem tristem*

3. *vitae brevēs*

4. *dominōs felicēs*

5. *vīta fēlix*

6. *rēx senex*

7. *mulier senex*

8. *fēlīcis*

9. *mīlitem fortem*

10. *rēs gravēs*

Substantives

Don't be surprised when you run across adjectives with no nouns around to agree with! The nouns they refer to are assumed. These are called substantives. We have them in English, too. Take the adjective *poor* for instance. If you talk about "the poor," the noun *people* is understood. Latin substantives are far more specific since Latin has distinct genders. A *bona*, for example, is "a good woman." The word *woman* is understood because the form is feminine. Likewise, *bonī* are "good men." The word *virī* isn't necessary since *bonī* is already masculine.

A substantive, then, is an adjective acting like a noun. Since it acts like a noun, that is to say it's independent and isn't agreeing with anything, you must treat it like a noun, using its case endings as regular noun functions.

Bonī in locō malō erant. (The good men were in a bad place.)

Bonī is nominative plural because it is the subject. *Malō* is ablative singular because it agrees with *locō*. (You'll learn about the ablative case in the next chapter.)

Substantives sometimes appear as just ordinary nouns. From the adjective *amicus, –a, –um* (friendly), you could make the substantive *amicus, –ī*, m. (male friend), or *amica, –ae*, f. (female friend). The most common substantive of all comes from the adjective *omnis, –e. Omnēs* is "everybody" ("all men") and *omnia* is "everything" ("all things").

Practice with Substantives

Translate the following substantives into English. Example: *alia* "another woman" or "other things"

1. *omnis*

2. *multa*

3. *dulcia*

4. *senem*

5. *tristēs*

6. *difficile*

7. *brevia*

8. *bonum*

9. *multī*

10. *aliae*

Chapter 7

Making Comparisons

Adjectives and adverbs (words that modify verbs) can be used to make comparisons between things: John's drawing was good, but Meg's painting was better. In English we often have to use the words "more" and "most" to make these comparisons—not so with an inflected language like Latin. This chapter introduces you to Latin adverb formations and shows you how to compare them.

Forming Comparisons with Adjectives

English hasn't held on to very many inflections over the centuries, but in the realm of adjectives and adverbs, there are some extremely common ones. We like to compare this to that, and in doing so we employ endings that are attached to the ends of adjectives, namely "–er" and "–est," as in tall, tall*er*, tall*est*. These are called comparative endings. Many English adjectives (e.g., "beautiful") use the words "more" and "most" to make the change. As you would expect, Latin uses endings.

There are three degrees of comparison. First is the positive degree, which is the regular form of an adjective. Next are the comparative and superlative degrees. Each of them has its own endings and special uses.

The comparative degree of adjectives does just what its name implies—it is used to make comparisons such as "Jeff is *stronger* than Pete." In Latin, the comparative does a bit more. In fact, when you usually see it, it's doing something other than strict comparison.

You may encounter Latin phrases that seem to be missing a verb, such as, "*Vita Brevis, ars longa.*" In most cases it is a form of the verb "to be" that is missing, and you'll need to fill it in when you translate: "Life (is) short, (but) art (is) long."

You will be glad to know that comparatives are easy to form and there is only one way to do it, no matter which kind of adjective (i.e., first/second or third declension) it started out as.

altus, alta, altum (tall) becomes *altior, altius* (taller)
longus, longa, longum (long) becomes *longior, longius* (longer)
fortis, forte (strong) becomes *fortior, fortius* (stronger)
ācer, ācris, ācre (fierce) becomes *ācrior, ācrius* (fiercer)

To form a comparative, all you need is an adjective's stem (changed stem if it undergoes a stem change), plus –*ior* for the masculine or feminine nominative singular and –*ius* for the neuter. If you guessed that all comparatives are third declension adjectives of two terminations, you're right. There is a slight twist in that they decline with normal third declension *noun* endings.

Here is a full declension of a comparative:

Table 7-1	Comparative Degree Declension of the Adjective *altus*, –a, –um ("tall, deep")		
Case	Masc.	Fem.	Neut.
	Singular		
Nominative	*altior*	*altior*	*altius*
Genitive	*altioris*	*altioris*	*altioris*
Dative	*altiorī*	*altiorī*	*altiorī*
Accusative	*altiorem*	*altiorem*	*altius*
Ablative	*altiore*	*altiore*	*altiore*
	Plural		
Nominative	*altiorēs*	*altiorēs*	*altiora*
Genitive	*altiorum*	*altiorum*	*altiorum*
Dative	*altioribus*	*altioribus*	*altioribus*
Accusative	*altiorēs*	*altiorēs*	*altiora*
Ablative	*altioribus*	*altioribus*	*altioribus*

It is not correct to say that *altior* means "taller" and leave it at that. It can be like the English "taller," but only if a direct comparison is being made.

Marcus erat altior quam Lucius. (Marcus was taller than Lucius.)

More often, the comparison is made simply to what you might expect.

Marcus erat altior.   (Marcus was rather tall.)
(Marcus was pretty tall.)
(Marcus was sort of tall.)
(Marcus was too tall.)

The word *quam* is used with adjectives and adverbs. It has different meanings depending on the degree of the adjective it is with. Examine the following examples and you will see.

Positive degree: *Quam celeriter cucurrit Marcus!*
                                    (**How** fast Marcus ran!)

Comparative degree: *Marcus celerius **quam** Titus cucurrit.*
                                    (Marcus ran faster **than** Titus.)

Superlative degree: *Gaius **quam** celerrimē currēbat.*
                                    (Gaius was running **as** fast **as he could**.)

The Superlative Degree

The superlative degree is easy to recognize and understand. The ending supplied to a noun is *–issimus*. Once again, it doesn't matter whether an adjective begins as a first/second or third declension adjective. All adjectives in the superlative degree are of the first/second declension variety (i.e., like *bonus, –a, –um*).

altus, alta, altum (tall) becomes *altissimus, –a, –um* (really tall)
longus, longa, longum (long) becomes *longissimus, –a, –um*
       (extremely long)
fortis, forte (strong) becomes *fortissimus* (very strong)

ALERT!

One important exception to the *–issimus* ending for superlatives applies to adjectives ending in *–er*. The adjective *ācer, ācris, ācre* (fierce), for instance, doubles the *r* on the unchanged stem and adds *–imus*, thus becoming *ācerrimus*. The adjectives *facilis* (easy), *difficilis* (difficult), *similis* (like), and *dissimilis* (unlike) do something similar with the final *l* on their stems (e.g., *facillimus*). Don't be fooled by them!

An adjective in the superlative degree represents a quality in the extreme. If a direct comparison is being made, then it can be like the English "–est."

> *Publius erat altissimus omnium puerōrum.*
> (Publius was the tallest of all the boys.)

As is the case with adjectives in the comparative degree, you will most commonly encounter superlatives on their own, showing nothing more than intense versions of themselves.

> *Publius erat altissimus.*   (Publius was very tall.)
> (Publius was extremely tall.)
> (Publius was unbelievably tall.)
> (Publius was how's-the-weather-up-there tall.)

Forming Comparatives

Translate the following noun phrases and substantives:

1. *hominem fortiorem* ....

2. *vitās longissimās* ....

3. *canis felicissimus* ....

4. *nihil gravius* ....

5. *difficillima* ....

6. *deōs fortiorēs* ....

7. *vir senior* ....

8. *rem faciliorem* ....

9. *diēs brevissima* ....

10. *mulierēs dulcissimae* ....

Irregular Comparison

English has some adjectives that don't behave themselves when forming the comparative and superlative. The degrees of the adjective "good," for instance, are not "gooder" and "goodest." They are, unpredictably, "good," "better," "best." Latin has its share of these irregulars as well. **TABLE 7-2** shows the most common of these adjectives that compare irregularly in Latin. They just have to be memorized. Most have English derivatives, which will help you remember them.

Table 7-2	Adjectives with Irregular Comparative Forms	
Positive	**Comparative**	**Superlative**
bonus (good)	*melior, melius*	*optimus*
malus (bad)	*peior, peius*	*pessimus*
magnus (big)	*maior, maius*	*maximus*
parvus (small)	*minor, minus*	*minimus*
superus (above)	*superior, superius*	*summus* (highest) or *supremus* (last)
inferus (below)	*inferior, inferius*	*īmus or infimus*
exter (foreign)	*exterior, exterius*	*extrēmus*
multus (much)	——, *plus**	*plurimus*
*prae*** (on front of)	*prior, prius*	*prīmus*
*prope*** (near)	*propior, propius*	*proximus*

* *Plus* is actually a noun in the singular (*plus, pluris*, n. —more), but in the plural it is a regular comparative adjective.
** The words *prae* and *prope* are prepositions, not adjectives. (You will learn about prepositions in Chapter 8.) The comparative and superlative degree forms of these prepositions, however, are adjectives.

See the following exercise for practice with irregular comparatives and superlatives.

Forming Irregular Comparatives and Superlatives

Translate the following noun phrases and substantives into English.

1. *canēs optimī* _____

2. *domus minor* _____

3. *locus extrēmus* _____

4. *pessimōs* _____

5. *nihil superius* _____

6. *rēgēs plurimī* _____

7. *maximum* _____

8. *loca īma* _____

9. *tempus prius* _____

10. *dominum meliorem* _____

Forming Adverbs

When you think of adverbs in English, you probably think of words ending in "–ly" (like "probably"). You're right. Those are adverbs. Adverbs are words that modify (i.e., clarify or say something about) either verbs or adjectives. In English, many adverbs are created from adjectives. The same is true for Latin. So, since you have just learned about adjectives, now is a very good time to see how Latin creates adverbs from adjectives and forms their comparative degrees.

Virtually any adjective can be made into an adverb in English by adding the suffix "–ly." "Thin" becomes "thinly," "slow" becomes "slowly," and so on. Latin also has suffixes that perform the same task. In Latin, though, there are two different endings, one for each of the two kinds of adjectives.

First/second declension adjectives add –ē to the modified stem:

Table 7-3   Adverb Formation for First/Second Declension Adjectives

Adjective	Adverb
lātus, lāta, lātum (wide)	*lātē* (widely)
lentus, lenta, lentum (slow)	*lentē* (slowly)
longus, longa, longum (long)	*longē* (far)
līber, lībera, līberum (free)	*līberē* (freely)
aeger, aegra, aegrum (sick)	*aegrē* (sickly)

Third declension adjectives add –iter to the modified stem:

Table 7-4   Adverb Formation for Third Declension Adjectives

Adjective	Adverb
gravis, grave (serious)	*graviter* (seriously)
fortis, forte (brave)	*fortiter* (bravely)
celer, celeris, celere (quick)	*celeriter* (quickly)
ācer, ācris, ācre (fierce)	*ācriter* (fiercely)
pār, paris (equal)	*pariter* (equally)
sapiens, sapientis (wise)	*sapienter* (wisely)

Note that if the modified stem ends in –nt–, you only need to add –er.

There is a handful of adjectives that don't form adverbs the way you would expect them to. They are easier to recognize than the English adverb for "good," which is "well" (not "goodly"!).

Table 7-5   Irregular Adverbs

Adjective	Adverb
bonus, –a, –um (good)	*bene* (well)
malus, –a, –um (bad)	*male* (badly)
facilis, –e (easy)	*facile* (easily)
multus, –a, –um (much)	*multum* (much)
parvus, –a, –um (little)	*parum* (not much)
magnus, –a, –um (great)	*magnopere* (greatly)

Comparison of Adverbs

If you can do something "well," you can do something "better"; and if that's the case, why not do it "extremely well"? Adverbs have comparative degrees just like adjectives. As a matter of fact, their comparative forms are based on the comparative forms of adjectives. If you already know how adjectives compare, then you already know how adverbs do, both in form and use.

Table 7-6 Comparison of Adverbs		
Positive	**Comparative**	**Superlative**
plānē (evenly)	*plānius* (rather evenly)	*plānissimē* (amazingly evenly)
miserē (miserably)	*miserius* (kind of miserably)	*miserrimē* (very miserably)
suāviter (sweetly)	*suāvius* (pretty sweetly)	*suāvissimē* (extremely sweetly)
potenter (powerfully)	*potentius* (sort of powerfully)	*potentissimē* (unbelievably powerfully)
bene (well)	*melius* (better)	*optimē* (best)
facile (easily)	*facilus* (rather easily)	*facillimē* (really easily)
saepe (often)	*saepius* (too often)	*saepissimē* (very often)
diū (for a long time)	*diūtius* (for a rather long time)	*diūtissimē* (for a very long time)
magnopere (greatly)	*magis* (more greatly)	*maximē* (most greatly)

If you examine these forms closely, you'll notice that they are either familiar or predictable. You already learned how to form adverbs from adjectives in the positive degree. The comparative degree is merely the neuter form of the comparative adjective (*–ius*). Since all adjectives in the superlative are first/second declension, all superlative adjectives make their adverbs by simply adding *–ē* to the stem (*–issimē* or *–imē*).

There are only two really important irregular adverbs that you should know. One is the adverb for *magnus: magnopere* ("greatly"). It has *magis* for a comparative, and its superlative is predictable: *maximē*. The other irregular adverb is the superlative of *multum* ("much"), namely *plurimum*.

Practicing Adverbs

Fill in the blanks in this adverb formation and comparison chart:

	Adjective	Adverb	Comparative	Superlative
1.	*fēlix*			
2.		*longē*		
3.			*peius*	
4.				*celerrimē*
5.			*brevius*	
6.	——	*diū*		
7.	*prūdēns*			
8.	*magnus*			
9.		*bene*		
10.		*facile*		

ALERT!

Don't forget that comparatives and superlatives are like adjectives in meaning. The comparative adverb *celerius* for example means "more quickly" only if a direct comparison is being made (e.g., Frank runs more quickly than George). Otherwise it only means "pretty quick." (e.g., Frank runs pretty quickly). The similar concept behind the superlative also applies.

Table 7-7   Vocabulary

aeternus, –a, –um	eternal
aqua, –ae, f.	water
aureus, –a, –um	golden
caput, capitis, n.	head
cōnsilium, consiliī, n.	plan, advice, assembly
dīversus, –a, –um	different, assorted
hūmānus, –a, –um	kind, human, civilized
iuvenis, iuvenis	young
laetus, –a, –um	fertile, happy, fat
lātus, –a, –um	wide
nātūra, –ae, f.	nature
nōbilis, –e	well known, upper class
paucī, –ae, –a	few
pauper, pauperis, paupere	poor (not wealthy)
pēs, pedis, m.	foot
quam, adv.	*see page 76*
simul, adv.	at the same time (*simul ac* [at the same time as])
singulus, –a, –um	individual, separate
tener, tenera, tenerum	soft, gentle, tender
valdē, adv.	very, intensely
varius, –a, –um	various, different, assorted
via, –ae, f.	road, way
virtūs, virtūtis, f.	manliness, courage, virtue, excellence
vīvus, –a, –um	living, alive
cadō, –ere, cecidī, cāsum	to fall, happen
discō, –ere, didicī,———	to learn
praecipiō, –ere, –cēpī, –ceptum	to teach, take beforehand
surgō, –ere, surrexī, surrēctum	to get up, rise
trādō, –ere, trādidī, trāditum	to hand over, surrender
cūrō, –āre, –āvī, –ātum	to care for
labor, labōris, m.	work
potestās, potestātis, f.	power
os, ossis, n.	bone

Latin-to-English Translations

Translate these Latin sentences into English.

1. *Tum mīlitēs Troiānī et deās et deōs offendērunt.*

2. *Iam tempora erant neque gravia neque difficilia.*

3. *Aliī canēs ācrius quam aliī latrābant.*

4. *Sīc habuit mulier vitam breviōrem sed dulcem.*

5. *Quam magnus fuit pater tuus!*

English-to-Latin Translations

Translate these English sentences into Latin:

1. The bad master cared for his slaves rather poorly.

2. My work used to be easier than your work.

3. The king held power for as long a time as he could.

4. The goddess was sad because she saw extremely difficult times.

5. Your dog used to love really big bones.

Chapter 8

Prepositions and the Ablative Case

Of all the parts of speech, prepositions are the hardest to define. In essence, they're the little words that show relationships between words, such as "the book *on* the table" as opposed to "the book *under* the couch" or "the book *about* Latin." To paraphrase Potter Stewart, you might not be able to define prepositions, but you know them when you see them.

Prepositional Phrases

A phrase is a group of words that expresses a thought but doesn't form a complete sentence. A prepositional phrase is a phrase that starts with a preposition. That sounds simple, doesn't it? In English that's all there is to it. Latin nouns, however, need to be in certain cases. The word that follows or goes with a preposition is called its object. Earlier you learned about direct objects of verbs and how Latin puts direct objects in the accusative case. Objects of prepositions are also in the accusative case. Well, most of them are.

There is another case, the ablative case, whose job it is to show many different kinds of relationships between words.

There are many prepositions. If some require their objects to be in the accusative case while others require their objects to be in the ablative case, how can you keep them all straight? **TABLE 8-1** should eliminate any confusion before it begins.

The objects of the seven prepositions in the first column are always in the ablative case. With the exception of *in* and *sub,* all other prepositions are followed by a word in the accusative case.

Table 8-1 Prepositions and Their Cases		
Prepositions That Take the Ablative Case	**Prepositions That Take Either Case**	**Prepositions That Take the Accusative Case**
ā/ab ([away] from)	*in* (in, on, into, onto)	all others!
ē/ex (out of)	*sub* (under, at the foot of)	
dē (down from, about)		
sine (without)		
cum (with)		
prae (in front of, before)		
prō (in front of, on behalf of, for)		

The prepositions *in* and *sub* are not ambivalent about which case their objects take. The choice depends on meaning. As you may recall, the basic idea behind the accusative case is to show the limit of an action. If you read a book, the reading is limited to the book, so in Latin, "book" would be in accusative case. If you go to the city, the "going" is limited to the city. When you get to the city you stop going, so "city" would be in the accusative case. One of the basic ideas behind the ablative case is location—where the action is taking place. If you live in the city, that's just where you live.

The preposition *ā* becomes *ab* when the next word begins with a vowel; for example, *ā silvā* ("away from the woods"), but *ab urbe* ("from the city"). The prepositions *ē* and *ex* do the same thing; for example, *ē silvā* ("out of the woods"), but *ex urbe* ("out of the city"). This is similar to the way the English word "a" becomes "an" before a word starting with a vowel; for example, "a tree" but "an apple."

How this applies to *in* and *sub* is simple: Use the accusative to show motion toward and the ablative to show the place where something is.

Catellus in domum cucurrit.
    (The puppy ran into the house.) (motion toward)
Catellus sub mensam cucurrit.
    (The puppy ran under the table.) (motion toward)

Catellus in domō dormiēbat.
    (The puppy was snoozing in the house.) (place where)
Catellus sub mensā dormiēbat.
    (The puppy was snoozing under the table.) (place where)

Why *domō* in the example instead of *domū*? The word *domus* is fourth declension, so it should be *domū*. Sometimes the word *domus* thinks it's second declension. Occasionally it is *domū,* but it usually appears as *domō*.

The prepositions that take *only* the accusative case are all the others. **TABLE 8-2** shows the most common ones.

Table 8-2	Prepositions		
ad	to, toward, near	*prope*	near
per	through	*circā*	around
inter	between, among	*circum*	around
ante	before, in front of	*praeter*	except for, beyond
post	before, behind	*trans*	across
super	on top of, above	*infrā*	beneath
apud	at the home of, among	*suprā*	above
propter	on account of	*intrā*	inside of
ob	on account of	*extrā*	outside of

The Ablative Case

Traditionally among students of Latin, the ablative case is the most confusing. Unlike the other cases, it seems to have 1,001 totally random uses, some of which require certain prepositions, others require no preposition at all. It doesn't help matters that, traditionally among teachers of Latin, the response to this confusion is: Don't ask. Just learn it. You won't get that treatment in *this* book!

It is true that the ablative case has myriad uses, but they aren't complete hodgepodge. The ablative case appears to have a few different, disconnected basic ideas because it is the result of the merger of three different cases.

How the Latin Ablative Case Became So Busy

Latin's grandmother tongue, Proto-Indo-European, possessed several cases, including an ablative case, an instrumental case, and a locative case. Each of these three cases had its own use.

The basic idea behind the original Proto-Indo-European "ablative case" was to show motion away from something. In this sense, you could think of it as the opposite of the accusative case. For example, if you went straight from the restaurant to the movies, "movies" would be in the accusative case because that's where you were heading. (Motion toward, right?) Meanwhile a Proto-Indo-European speaker would put "restaurant" in the ablative case because that's the place you went away from. In other words, it showed the source of your motion. So in Proto-Indo-European, you go toward the accusative and away from the ablative.

The Proto-Indo-European instrumental case went neither toward nor away from. Instead, it went right alongside. It showed something that was there at the beginning of an action and was there at the end. If you went *with Allison* straight from the restaurant to the movies, "movies" would be in the accusative, "restaurant" would be in the ablative, and "Allison" would be in the instrumental case because she came right along with you—she was there at the restaurant where you started, she was there at the movies where you were going.

The Proto-Indo-European locative case showed location. To continue our example, if you went with Allison straight from the restaurant to the movies *on Maple Road*, "Maple Road" would be in the locative case because that where the movies were.

This voyage into historical linguistics will help you cope with a case that has so many different uses. You will find that beyond the basic ideas of accompaniment, motion away, and place where, each specific use of the ablative case (and there are many!) has a formal name; for example, Ablative of Manner, Ablative of Means, Ablative of Accompaniment, et cetera. It is important that you learn the formal names of these uses. It helps to keep them straight.

In addition to distinct forms, the Proto-Indo-European ablative, instrumental, and locative cases each had distinct endings. Over time, Proto-Indo-European grew and changed into Classical Latin—which is what you are learning. Confusion came when all those distinct endings blurred into one. You couldn't tell which idea was intended: Source? Accompaniment? Location?

In the end, what used to be three separate sets of endings with three separate ideas became one set of endings with three separate ideas. Rather than give this new triple-duty case an original name, scholars lumped them all together under the name "ablative."

Ablative Case Forms

The ablative case may have a lot of uses, but its forms are easy and highly recognizable.

Case	First	Second	Third	Fourth	Fifth
Table 8-3	**Ablative Case Across the Declensions**				
			Singular		
Nominative	āla	ager	laus	exitus	aciēs
Genitive	ālae	agrī	laudis	exitūs	aciēī
Dative	ālae	agrō	laudī	exituī	aciēī
Accusative	ālam	agrum	laudem	exitum	aciem
Ablative	**ālā**	**agrō**	**laude**	**exitū**	**aciē**
			Plural		
Nominative	ālae	agrī	laudēs	exitūs	aciēs
Genitive	ālārum	agrōrum	laudum	exituum	aciērum
Dative	ālīs	agrīs	laudibus	exitibus	aciēbus
Accusative	ālās	agrōs	laudēs	exitūs	aciēs
Ablative	**ālīs**	**agrīs**	**laudibus**	**exitibus**	**aciēbus**

In the singular, the ablative case forms are not only simple vowels, but they are also the vowel that seems to be thematic within each declension. The plural ablative forms are quite distinctive as well—not to mention a tad repetitive.

See the following exercises for practice with ablative case forms and prepositional phrases.

Preposition Practice

Translate these prepositional phrases into English:

1. *prō homine* ....

2. *inter bella* ....

3. *trans silvam* ....

4. *per oppidum* ....

5. *sub arbore* ....

6. *sub arborem* ....

7. *ab urbe* ....

8. *dē monte* ....

9. *circum domum* ....

10. *propter pecuniam* ....

The Instrumental Ablative

The original Proto-Indo-European instrumental case—the one that showed something that goes from beginning to end alongside an action—survives in the Latin ablative case in six important ways. Those six ways fall into two groups. One group you could call the "with" group. It almost always appears in English with the preposition "with." The other group is a little more slippery. It basically points out in what respect something is true. We can call it the "respect" group.

The "With" Group

English phrases starting with the preposition "with" convey several different ideas. "With" can introduce a companion, as in "Ryan stayed *with me* the whole time." It can show a tool that is used to accomplish something, as in "I fixed it *with my hammer*." It can also describe the manner in which something is done, as in "They applauded the actors *with great enthusiasm*." Although these ideas may sound all alike to you in English, they're actually quite different. Latin recognizes the differences and uses different grammatical constructions to express them.

FACT

The English preposition "with" can also mean the opposite of itself! "He fought with his brother." Does that mean he fought alongside his brother or against him? There's no confusion in Latin. *Cum fratre suō pugnāvit* means that he fought with his brother at his side. If you mean "against," you say "against." *Contrā fratrem suum pugnāvit.*

Let's take a closer look at these distinctions that sound so alike in English. Consider this sentence: "The farmer was plowing the field with his son." This sentence could mean two different things. Either Junior was helping Pop in preparing the field, or Pop was cruelly dragging Junior through the dirt. One understanding of the sentence makes a little more sense, even without a context. There are times, however, that you do need context to figure out what is meant.

Here is another example: "The master beat the slave with a stick." It could mean two things, couldn't it? First, it could be that the master used the stick to beat the slave with. It could also be that of all the slaves, the one holding the stick got beaten. Latin has a grammatical way to clarify this confusion.

Different uses for the ablative case have formal names. The most common of these uses is the ablative of accompaniment. It uses the Latin preposition *cum* (with its object in the ablative case, of course) and shows exactly what its name suggests: accompaniment.

> *Vir **cum multīs senātoribus** vēnit.*
> (The man came **with many senators**.)

Not all ablative case uses are introduced by a preposition. Some uses never have any prepositions at all. They just appear all by themselves. The most common of these ablative uses that doesn't require a preposition is the ablative of means.

The phrase "ablative of means" doesn't indicate its use as well as many other ablative usage names do. It shows the "means" by which something is done; that is, the tool used.

> *Mīles hostem **gladiō** interfēcit.*
> (The soldier killed the enemy **with a sword.**)

The presence or absence of the preposition *cum* will guide your understanding.

There is one other ablative case use that usually employs the preposition *cum.* The ablative of manner shows the *manner* in which something is done.

> *Omnēs **cum studiō** clamābant.*
> (Everyone was cheering **with enthusiasm.**)

There are two peculiarities of the ablative of manner that occur when the noun in the phrase has an adjective with it. First, the adjective usually comes *before* the *cum.* Second, when there is an adjective, the *cum* becomes optional. (Without an adjective, you have to have the word *cum.*)

> *Omnēs **magnō cum studiō** clamābant.*
> (Everyone was cheering **with great enthusiasm.**)
> *Omnēs **magnō studiō** clamābant.*
> (Everyone was cheering **with great enthusiasm.**)

An ablative of manner phrase often sounds better when translated like an adverb: Everyone was cheering **enthusiastically** (*cum studiō*), or **very enthusiastically** (*magnō cum studiō*).

The Respect Group

There are three ablative case uses that show in what respect something is true. The fact that none of these uses requires a preposition is something else that they have in common. What distinguishes them most is where they occur and how you translate them.

The "ablative of respect" is the most common use of the ablative case to show respect.

> *Titus Tatius erat rēx **nomine**, sed nōn **potestāte**.*
>   (Titus Tatius was king **in name**, but not **in power.**)

Another way to look at that example is that Titus was king with respect to his name, but not with respect to power.

The "ablative of comparison" is simply an alternate way to express something you learned in the last chapter:

> *Marcus erat altior quam Lucius.* (Marcus was taller than Lucius.)
> *Marcus erat altior **Luciō**.* (Marcus was taller **than Lucius.**)

In other words, Marcus was pretty tall compared to Lucius. Whether you use the ablative of comparison or *quam,* the meaning is the same.

The "ablative of degree of difference" is a frequent companion to the ablative of comparison. When a comparison is being made, it can give you specifics as to how different the two things are.

> *Marcus erat **multō** altior quam Lucius.*
>   (Marcus was taller than Lucius **by much.**)
> *Marcus erat **multō** altior Luciō.*
>   (Marcus was taller than Lucius **by much.**)

As often happens, a word-for-word translation of the Latin into English sounds horrible. This example would be much easier on the ear if we said "Marcus was much taller than Lucius."

Forming the Ablative Case

Give the ablative case forms, singular and plural, for all the nouns in the vocabulary list in **TABLE 8-4.**

Table 8-4   Vocabulary

ambulō, –āre, –āvī, –ātum	to walk
animus, –ī, m.	spirit, mind, courage
annus, –ī, m.	year
bellum, –ī, n.	war
cēdō, –ere, cessī, cessum	to go, proceed, withdraw, yield
certus, –a, –um	certain, sure
cūra, –ae, f.	care, concern, worry, anxiety
equus, –ī, m.	horse
fīlius, –ī, m.	son
gerō, –ere, gessī, gestum	to bear, carry, accomplish, wage (war)
habitō, –āre, –āvī, –ātum	to live (in a place), dwell
hostis, hostis, m.	sing., an enemy; pl., the enemy
legō, –ere, lēgī, lectum	to choose, pick, gather, read
medius, –a, –um	middle, the middle of
mensis, mensis, m.	month
mittō, –ere, mīsī, missum	to send, throw (basic idea: to make something go away)
nōmen, nominis, n.	name
noster, nostra, nostrum	our
novus, –a, –um	new, strange (often with a bad connotation)
nox, noctis, f.	night
oppidum, –ī, n.	town
properō, –āre, –āvī, –ātum	to hurry
sacer, sacra, sacrum	sacred, holy
scrībō, –ere, scrīpsī, scrīptum	to write
terra, –ae, f.	land, earth
ubi	where, when
urbs, urbis, f.	city
vērus, –a, –um	true, real
vester, vestra, vestrum	your (pl.)
via, –ae, f.	road, way
vincō, –ere, vīcī, victum	to conquer, beat

Talking about Time

If Einstein didn't know it at the time (though he probably did), he would have been pleased to learn that for the Romans, there was little difference between time and space. Grammatically, anyway. Even *ubi*, the Latin question word for "where," can also mean "when"!

When talking about time, there are two different issues at hand. One issue deals with extent of time, or how long something lasted. The other issue is pinpointing exactly when, or at least within what time frame, an event occurred.

Accusative of Extent

In addition to its job marking direct objects of verbs and objects for most prepositions, the accusative case can also show extent of time or space.

> *In silvā **trēs horās** ambulābāmus.*
> (We walked in the woods **for three hours.**)
> *In silvā **tria milia passuum** ambulābāmus.*
> (We walked in the woods **for three miles.**)

It is worth noting that English requires the preposition "for" while Latin uses none at all. In fact, the accusative and ablative case uses discussed in this chapter require prepositions in English, though not always in Latin.

FACT

The smallest unit of time in the Roman world was the hour (*hōra*). The amount of time from sunrise to sunset was divided into twelfths using a sundial. An hour, then, was one-twelfth of the day. In the winter when days were short, so were the hours. In the summer the opposite was true. Nighttime was divided into four vigils (*vigiliae*). The end of the first vigil and the beginning of the second came when whatever constellation had been on the eastern horizon at sunset made it halfway up to the zenith.

Ablative of Time When or Within Which

You will recall that the locative case was one of the Proto-Indo-European cases that melded with the ablative in Latin. The job of the locative case was to show location. Given the Roman time/space equation, location on a calendar makes just as much sense as location on a map. The Ablative of Time When or Within Which does just that. It specifies a time or a time range. As with the other time expressions, no preposition is used in the Latin.

> *Decimā horā advēnit.* (He arrived **at the tenth hour.**)
> *Decem horīs advēnit.* (He arrived **within ten hours.**)

Talking about Places

Talking about places is a little more complicated than talking about time. There are more dynamics involved. You can go *to* a place, come *from* a place, or just be *at* a place. Earlier in this chapter you learned that ideas involving motion toward were the domain of the accusative case. You also saw how place where—staying put—went in the ablative case.

Confusion can arise because the "place where from" idea is also handled by the ablative case. Thus, the Latin ablative can show both location and point of origin. This potential confusion is resolved with prepositions.

ALERT!

The prepositions *ad* and *in* with the accusative have a not-so-subtle difference. *Ad* means "to" in the sense of "toward." *Ad Italiam navigāvērunt.* ("They sailed to Italy"—in that direction, maybe as a destination, but not necessarily.) *In Italiam navigāvērunt.* ("They sailed to Italy"—in that direction, got there, and went **on**shore. Mission completed!)

Going *to* a Place

Early in this chapter you saw how the prepositions *in* and *sub* take the accusative when they show motion toward. Even more common than those two prepositions to show motion toward is the preposition *ad* (to, toward; near). You can expect to see it a lot!

Coming *from* a Place

Many of the prepositions that require an object in the ablative case have a "from" idea: *ā* ("from, away from"), *ē* ("out of"), *dē* ("from, down from"), and even *sine* ("without"). These prepositions naturally have objects in the ablative.

> *Dē tectō cecidit iuvenis.* (The young man fell [down] from the roof.)

The formal name for this use is ablative of place where from.

Being *at* a Place

The most common prepositions to show location are *in* and *sub* with the ablative.

> *Mīlitēs castra **in monte** posuērunt.*
>   (The soldiers pitched camp **on the mountain.**)
> *Mīlitēs castra **sub monte** posuērunt.*
>   (The soldiers pitched camp **at the foot of the mountain.**)

The formal name for this use is ablative of place where.

Special Places

The English word "home" has a special place in grammar as well as in the heart. It often doesn't require a preposition. You can stay "home" or "at home" (place where). You can go "home," but not "to home" (motion toward). However, if you come "from home" (place where from), you have to use the preposition "from."

Latin is more consistent than that, which is a good thing because in Latin, "home" is not the only special place!

Cities, Towns, Small Islands . . .

The "special places" in Latin are exceptions to the coming, going, and staying rules you have been reading about. The list isn't very long:

- names of cities (e.g., *Roma*)
- names of towns (e.g., *Pompēiī*)
- names of small islands (e.g., *Malta*)
- the word *domus, –ūs,* f. when it means "home"
- the word *humus, –ī,* f. (the ground)
- the word *rūs, rūris,* n. (the country, as in the countryside as opposed to the city)

On the whole, their exceptions to the rules aren't very exceptional.

- To go **to** them, no preposition is needed. Just put them in the accusative. (*Romam*—"to Rome")
- To go **from** them, no preposition is needed. Just put them in the ablative. (*Romā*—"from Rome")
- To simply be **at** them, no preposition is needed. You need to put them in the locative case. . . .

Locative Case

Yes, the old Proto-Indo-European locative case did disappear into the ablative in Latin. However, the names of cities, towns, and small islands and the words *domus, humus,* and *rūs* held onto those antique forms.

As for those special words, they have special locative forms:

domus becomes *domī* (at home)
humus becomes *humī* (on the ground)
rūs becomes *rūrī* (in the country)

As for the names of cities, towns, and small islands, here are the locative forms:

Table 8-5		Locative Case Across the Declensions		
First	Second	Third	Fourth	Fifth
		Singular		
–ae	–ī	–e	–ū	–ē
		Plural		
–īs	–īs	–ibus	–ibus	–ēbus

Locative case endings really don't offer much new for you to learn. Here's a shortcut: All the locative forms are the same as the ablative. Only first and second declension singular place names (like *Roma*) are different.

QUESTION?

What makes an island "small"?
A small island is one that is so small that it has only one town on it, and the name of the town and the name of the island are the same.

TABLE 8-6 is a chart that summarizes everything in this section:

Table 8-6	Place Constructions		
Idea	*urbs, urbis,* **f. (city)**	*Roma, –ae,* **f. (Rome)**	*humus, –ī,* **f. (the ground)**
motion toward	*ad urbem*	*Romam*	*humum*
(accusative)	to the city	to Rome	onto the ground
motion away	*ab urbe*	*Romā*	*humō*
(ablative)	from the city	from Rome	from the ground
place where	*in urbe*	*Romae*	*humī*
(ablative or locative)	in the city	in Rome	on the ground

Latin-to-English Translations

Translate these sentences into English:

1. *Nuntius noster ad castra Romāna properāvit ubi hostēs vīdit.*

2. *Graecī bellum multōs annōs Troiae gessērunt.*

3. *Māter, nomine Livia, cum filiīs Veiōs saepius ambulābat.*

4. *Hominēs in illō oppidō vera nōn dicēbant.*

5. *Drusus unā diē Veronam equō celerrimō pervēnit.*

6. *Homō certus erat et minimē mendax.*

7. *Pater filium suum in terrās extrēmās mīsit.*

8. *Castra sub monte mediā nocte magnā cum dīligentiā posuimus.*

9. *Romānī et Gallōs et Germānōs post paucōs annōs vīcērunt.*

10. *Plurimī Athenae vīcīnōs in urbem suam propter timorem diū nōn accipiēbant.*

English-to-Latin Translations

Translate these sentences into Latin:

1. We used to go from Capua to Brundisium by means of the Via Appia.

2. The Romans were much luckier than the Germans.

3. The father sailed to Greece because he was looking for his son.

4. He found his son in Sparta.

5. All the people in Rome loved the new emperor named Titus.

Chapter 9

E Genitive Case and Dative Case

The genitive and the dative cases differ from the other cases, each in its own unique way. We still have a genitive in English. It should cause no problems at all. The dative, on the other hand, may require you to stretch your imagination a little.

What Is the Genitive?

The genitive is the only case that English retained for nouns as well as pronouns. You may recall that pronouns in English show three cases. Here is a chart that demonstrates the English forms:

Case	Singular	Plural	Singular	Plural
		Table 9-1 English Noun and Pronoun Declension		
Nominative	bird	birds	he	they
Genitive	**bird's**	**birds'**	**his**	**their**
Objective	bird	birds	him	them

For the English noun "bird," the nominative case and the objective case (i.e., all cases except the genitive rolled into one) change only going from singular to plural. The genitive, however, takes "–'s" in the singular and "–s'" in the plural. For the pronoun "he," the changes appear in every case and number.

Genitive Case Forms

Genitive case forms in Latin are peculiar to each declension. In fact, the way a noun forms its genitive is what determines the declension to which it belongs. The dictionary listing for a noun gives the nominative, genitive, gender, and meaning (e.g., *os, ossis,* n.—bone). The nominative form, *os,* has to be provided because it cannot always be predicted. The second word, *ossis,* is the genitive. From it you learn the stem change (*oss–*). The genitive ending *–is* tells you that it is third declension.

Table 9-2   Genitive Case Forms

Case	First	Second	Third	Fourth	Fifth
			Singular		
Nominative	āla	ager	laus	exitus	aciēs
Genitive	**ālae**	**agrī**	**laudis**	**exitūs**	**aciēī**
Dative	ālae	agrō	laudī	exituī	aciēī
Accusative	ālam	agrum	laudem	exitum	aciem
Ablative	ālā	agrō	laude	exitū	aciē
			Plural		
Nominative	ālae	agrī	laudēs	exitūs	aciēs
Genitive	**ālārum**	**agrōrum**	**laudum**	**exituum**	**aciērum**
Dative	ālīs	agrīs	laudibus	exitibus	aciēbus
Accusative	ālās	agrōs	laudēs	exitūs	aciēs
Ablative	ālīs	agrīs	laudibus	exitibus	aciēbus

Third Declension *i*-Stem Nouns

There is a group of third declension nouns that varies slightly from regular third declension nouns. The reason we have postponed discussing them is that their principal variation comes in the genitive plural.

Masculine and feminine *i*-stems have *–ium* for their genitive plural instead of the regular *–um*. Not much of a difference, is it? The neuters, however, add an *i* every place they can.

Table 9-3   Third Declension *i*-Stem Forms

Case	cīvis, cīvis, c. –(citizen)	mare, maris, n. –(sea)
	Singular	
Nominative	cīvis	mare
Genitive	cīvis	maris
Dative	cīvī	marī
Accusative	cīvem	mare
Ablative	cīve	marī

continued on following page

Table 9-3	Third Declension *i*-Stem Forms—*continued*	
Case	*cīvis, cīvis*, c. –(citizen)	*mare, maris*, n. –(sea)
	Plural	
Nominative	*cīvēs*	*maria*
Genitive	*cīvium*	*marium*
Dative	*cīvibus*	*maribus*
Accusative	*cīvēs*	*maria*
Ablative	*cīvibus*	*maribus*

ALERT!

The abbreviation "c." is short for "common gender." It is used for nouns like *cīvis* that can be masculine or feminine (i.e., "A citizen can be a man or a woman").

It isn't difficult to tell which third declension nouns are *i*-stems. They fall into three groups based on certain patterns.

- **Parasyllabic Third Declension *i*-Stems.** Words with a nominative ending in –*is* or –*es* and a genitive with the same number of syllables:
  nāvis, nāvis, f. (ship)
  nūbes, nūbis, f. (cloud)
- **Monosyllabic Third Declension *i*-Stems.** Words with a nominative in one syllable and a base ending in two (or more) consonants:
  urbs, urbis, f. (city)
  nox, noctis, f. (night)
- **Neuter Third Declension *i*-Stems.** Neuter third declension words ending in –*e*, –*al*, or –*ar*:
  mare, maris, n. (sea)
  animal, animalis, n. (animal)

If the peculiarities of third declension *i*-stem endings—especially those of the neuters—look familiar, they should. You've already seen them in the endings of third declension adjectives.

The Uses of the Genitive Case

What is special about the genitive case is that it lets one noun modify another noun or show a close link between two nouns without saying that they are the same thing. For instance, "Chris's truck" shows a close link between Chris and a truck, but it doesn't say that they are the same thing. This example shows possession, but the genitive case shows more than just possession. If you refer to "a tablespoon of vinegar," "tablespoon" and "vinegar" certainly aren't the same thing, nor does the tablespoon own the vinegar. There is merely a close link between those two nouns.

You can link two nouns and mean that they *are* the same thing. This is called apposition. All you have to do is put the second noun in the same case as the first. For example, to say "I saw your mother, Aurelia, yesterday" would be *herī matrem tuam Aureliam vīdī*.

Possessive Genitive

The most common—and most obvious—use of the genitive case is to show possession. English has two ways to do this. One is through English's own genitive case endings (i.e., "–'s" or "–s'"). The other is with the preposition "of." "The farmer's fields" means the same as "the fields of the farmer."

> *Iter **Marcī** erat longum et difficile.*
> (Mark's journey was long and difficult.)

Like most modifiers in Latin, words in the genitive case tend to follow the nouns they modify.

The Latin words *meus* ("my"), *tuus* ("your"), *noster* ("our"), *vester* ("your"), *suus* ("his, her, its, their") are possessive adjectives. They already have the idea of possession in their meanings, and being adjectives, they must agree in gender, case, and number with the noun they modify; for example, *canis meus* (my dog), *canēs meī* (my dogs).

Partitive Genitive

Another common use of the genitive case is called the partitive genitive. This use shows something of which a part is taken. For example, in the phrase "a cup of sugar," "sugar" would be in the genitive because it is the something of which a "cup" is taken.

*Pars **exercitūs** extrā urbem manēbat.*
> (Part **of the army** stayed outside the city.)

At times, what is partitive in English is not partitive in Latin and *vice versa.* In English you can say "all the people" or "all of the people" and it means the same thing. In Latin, you could say only *omnēs hominēs.* On the other hand, the Latin word *nihil* (nothing) uses a partitive genitive, so *nihil cibī* literally translates as "nothing of food," meaning "no food."

ALERT!

Watch out for the comparative of the adjective *multus*! In the singular, *plūs* is a third declension neuter noun (*plūs, plūris,* n.— more) and always takes a partitive genitive. *Plūs cibī* literally says "more of food" meaning "more food." The English word "more" can use a partitive or not; in Latin it is always partitive.

Subjective and Objective Genitives

The subjective and objective genitive case uses can be tricky. These two genitive case uses both involve a noun in the genitive paired with a noun that has a verbal idea like "love." "Love" can be a noun or a verb. More often than not, however, the noun and the verb are closely related, but not identical. Take for instance the word "growth." It is a noun, but it is clearly related to the verb "grow."

The terms "subjective" and "objective" have something to do with verbs as well, don't they? Subjects perform actions, objects receive them. Consider this sentence:

Augur mōtum avium in caelō spectābat.
> (The augur was watching the movement of birds in the sky.)

The genitive phrase is *mōtum avium* ("the movement of birds"). The birds don't own movement. Movement is not a quantity of birds. But the birds are moving—they are the *subjects* of the verbal idea of the noun *mōtum* ("movement"). *Avium,* then, is a subjective genitive.

Now we can turn this around. Here is another sentence:

Odium bellī in oppidō erat magnum.
(The hatred of war in the town was great.)

Odium ("hatred") has an obvious link to the verb "to hate." But is the war doing the hating, or is war what is hated? In this example, the word in the genitive is receiving the action. That is to say, it is the object. *Bellī,* then, is an objective genitive.

Genitive of Description

A noun in the genitive case can be used to describe another noun.

Melissa erat mulier animī bonī.
(Melissa was a woman of good spirit.)

The only restriction in this construction is that the noun in the genitive must be accompanied by an adjective, just as *bonī* agrees with *animī* in the example above.

As an alternative to a noun with an adjective in the genitive, you can use the ablative case without a preposition instead. *Melissa erat mulier animō bonō.* The meaning is exactly the same; the only difference is stylistic. This ablative use is predictably called the Ablative of Description.

The Dative Case

The dative case is the most elusive of all the cases. Understanding it truly takes some effort. What makes the dative case challenging is that there is no single way to translate it. There are many ways to express the ideas it represents in English, so context is the real key. The most important thing for you to do is try to capture the dative's *central idea*.

Once you have learned the forms for the dative case, you will have learned all the cases! The most obvious feature of the dative singular is the ending –*ī*. First and second declension are the only places you don't see it. In fact, you will be introduced to some special declension words later in the book, and they all show this –*ī* as well.

As for the dative plural, you already know it. Dative and ablative plurals are always the same.

Case	First	Second	Third	Fourth	Fifth
Table 9-4		**Dative Case Forms**			
		Singular			
Nominative	āla	ager	laus	exitus	aciēs
Genitive	ālae	agrī	laudis	exitūs	aciēī
Dative	**ālae**	**agrō**	**laudī**	**exituī**	**aciēī**
Accusative	ālam	agrum	laudem	exitum	aciem
Ablative	ālā	agrō	laude	exitū	aciē
		Plural			
Nominative	ālae	agrī	laudēs	exitūs	aciēs
Genitive	ālārum	agrōrum	laudum	exituum	aciērum
Dative	**ālīs**	**agrīs**	**laudibus**	**exitibus**	**aciēbus**
Accusative	ālās	agrōs	laudēs	exitūs	aciēs
Ablative	ālīs	agrīs	laudibus	exitibus	aciēbus

Practice Your Declensions

Decline (make charts for) the following nouns in each of the Latin cases:

1. *cor, cordis,* n. (heart)

2. *ignis, ignis,* m. (fire)

3. *villa, villae,* f. (farmhouse)

4. *fidēs, fideī,* f. (trust)

5. *squālor, squāloris,* m. (roughness)

6. *nāsus, nāsī,* m. (nose)

7. *iubar, iubaris,* n. (lightbeam)

8. *rītus, rītūs,* m. (ceremony, rite)

The Uses of the Dative Case

In essence, the dative case shows a person or thing—usually a person—who has a vested interest in the outcome of the action of the verb in a sentence; someone who stands to gain or lose, is benefited, harmed, or otherwise *indirectly* affected. It can pop up in some fairly unexpected places. Sometimes it translates easily, other times it defies translation altogether. Either way, the dative case is a peculiarity of Latin that adds a dash of flavor to the language.

Indirect Object

In addition to a direct object, some verbs take what is called an *indirect object*. An indirect object is a sort of secondary object. In Latin, indirect objects are put into the dative case. The verbs that usually have a dative indirect object are ones of:

- saying: *Imperātor rem **senātoribus** explicāvit.*
  (The emperor explained the situation **to the senators.**)
- showing: *Imperātor rem **senātoribus** monstrāvit.*
  (The emperor showed **the senators** the problem.)
- giving: *Senātorēs **consilium imperātorī** dedērunt.*
  (The senators gave **the emperor** advice.)
- entrusting: *Senātorēs rem **imperātorī** mandāvērunt.*
  (The senators entrusted the matter **to the emperor.**)

In any of these examples, the dative indirect object could be left out and the sentence would continue to function. Although the sentences could work grammatically, they would still be crying for a little more information. "The emperor explained the situation . . ." to whom? Who cared? The senators did. "The senators gave advice . . ." to whom? Who stood to gain or lose from this advice? The emperor did.

Dative of Possession

Isn't it the genitive case that shows possession? Well, yes, but the dative can also under certain conditions, the principal one being that the main verb of the sentence is a form of the verb "to be." The "dative of possession" is actually more of a "dative of reference."

*Nomen **illī mulierī** Tanaquil erat.*
　　(**With reference to that woman,** the name was Tanaquil.
　　As for that woman, the name was Tanaquil.)

It's just easier to say:

That woman's name was Tanaquil.

Body parts and other personal effects often use the dative of possession instead of a genitive. For example: *Dominus caput servō percussit* literally means "The master hit the head with reference to the slave" meaning "The master hit the slave on the head." Obviously this was to the slave's disadvantage, so a dative works best in this sentence.

Dative with Adjectives

Certain adjectives take the dative case in Latin. They are easy to understand because they use a dative sort of construction in English, too.

*Rēgem similem **deō** habēbant.*
   (They considered the king similar **to a god.**)
*Spectāculum idoneum **puerīs** nōn erat.*
   (The show was not suitable **for children.**)

Dative with Intransitive Verbs

There are two kinds of verbs, transitive and intransitive. Transitive verbs show a subject performing an action directly on an object. Not only *can* they take a direct object, but they *must* have one to form a complete thought. Intransitive verbs show states of being or motion from place to place. They *cannot* have a direct object.

This distinction between transitive and intransitive verbs becomes extremely important when studying Latin. There are some verbs that are transitive in English but intransitive in Latin. The objects intransitive verbs take in Latin are dative rather than accusative.

It can be hard to understand how this can be true. The secret behind this mystery lies in what the verbs actually mean. For instance, the Latin verb for "obey" is *pāreō*. It takes a dative object because it really means "to be obedient." The sentence *Publius **patrī suō** pārēbat* translates literally as "Publius used to be obedient **to his father.**" The English verb "obey" is transitive, so you would expect an accusative object. Its Latin counterpart, however, is intransitive, so its object becomes a matter of reference: "Publius used to be obedient **with reference to his father.**" It sounds much less awkward in English to treat the Latin as if it were transitive and say "Publius used to obey **his father**."

The Word "And"

Latin has three words for "and." Each treats the items being connected a little differently: "Here are some examples of dogs and cats."

- *canēs et fēlēs*: *et* joins two things without making any inference. There are dogs, and there are some cats, too.
- *canēs atque fēlēs*: *atque* (or *ac*) joins two things, inferring that they are natural companions. There are dogs, so of course there are cats there as well. Where there's smoke, there's fire.
- *canēs fēlēsque*: *–que* joins two things that are pairs or opposites and together they complete a set, like salt 'n' pepper, top 'n' bottom, or raining cats 'n' dogs.

The ending *–que* is an enclitic. An enclitic is more of a half-word than a word. It cannot stand on its own; it must be attached to the end of another word. The enclitic *–que* is also strange in that it is attached to the end of the *second* of the two things being joined.

Table 9-5 Vocabulary	
amor, amōris, m.	love
atque (ac), conj.	and, and so, and naturally, and of course
autem, conj.	moreover, on the other hand, but, however
carcer, –is, m.	jail
cēterus, –a, –um	the rest, the other
corpus, corporis, n.	body
crēdō, –ere, crēdidī, crēditum (+ dative)	to believe, trust, rely on (lit. to have trust)
cunctus, –a, –um	all
doceō, –ēre, docuī, doctum	to teach
ergō, conj.	therefore, so

continued on following page

Table 9-5   Vocabulary—*continued*

et, conj.	and, also, too, even
fugiō, –ere, fūgī, fugitum	to run away, flee, escape
hīc, adv.	here, in this place
ibi, adv.	there, in that place
invītus, –a, –um	unwilling
itaque, conj.	and so, and therefore (*ita* + *–que*)
mēns, mentis, f.	mind
miser, misera, miserum	poor, unfortunate, wretched
modus, –ī, m.	way, method
mors, mortis, f.	death
mōs, mōris, m.	habit, custom, ways (in the plural, character)
moveō, –ēre, mōvī, mōtum	to move (physically or emotionally)
nē ____ quidem, adv.	not even ____ (e.g., *nē pecunia quidem*—"not even money")
nimis, adv.	too much, very much
pār, paris	equal, even
pars, partis, f.	part, some, direction
paucī, –ae, –a	few
plēnus, –a, –um	full
–que, enclitic	and (*see page 114*)
quidem, adv.	at least, even, in fact (used for emphasis)
relinquō, relinquere, relīquī, relictum	to leave behind, abandon
respondeō, –ēre, respondī, respōnsum	to answer, respond (usually with a dative)
sanctus, –a, –um	holy, consecrated, inviolable
satis, adv.	enough
similis, –e	similar, like
stō, stāre, stetī, statum	to stand
ut (utī), conj.	like, as, when
valeō, –ēre, –uī, –itum	to be strong, be well
vīvō, –ere, vīxī, vīctum	to live
vocō, –āre, –āvī, –ātum	to call, summon

Latin-to-English Translations

Translate these Latin sentences into English:

1. *Mens virī nōn valēbat.*

2. *Amor mātris filiō aegrō mē permōvit.*

3. *Deī deaeque hominēs urbium, quī rītūs sanctōs atque sacrōs numquam observābant, saepe relīnquebant.*

4. *In mediō oppidō stābant et corpus rēgis mortuī omnibus monstrāvit.*

5. *Pars civium lacrimābant, cēterī gaudēbant.*

English-to-Latin Translations

Translate the following sentences into Latin:

1. After a few months they caught the sad man in the country near Cumae.

2. Cumae was closer to Rome than Brundisium.

3. They took the man by ship across the sea.

4. He came home very unwillingly.

5. He stayed in jail for many days with the others.

Chapter 10
Grammatical Mood

The traditional approach to learning Latin offers students everything there is to know about Latin's verb system before touching on the concept of grammatical mood. But Latin is full of phrases and constructions that require a deep understanding of the concept of what's known as the subjunctive mood. Read on to learn what ideas are expressed using this mood.

What Is Grammatical Mood?

The term "mood," when used in a grammatical sense, refers to verb forms that illustrate the way the speaker is treating an action. In Proto-Indo-European, there were four moods:

- Indicative mood—fact
- Subjunctive mood—idea
- Optative mood—wish
- Imperative mood—command

The indicative mood treats an action as a fact. The word "treats" is important because whether an action is indeed a fact or not is beside the point. When a speaker uses the indicative mood, he or she is only *treating* the action as a fact.

> *Rōmānī hostēs vīcērunt.*
>   (The Romans conquered the enemy.)

The two verb tenses you've learned so far—the imperfect and the perfect—have both been in the indicative mood. In this chapter you will learn two tenses—the imperfect and the pluperfect—but in the subjunctive mood.

With the subjunctive mood, the speaker is treating an action as an *idea*. That is to say, as a sort of hypothetical situation.

> *Si Rōmānī hostēs vincerent, . . .*
>   (If the Romans conquered the enemy, . . .)

Once again, the factual or potential truth of what is being said doesn't really matter.

Just like the old Proto-Indo-European ablative, instrumental, and locative cases merged into one case (the ablative) in Latin, the old optative mood combined with the subjunctive in Latin. This gives Latin one mood, the subjunctive, that does the work of two.

Utinam Rōmānī hostēs vincerent.
(I wish that the Romans conquered the enemy.)
(If only the Romans conquered the enemy.)
(Would that the Romans conquered the enemy.)

Since wishes are ideas and not facts, it's easy to see how the subjunctive and optative moods were able to merge.

The fourth mood, the imperative, simply expresses a command.

Rōmānī, vincite hostēs! (Romans, conquer the enemy!)

The imperative mood is covered in detail in Chapter 18.

The subjunctive is used occasionally in English. For example, in the sentence "She insists that you be ready by noon," why is it "you be" rather than "you are"? "She insists" is a fact, "you be" is a wish. Some other examples are "I wish Katie *were* my physician" and "*come* hell or high water."

There is a fifth category that isn't exactly a mood, but it's worth mentioning here. This group contains forms that are called "infinitives." Infinitives are verb forms that don't treat actions as anything at all. They don't even have a person or number! In English, infinitives are usually preceded by the word "to," as in "to walk," "to cry," "to sweep," and so on. Infinitives are covered in detail in Chapter 17.

The Imperfect Subjunctive

What you already know about the present system (i.e., continuous aspect) and the perfect system (i.e., completed aspect) for the indicative mood still applies for the subjunctive mood. The first two principal parts of a verb are needed to form the present system tenses. The last two principal parts are needed for the perfect system.

There are only four tenses in the subjunctive mood: present, imperfect, perfect, and pluperfect. There is no future or future perfect tense.

Of all the verb tenses in the subjunctive mood, the imperfect subjunctive is by far the most common. It is also fairly easy to form and recognize. It consists of the second principal part of a verb plus regular personal endings.

Table 10-1	The Imperfect Subjunctive			
Person	*amō, amāre*	*habeō, habēre*	*mittō, mittere*	*veniō, venīre*
1st, sing.	*amārem*	*habērem*	*mitterem*	*venīrem*
2nd, sing.	*amārēs*	*habērēs*	*mitterēs*	*venīrēs*
3rd, sing.	*amāret*	*habēret*	*mitteret*	*venīret*
1st, pl.	*amārēmus*	*habērēmus*	*mitterēmus*	*venīrēmus*
2nd, pl.	*amārētis*	*habērētis*	*mitterētis*	*venīrētis*
3rd, pl.	*amārent*	*habērent*	*mitterent*	*venīrent*

There isn't any good, single, predictable way to translate the subjunctive. How to read, understand, or translate it will depend on how it is being used in a sentence.

The most important thing to remember about the imperfect subjunctive is that it always shows an action taking place at the *same time* or *after* the time of the main verb.

The Pluperfect Subjunctive

The second most common tense is the pluperfect subjunctive. While it may not be the most common, it *is* the most easily recognizable. Since the pluperfect is a perfect system tense, you use the perfect stem. The perfect stem is the third principle part of a verb minus the final –ī. Once you have the stem, add the tense/mood indicator for the pluperfect subjunctive, –*isse*–, then add the regular personal endings.

Table 10-2   The Pluperfect Subjunctive

Person	amō, amāre	habeō, habēre	mittō, mittere	veniō, venīre
1st, sing.	amāvissem	habuissem	mīsissem	vēnissem
2nd, sing.	amāvissēs	habuissēs	mīsissēs	vēnissēs
3rd, sing.	amāvisset	habuisset	mīsisset	vēnisset
1st, pl.	amāvissēmus	habuissēmus	mīsissēmus	vēnissēmus
2nd, pl.	amāvissētis	habuissētis	mīsissētis	vēnissētis
3rd, pl.	amāvissent	habuissent	mīsissent	vēnissent

Once again, the only way to translate a subjunctive is to see it in context. It nearly always translates into English with the helping verb "had" (e.g., *mīsissent*, "they had sent"). The most important thing to remember about the pluperfect subjunctive is that it always shows something that happened *before* the main verb.

ALERT!

The special perfect tense personal endings *–ī, –istī, –it, –imus, –istis,* and *–ērunt* are only for the perfect indicative, which you learned in Chapter 4. These personal endings appear no place else.

Conjugating the Subjunctive

Conjugate the following verbs in the imperfect and pluperfect subjunctive.

1. *canō, canere, cecinī, cantum*

2. *absum, abesse, āfuī, āfutūrus*

3. *fleō, flēre, flēvī, flētum*

Showing Purpose

A purpose clause is a clause that shows the purpose of the action of the main clause of a sentence. In the sentence "I ran to the store to buy some cocktail wienies," for example, "I ran to the store" expresses a fact—something that happened—so in Latin it would be in the indicative mood. The "to buy cocktail wienies" part, however, tells *why* "I ran to the store." It doesn't say whether or not I actually bought any wienies. Since buying wienies was the *idea* behind the trip, in Latin it would be cast into the subjunctive mood.

Let's take a closer look at the way English expresses purpose. It is important to understand how the English construction works, because Latin takes a different tack.

I ran to the store	to buy cocktail wienies.
In macellum properāvī	*ut tomācula emerem.*

In English, the main clause is independent, but the purpose clause isn't even a clause (a phrase with both a subject and a verb)! English uses an infinitive phrase instead. Latin *never* uses an infinitive to express purpose. You could use a construction in English that more or less parallels the Latin approach to expressing purpose, but it sounds awkward: "I ran to the store in order that I might buy cocktail wienies."

The Latin version has two clauses: Both the first and the second part have subjects (via personal endings) and predicates. The first part is the main clause. Its verb is in the indicative mood because it relates a fact. The second part, the subordinate clause, has a verb in the subjunctive because it doesn't describe a fact. It illustrates a wish or idea.

The subordinating conjunction that introduces a purpose clause in Latin is the word *ut*. However, if the purpose clause is negative it is introduced by the word *nē* instead.

Tomācula ēmī	*nē in convictū ēsurīrēmus.*
I bought cocktail wienies	so that we wouldn't be hungry at the party.

Once again, Latin has two clauses, a main, independent one, then the subordinating conjunction *nē*, and finally a subordinate clause in the subjunctive. As far as the grammatical constructions are concerned, the only difference between a positive versus a negative purpose expression in Latin is the use of *nē* instead of *ut*.

The English, on the other hand, does a flip-flop. In the earlier example of a positive purpose expression, there was an infinitive phrase ("to buy . . .") and the subordinated clause version sounded awkward ("in order that I might buy . . ."). This time, with a negative purpose expression, English uses a subordinate clause. You could use an infinitive phrase, but it sounds funny: "I ran to the store for us not to be hungry at the party."

Latin is consistent and logical. English isn't. In fact, there are many ways to translate purpose clauses into English. When you become more familiar with the gist of the Latin, you will be able to find many ways that sound better than the suggestions offered above.

The tiny word *ut* has more uses than just as a subordinating conjunction for the subjunctive. With the indicative it can mean "when" or "because" (*ut vēnistī*, "when you came"), with a noun it can be translated "like" or "as" (*ut avēs*, "like birds"), with an adjective or adverb it can take the place of *quam* (*ut venustus erat!* "How sexy he was!").

Showing a Result

In addition to purpose clauses, the subordinating conjunction *ut* can introduce a result clause. A result clause is a clause that shows the result of the action of the main verb. Like purpose clauses, the verb of a result clause is in the subjunctive.

> *Tam celeriter currēbat ut in lutum caderet.*
> (He was running so fast that he fell in the mud.)

Don't worry about getting confused over recognizing a purpose clause versus a result clause. Context aside, there are a couple of things to look for that set the two uses apart. The first clue appears if the result clause is negative. Instead of switching the *ut* to *nē*, result clauses keep the *ut* and add a negative word inside the clause itself.

> *Ita currēbat ut in lutum nōn caderet.*
>> (He was running in such a way that he didn't fall in the mud.)
> *Tam celeriter currēbat ut in lutum numquam caderet.*
>> (He was running so fast that he never fell in the mud.)

The second surefire way to recognize a result clause actually appears in the main clause. Look at the examples above and you will notice a "so" word. The main clause preceding a result clause is reminiscent of the old joke sequence: "My sister is so skinny . . ." to which the audience interrupts: "How skinny is she?!"

The "so" word isn't a requirement, but it's almost always there to tip you off. Here is a list of the most common "so" words:

ita (in such a way)
sīc (like this, in such a way)
tālis (of such a kind)
tam (so)
tantus (so big, so great)
tot (so many)

FACT

It is rather puzzling that the verb in a result clause takes the subjunctive. *Tam celeriter currēbat* is in the indicative mood because it describes a fact. Yet "that he fell in the mud" is also a fact, not a wish or idea. So why the subjunctive? No one really knows. That's just the way it is.

Cum Clauses

The subjunctive usually appears in sentences where the speaker intends for the action to be understood as a wish or simply an idea. Sometimes, however, the nonfactual "feel" that the subjunctive mood provides is used for something else. The subjunctive mood can also push an action into the background so that the action illustrated by the main verb (i.e., the verb in the indicative mood) can be made more vivid. This is what *cum* clauses do.

Cum clauses are subordinate clauses. There are four different ways to read them. Three of those ways use a verb in the subjunctive mood; the other one is indicative.

- *cum* temporal clause: *Cum advēnit, laetī erāmus.*
  (When he arrived, we were happy.)
- *cum* circumstantial clause: *Cum advenīret, laetī erāmus.*
  (When he arrived, we were happy.)
- *cum* causal clause: *Cum advenīret, laetī erāmus.*
  (Because/Since he arrived, we were happy.)
- *cum* concessive clause: *Cum advenīret, laetī tamen erāmus.*
  (Even though/although he arrived, we were happy [anyway].)

Cum temporal and *cum* circumstantial clauses translate the same way ("when . . ."), but they use different moods because they emphasize different things. Temporal clauses put their verbs in the indicative. They stress the *time* the main clause took place. (The word "temporal" comes from the Latin *tempus, temporis,* n.—time.) Circumstantial clauses have verbs in the subjunctive. They show the *circumstances* under which the main clause takes place. By using the subjunctive instead of the indicative, they downplay the importance of their clauses, which in turn emphasizes the main clause.

Cum causal clauses do exactly what their name suggests. They show the *cause* or reason for whatever the main clause says. The subjunctive stresses the possibility of cause rather than the fact of the matter.

Cum concessive clauses aren't very common, but they are easily recognized by the inclusion of the word *tamen* ("but, anyway, nevertheless") in the main clause. Another way to translate the above example could be: "He arrived, but we were happy anyway." The *cum* clause sets up the circumstances, but it's the *tamen* in the main clause that provides the gist of the entire sentence.

So, when you're reading, how do you know which kind of *cum* clause it is? If it's temporal, the verb will be in the indicative mood. If *tamen* appears in the main clause, it's concessive. That leaves circumstantial and causal. To tell them apart you need to rely on context.

ALERT!

The conjunction *cum* is not the same as the preposition *cum* meaning "with." They are totally different words. The conjunction was *quom* in archaic Latin. That it evolved to look like the preposition is a coincidence. If you see the word *cum* followed by an ablative, you've got the preposition. If *cum* starts a clause that has a verb in the subjunctive (as they usually do), then it's the *cum* we just discussed.

Table 10-3 Vocabulary	
absum, abesse, āfuī, āfutūrus	to be away
adsum, adesse, adfuī, ———	to be present
āmissus	lost
caelum, –ī, n.	sky, heaven
canō, –ere, cecinī, cantum	to sing, play (a musical instrument), recite (poetry)
carmen, carminis, n.	poem, song
causa, –ae, f.	reason, cause (*causā* + gen. for the sake of)
clārus, –a, –um	clear, bright, famous
dignus, –a, –um	worthy
dūrus, –a, –um	hard, harsh, rough
enim, conj.*	that is to say, for instance
ferus, –a, –um	wild, untamed
fleō, –ēre, flēvī, flētum	to cry, weep
igitur, conj.	therefore
intrō, –āre, āvī, ātum	to enter

continued on following page

Table 10-3	Vocabulary—*continued*
itaque, conj.	and so
mereō, –ēre, –uī, itum	to deserve
mox, adv.	soon
nēmō, nēminis, m.	no one
numquam, adv.	never
perīculum, –ī, n.	danger
puella, –ae, f.	girl
puer, puerī, m.	boy
quālis, –e	what kind (of)?
quantus, –a, –um	how big? how great?
quot, adv.	how many?
stella comāta, –ae, f.	comet (literally "a star with long hair"!)
tālis, –e	such, of such a kind
tam, adv.	so
tamen, conj.	but, however, nevertheless, anyway
tantus, –a, –um	so big, so great
timeō, –ēre, –uī, ———	to fear, be afraid of
tot, adv.	so many
tunc, adv.	then, at that time
vel, conj.**	or
verbum, –ī, n.	word
vīs, vīs, f.	force, strength, power

* The conjunction *enim* is used to clarify or re-explain something that was just said. Here is an example in English to help you get a feeling for what *enim* means: "I was late to work this morning because of traffic; *you see,* there was an accident."
** The conjunction *vel* means "or," but not in the same way *aut* means "or." *Aut* offers a choice between things where only one thing can be chosen (e.g., life *or* death). *Vel* offers a choice where choosing one does not exclude the other (e.g., chocolate *or* vanilla).

Latin-to-English Translations

Identify which subjunctive use is illustrated—if there is one—in each sentence; then translate into English. Use the vocabulary from **TABLE 10-3** to help you.

1. *Puella caelum omnī nocte spectābat ut stellās comātās invenīret.*

2. *Cum corde tam gravī filium āmissum exspectābat pater infelix ut mox exspīrāret.*

3. *Cum rēx clārus Romam advēnisset, senātorēs epulās maximās posuērunt.*

4. *Vergilius erat poeta tālis ut nēmō carmina nōn caneret.*

5. *Graecī Troiam multīs navibus advēnērunt ut urbem caperent.*

English-to-Latin Translations

Identify which subjunctive use is illustrated—if there is one—in each sentence; then translate into Latin.

1. Since the slave feared his master, he ran away.

2. The dogs were so fierce that no one would enter the house.

3. The Greeks came to Troy to conquer the Trojans.

4. The women of the town left their houses in the middle of the night.

5. They walked for many days so the evil men wouldn't capture them (*eās*).

Chapter 11

Time and Tense

In this chapter you will be introduced to the remaining four tenses of the indicative mood: the present, the future, the pluperfect, and the future perfect indicative. By now you should be comfortable with stems and personal endings, so learning four tenses all at once should not be daunting. You will quickly discover that they are only variations on things you have been practicing for quite some time now.

The Present Indicative

The present is right now. But "right now" as you read this is not the same "right now" as when these words were being written. Obviously, the idea of present tense is not as simple as it might seem, is it? Your concept of the present is relative to your reading this sentence. In an hour, your "present" will have changed and your reading of the last sentence will have faded into the past.

Of the six tenses in Latin, the present tense is the only one that has different formation rules for each conjugation. The first two principal parts give you all the information you need to form the present tense. As you may recall, the conjugation to which a verb belongs is governed by its infinitive ending (i.e., the ending on its second principal part). The breakdown goes like this:

- First conjugation: *–āre* (e.g., *stō, stāre* [to stand])
- Second conjugation: *–ēre* (e.g., *moneō, monēre* [to warn])
- Third conjugation: *–ere* (e.g., *mittō, mittere* [to send])
- Third conjugation *–iō*: *–ere* (e.g., *capiō, capere* [to take])
- Fourth conjugation: *–īre* (e.g., *sentiō, sentīre* [to feel])

Examine the above list and you will notice that before the *–re* of each infinitive ending is a "theme" vowel: *–ā–* for first conjugation, *–ē–* for second, and so on. The theme vowels are the distinguishing features among the conjugations in the present tense.

Table 11-1		Present Tense Across the Conjugations			
Person	**First**	**Second**	**Third**	**Third** *–iō*	**Fourth**
1st, sing.	*stō*	*moneō*	*mittō*	*capiō*	*sentiō*
2nd, sing.	*stās*	*monēs*	*mittis*	*capis*	*sentīs*
3rd, sing.	*stat*	*monet*	*mittit*	*capit*	*sentit*
1st, pl.	*stāmus*	*monēmus*	*mittimus*	*capimus*	*sentīmus*
2nd, pl.	*stātis*	*monētis*	*mittitis*	*capitis*	*sentītis*
3rd, pl.	*stant*	*monent*	*mittunt*	*capiunt*	*sentiunt*

First and second conjugation verbs are fairly unremarkable in the present indicative. All you have to do is drop the –*re* from the infinitive and attach personal endings to the theme vowel. The only thing to watch out for is in the first person singular of first conjugation verbs. There, the theme vowel and the personal ending combine, leaving you with just –*ō*.

ALERT!

The personal endings in the present tense are the same as the ones you learned for the imperfect tense. There is, however, one exception. The –*m* for the first person singular (i.e., the "I" form) is replaced with an –*ō*. The present indicative is one of the few places you will see –*ō* instead of –*m*.

Third and fourth conjugation are not as predictable. In third conjugation, the short vowel –*e*–combines with the –*ō* in the first person singular, then weakens to an –*i*–, and eventually bottoms out to a –*u*– in the third person plural. If a verb has a first principal part that ends in –*iō*—which is true for some third and all fourth conjugation verbs—then it forms the present tense the same way as third. The only difference is that wherever the third conjugation doesn't have an –*i*–, these –*iō* verbs add one, so –*ō* becomes –*iō* and –*unt* becomes –*iunt*.

ESSENTIAL

The subjunctive mood also has present tense forms—perfect tense, too—but they aren't very common. You will learn them along with the subjunctive uses where they are used most often.

Using the Present Indicative

As you will recall, the perfect tense can make a general reference to something that happened in the past ("You wrote the sentence"), or it can show an action that was completed at the time of writing or speaking ("You have [now] written the sentence"). This latter use of the perfect tense emphasizes the "as of the present time" component of a "completed" action in the past. Previously, you learned that we use the term "completed aspect" to indicate the completed nature of an action. The other two aspects are included in the list below.

- Continuous aspect: something in the process of happening as of right now (e.g., "I am going")
- Completed aspect: something that is finished happening as of right now (e.g., "I have gone")
- Aorist aspect: neither process nor completion, just something generally happening round about now (e.g., "I go" or "I do go")

In Latin, when we want to stress that the action is actually taking place "as of the present time," we use the present tense ("I am [now] writing the sentence"). We use the present tense for the continuous and aorist aspects when we want to show "present time" action. (Note: There is no such thing as the present tense with the completed aspect; that action has to be expressed by the perfect tense.) Because it has this double duty, it can be translated more than one way. As a continuous aspect tense, *mittunt* can be translated "they are sending." As an aorist aspect tense, it can be read "they send" or "they do send." (Adding the "do" in English simply shows emphasis.)

Forming the Future Indicative

Now that you have the present tense under your belt, you will find the future tense a breeze. The concepts that apply to the present can also apply to the future with only a few twists. Once again, the key will be relativity.

Present tense forms can be a little challenging because they vary depending on the conjugation of the verb. You may have also noticed in our discussion of present tense forms that first and second conjugations have an affinity. Third and fourth conjugation verbs also share some characteristics.

This pairing of first/second and third/fourth is seen again in future tense forms. For the future tense though, there are two utterly distinct ways to form future tense.

Person	First	Second	Third	Third –iō	Fourth
	Table 11-2	**Future Tense Across the Conjugations**			
1st, sing.	stābō	monebō	mittam	capiam	sentiam
2nd, sing.	stābis	monēbis	mittēs	capiēs	sentiēs
3rd, sing.	stābit	monēbit	mittet	capiet	sentiet
1st, pl.	stābimus	monēbimus	mittēmus	capiēmus	sentiēmus
2nd, pl.	stābitis	monēbitis	mittētis	capiētis	sentiētis
3rd, pl.	stābunt	monēbunt	mittent	capient	sentient

First and second conjugation verbs do their own, distinctive thing. The verb stem shows the theme vowel of the conjugation; then there is a tense indicator and personal ending combination that is quite reminiscent of the –ba– + –m, –s, et cetera, of the imperfect tense. The vowel that fills the –b_m is significant. While the imperfect tense has an –a– straight down the line, the future tense has a vowel that changes as it goes. On reflection, however, the vowel pattern should look familiar. It is the same odd pattern you see in the present tense of third conjugation verbs!

Third and fourth conjugation verbs in future tense march to an entirely different drummer. In third conjugation, the short vowel –e– remains and only shifts to –a– in the first person singular where the old personal ending –m returns. Once again, –iō verbs form future tense the same way as third conjugation verbs, but add an –i– wherever regular third conjugation verbs don't have one. For the future tense, regular thirds *never* do, so –iō verbs in the future tense always have the stem –iē– onto which the personal endings are attached.

FACT

You will never learn the future subjunctive because it does not exist. By nature, the future is only an idea. Since the subjunctive mood already treats action as an idea, there is no need for a future subjunctive. So how can the indicative (the "fact" mood) have a future tense? Remember: grammatical mood shows how action is *treated,* so the future indicative only *treats* a future event as a "fact."

Using the Future Indicative

You read earlier in this chapter how present "time" and present "tense" are relative concepts. The future tense is also relative, since it takes the present as its reference point and shows something that happens *after* it. It doesn't matter exactly *when* the reference point is, the future tense simply follows it. It could just as easily be called the "later-on tense."

With respect to aspect, **TABLE 11-3** shows that the future tense functions like the present tense does. The form *curret*, then, can be translated "he will be running" as a continuous aspect tense, or "he will run" for the aorist aspect. (Unlike it does for the aorist present, English does not have a corresponding emphatic form "he do will run" or "he will do run"!)

Table 11-3	Action and Aspects		
Time/Aspect	Continuous (Present System)	Completed (Perfect System)	Aorist
	Present Tense	Perfect Tense	Present Tense
Now	*currit*	*cucurrit*	*currit*
	he is running	he has run	he runs
	Imperfect Tense	Pluperfect Tense	Perfect Tense
Earlier	*currēbat*	*cucurreat*	*cucurrit*
	he was running	he had run	he ran
	Future Tense	Future Perfect Tense	Future Tense
Later	*curret*	*cucurrerit*	*curret*
	he will be running	he will have run	he will run

The Pluperfect and Future Perfect Indicative

The last two Latin tenses, the pluperfect indicative and the future perfect indicative, are so similar in form and use that they are best spoken of together rather than as separate sections. Their functions are also relative to such an extent that they almost always require the presence of another verb as a reference point.

All the tenses of the perfect system are formed on the same stem. This stem is the third principal part of a verb minus the final –ī. The perfect tense has its own set of special personal endings that you have already learned and have been working with in the exercises. The pluperfect and future perfect tenses are formed on the same stem, of course, but they follow a tense construction model similar to that of the imperfect tense. That is to say, on the stem you add a tense indicator followed by a personal ending. The stem tells you that the tense is in the perfect system, the tense indicator tells you which tense it is, and the personal ending finishes the verb off by providing person and number information.

Here are some paradigms (i.e., charts showing the different forms) of the following verbs in the pluperfect and future perfect tenses:

*stō, stāre, **stetī**, statum* (to stand)
*moneō, monēre, **monuī**, monitum* (to warn)
*mittō, mittere, **mīsī**, missum* (to send)
*capiō, capere, **cēpī**, captum* (to take)
*sentiō, sentīre, **sēnsī**, sēnsum* (to feel)

Table 11-4   Pluperfect Tense Across the Conjugations

Person	First	Second	Third	Third –iō	Fourth
1st, sing.	*steteram*	*monueram*	*mīseram*	*cēperam*	*senseram*
2nd, sing.	*steterās*	*monuerās*	*mīerās*	*cēperās*	*senserās*
3rd, sing.	*steterat*	*monuerat*	*mīserat*	*cēperat*	*senserat*
1st, pl.	*steterāmus*	*monuerāmus*	*mīserāmus*	*cēperāmus*	*senserāmus*
2nd, pl.	*steterātis*	*monuerātis*	*mīserātis*	*cēperātis*	*senserātis*
3rd, pl.	*steterant*	*monuerant*	*mīserant*	*cēperant*	*senserant*

Table 11-5   Future Perfect Tense Across the Conjugations

Person	First	Second	Third	Third –*iō*	Fourth
1st, sing.	*steterō*	*monuerō*	*mīserō*	*cēperō*	*senserō*
2nd, sing.	*steteris*	*monueris*	*mīeris*	*cēperis*	*senseris*
3rd, sing.	*steterit*	*monuerit*	*mīserit*	*cēperit*	*senserit*
1st, pl.	*steterimus*	*monuerimus*	*mīserimus*	*cēperimus*	*senserimus*
2nd, pl.	*steteritis*	*monueritis*	*mīeritis*	*cēperitis*	*senseritis*
3rd, pl.	*steterint*	*monuerint*	*mīserint*	*cēperint*	*senserint*

The pluperfect tense forms are the same across the conjugations. In the perfect system, the conjugation to which a verb belongs doesn't matter. But however a perfect system tense is formed, it is the same across the board. The perfect stem has the tense indicator –*era*– and a personal ending.

The future perfect tense forms are also the same from conjugation to conjugation. To form the future perfect, the tense indicator –*eri*– is used. The only little exception to that rule is in the first person singular where the –*i*– is absorbed into the –*ō*. Otherwise, it's –*eri*– all the way down.

Conjugating the Six Tenses

Conjugate the following verbs in each of the six tenses—present, imperfect, future, perfect, pluperfect, and future perfect.

1. *iaciō, iacere, iēcī, iactum* (to throw)

2. *iaceō, iacēre, iacuī, itum* (to lie, i.e., maintain a horizontal position)

Using These Two Tenses

The pluperfect indicative is a fairly common tense. The future perfect indicative, on the other hand, is among the least commonly seen tenses in

Latin. They are presented together here because their function in the language is virtually the same. Their purpose and sole reason for existence is to show something that happened *before* something else happened. Take another look at where these two tenses appear on the aspect chart in **TABLE 11-3**. The pluperfect represents the past time tense for the completed aspect. The future perfect tense does the same thing, but in the future.

Earlier in this chapter you read about the relativity of tense use. The pluperfect and future perfect tenses are also relative, but they are relative to other tenses more than they are to a fixed point in time. In fact, they rely on the presence of another verb in a different tense to have meaning. This graphic will help illustrate all the tenses and their relative positions:

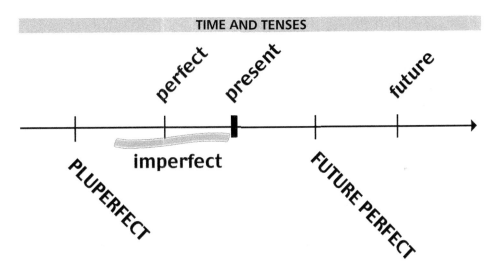

TIME AND TENSES

In this graphic, the arrow and its ticks represent time. The thick tick in the center is "right now." The ticks before it show "before now" (i.e., past time), and the ticks after it show "after now" (i.e., future time).

The words in the figure represent verb tenses. The present tense represents "right now." It is the reference point for the other tenses written above the line. The perfect and imperfect tenses show past actions, that is to say, actions that happened before "right now." The future tense shows actions yet to happen.

Beneath the line are the pluperfect and future perfect tenses. These two tenses are used to sequence events in the past or in the future respectively.

Given the placement of the pluperfect tense on the timeline, it looks like a super double past. In fact, it is. Sort of. The pluperfect is a past tense that takes as its reference point another past tense, either the perfect or imperfect tense. The perfect and the imperfect show something that happened before the present. The pluperfect shows something that happened before the perfect or imperfect.

> *Domum quam primum revēnī, sed commisātiō iam incēperat.*
> (I returned home as soon as possible, but the party had
> already started.)

Consider the sequence of events that this sentence lays out. First, the party started (pluperfect); then I came home (perfect). Both things took place in the past, but one did before the other.

Now look at the right side of the timeline. There you see two tenses, first the future perfect, then the future. The future perfect tense sits before the future tense just as the pluperfect tense sits before the perfect and imperfect tenses—and for the same reason. Here's our sentence again, *mutatis mutandis* (with the things that needed to be changed having been changed—sounds better in Latin, doesn't it?).

> *Domum quam primum reveniam, sed commisātiō iam incēperit.*
> (I will return home as soon as possible [future], but the
> party will have already started [future perfect].)

Both the pluperfect and the future perfect tenses need another verb in the past or future for them to make sense. You will rarely see them alone, and when you do, there is another action, past or future, that is implied.

FACT

English can be rather sloppy with expressing future events. The use of "will" and "will have" for translating the future and future perfect tenses may be grammatically correct, but sometimes we use the present tense to refer to a future event! For example, "While I am going to work tomorrow morning, . . ."

Table 11-6   Vocabulary

adhūc, adv.	to this point, still
arma, armōrum, n. pl.*	weapons
ars, artis, f.	skill, art
at (ast), conj.	but
beātus, –a, –um	blessed, happy
bibō, –ere, bibī, bibitum	to drink
cārus, –a, –um	dear, expensive
castra, castrōrum, n. pl.*	camp
cognōscō, –ere, cognōvī, cognitum	(*in present system*) to get to know, learn, recognize; (*in perfect system*) to know, be familiar with
deinde, adv.	then, next
dīvus, –a, –um	divine, deified
dum, conj.	while
frāter, frātris, m.	brother
genus, generis, n.	type, kind, sort
iter, itineris, n.	route, journey, way
iterum, adv.	again
labor, labōris, m.**	work, suffering
lābōrō, –āre, –āvī, –ātum	to work
levis, –e	light
līber, –a, –um	free
māter, mātris, f.	mother
nam, conj.	since, because
noscō, –ere, nōvī, nōtus	(*in present system*) to get to know, learn, recognize; (*in perfect system*) to know, be familiar with
nōtus, –a, –um	known, famous
occīdō, –ere, occīdī, occīsum	to kill
opus, operis, n.**	work
ōs, ōris, n.	mouth, face
os, ossis, n.	bone

continued on following page

parō, –āre, –āvī, –ātum	to prepare, get
pius, pia, pium	respectful, dutiful, pious
prīmus, –a, –um	first; (*quam prīmum* "as soon as possible")
pulcher, pulchra, pulchrum	beautiful, handsome
quasi, adv.	just as, as if
quod, conj.	since, because
reddō, –ere, reddidī, redditum	to give back, deliver
rivus, –ī, m.	stream
secundus, –a, –um	second, following, favorable
sīcut, adv.	like, as
solvō, –ere, solvī, solūtum	to untie, loosen, weaken; pay
soror, –ōris, f.	sister
statim, adv.	immediately
tandem, adv.	finally
turpis, –e	ugly, shameful
ubi, conj.	when, where
vera, n. pl.	truth
vix, adv.	hardly
vōx, vōcis, f.	voice

* *arma/castra*: These words are always plural in Latin. English also has words that only appear in the plural, such as "scissors."

** *labor/opus*: *Labor* means "work" in the sense of suffering or effort expended. *Opus* is "work" in the sense of the result of *labor*.

Latin-to-English Translations

Translate these Latin sentences into English.

1. *Verba Lātina tam bene discēbat ut omnia sīcut mātrem suam cognōvit.*

2. *Cum ācria nōn essent, arma servīs reddidimus.*

3. *Puellae plus aquae bibērunt nē sitīrent.*

4. *Canis miser os petet, alius tamen canis os facile invēnerit.*

5. *Ubi canis quidem fēlix os invēnerit, ōre domum feret.*

6. *Pecuniam reddit, nam tale praemium nōn meret.*

7. *Iter brevissimum capiētis ut Brundisium quam primum perveniātis.*

8. *Post mortem imperātoris, exercitus urbem vī et igne rapiet.*

9. *Cum civēs rēgem dīvum nōn habērent, dona tamen sacerrima atque cārissima dābant.*

10. *Cenābis bene apud mē.*

English-to-Latin Translations

Translate these sentences into good Latin.

1. Finally they will tell the women everything.

2. When the slave had worked for a fairly long time, his master said, "Enough."

3. The horses are drinking water out of the stream.

4. You learn things faster than your sister.

5. The soldiers killed the men so they wouldn't tell the truth.

Chapter 12

Vocabulary Building

Now is a good time to take a break from Latin grammar. This chapter offers you a chance to work on your vocabulary. We'll start with the most important verbs in the language—the irregular verbs—and then give you the opportunity to multiply your vocabulary by a factor of, as the Romans would say, the number of sands on the Libyan shore!

The Essential Verb "to Be"

The most notoriously irregular verb in any language is the verb that means "to be." In some languages, like English, it is actually cobbled together from a few different verbs. In other languages, like Russian, the present tense of the verb "to be" self-destructed and is no longer in use.

FACT

The wildly different forms of the English verb "to be" come from three Proto-Indo-European roots. The English present tense ("am," "is," and "are") are from the old root es–. The English infinitive and participles ("be," "being," "been") are from bhu–. The past tense ("was," "were") is from wes– meaning "dwell." Latin doesn't use this root.

Sum

The Latin verb *sum* is also cobbled together from descendants of the two Proto-Indo-European roots *es–* and *bhu–*, even though it doesn't quite look that way. In Latin, the stem for the whole present system is from *es–*, and the perfect system stem is from *bhu–*.

Table 12-1   The Verb *sum, esse, fui, futūrus* (to be)

Person	Present System — Present		Perfect System — Perfect	
	SINGULAR	PLURAL	SINGULAR	PLURAL
1st	sum	sumus	fuī	fuimus
2nd	es	estis	fuistī	fuistis
3rd	est	sunt	fuit	fuērunt

Person	Imperfect		Pluperfect	
	SINGULAR	PLURAL	SINGULAR	PLURAL
1st	eram	erāmus	fueram	fuerāmus
2nd	erās	erātis	fuerās	fuerātis
3rd	erat	erant	fuerat	fuerant

continued on following page

Table 12-1 The Verb *sum, esse, fui, futūrus* (to be)—*continued*

Person	Future		Future Perfect	
	SINGULAR	PLURAL	SINGULAR	PLURAL
1st	erō	erimus	fuerō	fuerimus
2nd	eris	eritis	fueris	fueritis
3rd	erit	erunt	fuerit	fuerint

The stem for the imperfect and future tenses experienced what linguists call rhotacism. It often happens in Indo-European languages that when an *s* finds itself sitting between two vowels, that *s* changes to an *r*. You can see this in English with the plural of "**is**" being "**are**," and the plural of "**was**" being "**were**." That's why *esam* became *eram*.

There are a couple more linguistic sleight-of-hand maneuvers that you might find interesting. For the imperfect of *sum,* cover the *er–* and replace it with a *b–*. Look familar? The same thing will happen if you do this with the future. Now cover the *fu–* in the pluperfect and future perfect and compare them with the imperfect and future. Presto! (Well, except for the *–i–* in *erint*.)

The forms for the perfect system don't need any explanation. The endings are regular. It's only the stem that is strange.

FACT

The English "be" and the Latin *fu–* don't look like they have anything to do with each other until you consider the relationship the letters *b* or *p* and *f* have between the languages. It usually happens that where one has a *b* or a *p*, the other has an *f* (e.g., *frāter* ["brother"], *pater* ["father"], *ferō* ["bear/bring"]).

Possum

Read the following dialog out loud:
"Jeet jet?"
"Naw, jew?"
Here's the same dialog slowed down:
"Did you eat yet?"
"No, did you?"

The Latin verb *possum* was born from this very same phenomenon. In the case of *possum*, the slurring is between the adjective *potis* ("able") and *sum* ("to be").

Table 12-2	The Verb *possum, posse, potui,* ——— (to be able)			
	Present System		**Perfect System**	
Person	**Present**		**Perfect**	
	SINGULAR	PLURAL	SINGULAR	PLURAL
1st	possum	possumus	potuī	potuimus
2nd	potes	potestis	potuistī	potuistis
3rd	potest	possunt	potuit	potuērunt
Person	**Imperfect**		**Pluperfect**	
	SINGULAR	PLURAL	SINGULAR	PLURAL
1st	poteram	poterāmus	potueram	potuerāmus
2nd	poterās	poterātis	potuerās	potuerātis
3rd	poterat	poterant	potuerat	potuerant
Person	**Future**		**Future Perfect**	
	SINGULAR	PLURAL	SINGULAR	PLURAL
1st	poterō	poterimus	potuerō	potuerimus
2nd	poteris	poteritis	potueris	potueritis
3rd	poterit	poterunt	potuerit	potuerint

The slurring of *potis* into *sum* follows some simple rules. There are only three things to remember:

1. The formula is: *pot* + a form of *sum*.
2. If the form of *sum* begins with an *s*, change the *t* to an *s*.
3. If the form of *sum* begins with an *f*, drop the *f*.

The only exception to these rules is the infinitive *posse*.

Imperfect and future tense forms of *possum* can be easily confused with forms of the pluperfect and future perfect tenses of *possum*. Furthermore, they can all be confused with perfect system forms of *pōnō* ("to put"). Compare, for example, *poteram* ("I was able," "I could"), *potueram* ("I had been able"), and *posueram* ("I had put").

The Small but Useful Verb "Go"

Perhaps the most beguiling verb in the entire Latin language is *eō*, the verb meaning "to go." It is tiny. In fact, it looks like a set of endings in search of a stem!

Table 12-3   The Verb *eō, īre, iī, itum* (to go)

	Present System		Perfect System	
Person	**Present**		**Perfect**	
	SINGULAR	PLURAL	SINGULAR	PLURAL
1st	*eō*	*īmus*	*iī*	*imus*
2nd	*īs*	*ītis*	*iistī*	*itis*
3rd	*it*	*eunt*	*iit*	*iēruent*
Person	**Imperfect**		**Pluperfect**	
	SINGULAR	PLURAL	SINGULAR	PLURAL
1st	*ībam*	*ībāmus*	*ieram*	*ierāmus*
2nd	*ībās*	*ībātis*	*ierās*	*ierātis*
3rd	*ībat*	*ībant*	*ierat*	*ierant*
Person	**Future**		**Future Perfect**	
	SINGULAR	PLURAL	SINGULAR	PLURAL
1st	*ībō*	*ībimus*	*ierō*	*ierimus*
2nd	*ībis*	*ībitis*	*ieris*	*ieritis*
3rd	*ībit*	*ībunt*	*ierit*	*ierint*

There are a few noteworthy points for this verb:

- *Eō* is the only verb whose stem for the imperfect and perfect tenses ends in *–i–*.
- The perfect stem is occasionally *iv–* instead of *i–* (e.g., *ivit* for *iit*).
- It is usually seen with a prefix. (e.g., *exeō*, "to go out")

Because of the clipped nature of *eō*, most Romance languages opted to keep a different verb—*vadō, vadere* (to plod)—in many or most of the forms for their verb meaning "to go." For example, to say "you go" in Spanish is *tú vas;* Italian, *tu vai;* French, *tu vais.*

The Verb "to Bring"

The Latin verb "to bring" (*ferō*) is what is called an athematic verb. That means that unlike regular verbs, it doesn't have a theme vowel. *Ferō* did have one, but only partially.

Table 12-4 The Verb *ferō, ferre, tulī, lātum* (to carry, bring, bear)

	Present System		Perfect System	
Person	**Present**		**Perfect**	
	SINGULAR	PLURAL	SINGULAR	PLURAL
1st	*ferō*	*ferimus*	*tulī*	*tulimus*
2nd	*fers*	*fertis*	*tulistī*	*tulistis*
3rd	*fert*	*ferunt*	*tulit*	*tulērunt*
Person	**Imperfect**		**Pluperfect**	
	SINGULAR	PLURAL	SINGULAR	PLURAL
1st	*ferēbam*	*ferēbāmus*	*tuleram*	*tulerāmus*
2nd	*ferēbās*	*ferēbātis*	*tulerās*	*tulerātis*
3rd	*ferēbat*	*ferēbant*	*tulerat*	*tulerant*
Person	**Future**		**Future Perfect**	
	SINGULAR	PLURAL	SINGULAR	PLURAL
1st	*feram*	*ferēmus*	*tulerō*	*tulerimus*
2nd	*ferēs*	*ferētis*	*tuleris*	*tuleritis*
3rd	*feret*	*ferent*	*tulerit*	*tulerint*

On the whole, *ferō* is formed just like a regular third conjugation verb. Where it truly departs from the pack is in the present tense; some of the forms are lacking a vowel. The most trouble *ferō* might give you is simply that its principal parts are so strange. The form *tulistī* doesn't immediately conjure "*ferō*."

Willing or Not

The Latin verb "to be willing" or "to wish" is highly irregular. It also has a pair of related verbs that are the result of slurring, like *possum*.

The verb *volō, velle, voluī* is very old and very strange. It is not sure whether it wants to be regular, third conjugation, or athematic!

The basic meaning behind this verb is *willingness*, not *need* or *desire*. (Think about the *vol*– in the English word "*vol*unteer.") Still, it sometimes sounds better to translate it as "to wish" or "to want" rather than "to be willing."

Table 12-5   The Verb *volō, velle, voluī*, ———
(to be willing, wish, want)

	Present System		Perfect System	
Person	**Present**		**Perfect**	
	SINGULAR	PLURAL	SINGULAR	PLURAL
1st	*volō*	*volumus*	*voluī*	*voluimus*
2nd	*vīs*	*vultis*	*voluistī*	*voluistis*
3rd	*vult*	*volunt*	*voluit*	*voluērunt*
Person	**Imperfect**		**Pluperfect**	
	SINGULAR	PLURAL	SINGULAR	PLURAL
1st	*volēbam*	*volēbāmus*	*volueram*	*voluerāmus*
2nd	*volēbās*	*volēbātis*	*voluerās*	*voluerātis*
3rd	*volēbat*	*volēbant*	*voluerat*	*voluerant*
Person	**Future**		**Future Perfect**	
	SINGULAR	PLURAL	SINGULAR	PLURAL
1st	*volam*	*volēmus*	*voluerō*	*voluerimus*
2nd	*volēs*	*volētis*	*volueris*	*volueritis*
3rd	*volet*	*volent*	*voluerit*	*voluerint*

There are two verbs that have a relationship to *volō* similar to the one *possum* has with *sum*.

The opposite, or negative of *volō* is the verb *nōlō, nōlle, nōluī*—"to be unwilling," "not to wish," "not to want." As you might have already guessed, it is the fusion of the negative *nōn* with the front end of *volō*.

Table 12-6   The Verb *nōlō, nōlle, nōluī,* ——— (to be unwilling, not to wish, not to want)

	Present System		Perfect System	
Person	**Present**		**Perfect**	
	SINGULAR	PLURAL	SINGULAR	PLURAL
1st	*nōlō*	*nōlumus*	*nōluī*	*nōluimus*
2nd	*nōn vīs*	*nōn vultis*	*nōluistī*	*nōluistis*
3rd	*nōn vult*	*nōlunt*	*nōluit*	*nōluērunt*
Person	**Imperfect**		**Pluperfect**	
	SINGULAR	PLURAL	SINGULAR	PLURAL
1st	*nōlēbam*	*nōlēbāmus*	*nōlueram*	*nōluerāmus*
2nd	*nōlēbās*	*nōlēbātis*	*nōluerās*	*nōluerātis*
3rd	*nōlēbat*	*nōlēbant*	*nōluerat*	*nōluerant*
Person	**Future**		**Future Perfect**	
	SINGULAR	PLURAL	SINGULAR	PLURAL
1st	*nōlam*	*nōlēmus*	*nōluerō*	*nōluerimus*
2nd	*nōlēs*	*nōlētis*	*nōlueris*	*nōlueritis*
3rd	*nōlet*	*nōlent*	*nōluerit*	*nōluerint*

If you study the previous paradigm, you will quickly recognize a pattern. The adverb *nōn* merges to replace the initial *v* with an *n* everywhere the form of *volō* begins *vol–*. The one exception to this rule is in the infinitive *nolle*.

The verb *mālō, malle, māluī* is not among the more common irregular verbs in Latin literature, even though it would have been quite common in the everyday speech of the ancient Romans. *Mālō* is the merger of the comparative adverb *magis* ("more") and *volō*. The result of this contraction is a verb that literally means "to be more willing," "to want more," but it is used in the sense of "to prefer."

Table 12-7 The Verb *mālō, mālle, mālui,* ——— (to prefer to be more willing, to want or like more)				
	Present System		**Perfect System**	
Person	**Present**		**Perfect**	
	SINGULAR	PLURAL	SINGULAR	PLURAL
1st	*mālō*	*mālumus*	*māluī*	*māluimus*
2nd	*māvīs*	*māvultis*	*māluistī*	*māluistis*
3rd	*māvult*	*mālunt*	*māluit*	*māluērunt*
Person	**Imperfect**		**Pluperfect**	
	SINGULAR	PLURAL	SINGULAR	PLURAL
1st	*mālēbam*	*mālēbāmus*	*mālueram*	*māluerāmus*
2nd	*mālēbās*	*mālēbātis*	*māluerās*	*māluerātis*
3rd	*mālēbat*	*mālēbant*	*māluerat*	*māluerant*
Person	**Future**		**Future Perfect**	
	SINGULAR	PLURAL	SINGULAR	PLURAL
1st	*mālam*	*mālēmus*	*māluerō*	*māluerimus*
2nd	*mālēs*	*mālētis*	*mālueris*	*mālueritis*
3rd	*mālet*	*mālent*	*māluerit*	*māluerint*

With *mālō*, the initial *vo–* or *ve–* of *volō* is changed to *mā–* throughout the verb. Wherever the form of *volō* does not begin with *vo–* or *ve–*, the *mā–* is simply attached.

There is one peculiar thing to note about this verb. Since it is formed by the addition of a comparative, it takes comparative constructions. That is to say, rather than requiring an accusative object as transitive verbs usually do, you see it with *quam* or an ablative of comparison.

Aurēlia fēlēs māvult. (Aurelia prefers cats.)
Aurēlia fēlēs canibus māvult. (Aurelia prefers cats to dogs.)
Aurēlia fēlēs quam canēs māvult. (Aurelia likes cats better than
     [she likes] dogs.)

There are two other irregular verbs in Latin. You will learn about one, *fīō* ("to become"), in a later chapter. The other, *edō, ēsse, ēdī, ēsum* ("to eat"), isn't common enough to deal with, though you should be aware of it. Its present tense can cause trouble as you might imagine: *edō, ēs, ēst, edimus, ēstis, edunt.* In Latin you really are what you eat!

Infinitives

You have been reading references to infinitives since you first read about verbs. They are the second principal part of a verb, and their endings determine the conjugation of that particular verb. You can spot them in English as the "to" form of a verb (e.g., to walk, to snooze, to fly, et al.).

There are four infinitive uses in Latin. Chapter 17 deals in more detail with infinitives. At the moment, however, you need to be acquainted with only one. This is called the complementary infinitive.

There are certain verbs that don't quite express an entire thought on their own. When an infinitive is used to complete the thought of such a verb, it is called a complementary infinitive. For example:

*Romam **īre** volō.* (I want **to go** to Rome.)
*Neque **legere** neque **scribere** poterant.* (They weren't able **to read** or **write.**)

Some verbs—*possum* is a prime example—are rarely seen *without* a complementary infinitive.

Vocabulary Building

The Latin language really doesn't have that many words in its vocabulary. The majority of Latin's vocabulary is the result of mix-and-match with prefixes, suffixes, and bases. There are also a few ways to tweak verbs to give them new, special meanings. If you learn bases and prefixes, you'll be able to multiply your Latin (and English!) vocabulary knowledge tremendously.

Adding Prefixes

Here is a list of the most common prefixes and their meanings. You should find them easy to learn because they are almost all closely related to prepositions. Some prefixes don't have an easily translatable word or phrase. They have a general idea, or flavor, that they add to the meaning of the base. For example, the verb *caedō* means "to cut," and the prefix *ob* has an "opposing," "up close and personal" flavor. Put them together and you get *occīdō, –ere, occīdī, occīsum* ("to kill").

Table 12-8   Latin Prefixes

Prefix	English	Example
ā, ab	away, from	*abeō* (to go away)
ad	to, toward, near	*adsum* (to be present)
ante–	before, in front	*antecedō* (to go ahead)
con–	with, together, intense	*conveniō* (to gather)
dē–	down, from, bad	*dērideō* (to mock)
dis–	scattered, apart, bad	*discumbō* (to sprawl)
ē–/ex–	out	*exeō* (to leave)
in	in, on, against	*ineō* (to enter)
in	not	*infirmus* (weak)
ob–	opposing, counter, blocking	*obvius* (evident) (*ob + via*, "blocking the road")
per–	thorough, intense	*perterritus* (thoroughly frightened)
prae–	ahead	*praesum* (to be in charge)
praeter–	except, beyond	*praetereō* (to pass by)
prō–	forward, in front	*prōcēdō* (to go ahead)
re–, red–	again, back	*redeō* (to return)
sub–	under, subtle	*subrideō* (to grin)
super–	over, above	*supersum* (to be left over, survive)
trans–, trā–	across	*trādō* (to hand over)

Some prefixes change their spelling slightly when attached to a word. The main reason this occurs is to make the word easier to say. These changes can make prefixes difficult to recognize.

A good example of these phenomena is the verb *accipiō* ("to welcome"; literally, "to take to one's self"). It is made of the prefix *ad–* ("to, toward") and the verb *capiō* ("to take"). The *d* on *ad* changes to *c* to make it easier to say. This process is called assimilation.

ALERT!

Be aware of vowel weakening. Sometimes the vowel in a verb base changes a little when a prefix is attached. This is most common when a verb has an *a* or *ae* in its base. For example, add the prefix *per–* to *faciō, facere, fēcī, factum* and you get *perficiō, perficere, perfēcī, perfectum*.

Adding Suffixes

A suffix is a syllable or two that can be added to the stem of a word to create another word related in meaning. Suffixes usually produce nouns or adjectives. Of course, the nouns they form have their own genitive and gender, and the adjectives have masculine, feminine, and neuter forms.

Here is a list of the most common suffixes:

Table 12-9 Latin Suffixes	
ability or worth:	
–bilis, –bile	*memorābilis, –e* (memorable)
full of:	
–ōsus, –a, um	*gloriōsus, –a, –um* (braggart)
–bundus, –a, um	*cantabundus, –a, um* (full of song)
pertaining to or from:	
–ālis, –e or *–āris, –e*	*vērnālis, –e* (pertaining to spring); *solaris, –e* (pertaining to the sun)
–ānus, –a, um or *–īnus, –a, um*	*Rōmānus, –a, um* (from Rome); *canīnus, –a, –um* (pertaining to dogs)
–icus, –a, –um	*rūsticus, –a, um* (pertaining to the country)

continued on following page

Table 12-9   Latin Suffixes—*continued*

condition or state:	
–ia, –iae, f.	*laetitia, laetitiae,* f. (happiness)
–tūdō, –tūdinis, f.	*multitūdō, multitūdinis,* f. (multitude)
–tās, –tātis, f.	*nuditās, nuditātis,* f. (nudity)

small, cute, dear: (This kind of suffix is called a diminutive.)	
–illus, –a, –um	*Iulilla, –ae,* f. (Julie, instead of Julia)

The following suffixes can be added to the stem of the fourth principal part of a verb:

A person who does an action:

–or, –ōris, m. or *–trīx, –trīcis,* f.
narrātor, narrātōris, m. (a male storyteller);
narrātrīx, narrātrīcis, f. (a female storyteller)

The act or result of an action:

–iō, –iōnis, f.   *actiō, actiōnis,* f. (action, the act or result of doing);
visiō, visiōnis, f. (vision, the act or result of seeing)

Making Verbs

There are a few ways for you to increase your verb knowledge. Verbs can take suffixes to create new verbs with special twists on their original meanings. Verbs can also be made from nouns or adjectives.

Frequentative verbs show an action that is repeated or sustained over time. Their meaning is quite similar to that of the continuous aspect. They are made by turning the fourth principal part of a verb into a first conjugation verb.

capiō, –ere cēpī, ***capt****um* (to take)
capt*ō, captāre* (to keep grabbing at)

Inceptive verbs show an action in its early stages. They are formed by adding *–scō, –scere* to the present stem of a verb.

candeō, **candēre,** *canduī* (to shine)
cande*scō, candescere* (to begin to shine, to glow)

Denominative verbs are verbs that are made from nouns or adjectives. We often use nouns in English as if they were verbs. For example, "tree" is a noun, but dogs "tree" cats every day. In Latin they are formed by taking the stem of a noun or adjective and treating it like a first conjugation verb.

nōmen, **nomin***is,* n. (a name)
nōminō, *nōmināre* (to name)

Latin-to-English Translations

Translate the following Latin sentences into English.

1. *Cum Carthagine rediissent, multa dē urbe narrābant.*

2. *Parum sapientiae habēre nolō.*

3. *Tot arma in hostēs intulērunt nostrī ut hostēs statim fūgerent.*

4. *Mīlitēs autem in castra redīre nolunt quod fortissimī sunt et minimē ignāvī.*

5. *Puerī domum properāre voluērunt nam in ludō totum diem esse nolēbant.*

continued on following page

Latin-to-English Translations—*continued*

6. *Cum Graecī urbem Trōiam perdidissent, multī hominēs tamen superfuērunt.*

7. *Ubi dea miserōs in periculō vīderat, adiuvāre volēbat at nōn poterat.*

8. *Soror perterrita fuit, cum frāter suus periit.*

9. *Omnia multā arte cūrāque conficere poteris.*

10. *Paucī tanta tam facillimē gerere possunt.*

Figuring Out Meaning

What do you think these words mean? (Guess, before you look them up!)

1. *conveniō*

2. *perambulō*

3. *praeterdūcō*

4. *superpōnō*

5. *absum*

6. *suscipiō*

7. *praedīcō*

continued on following page

Figuring Out Meaning—*continued*

8. *suburbānus*

9. *perfacile*

10. *ingerō*

11. *transferō*

12. *incredibilis*

13. *obsum*

14. *discēdō*

15. *inventor*

16. *repugnō*

17. *ignoscō*

18. *excipiō*

19. *praeparō*

20. *remaneō*

Chapter 13

Pronouns

Pronouns are those little words that stand in for nouns. We take pronouns for granted, though we shouldn't. Without them we would have to keep repeating nouns. That would be terribly tedious. Latin pronouns are declined almost identically to one another, and you know virtually all the endings already.

Personal Pronouns

As their name suggests, these pronouns refer to grammatical persons: first ("I"), second ("you"), and third ("he," "she," "it").

Table 13-1 First Person Pronouns			Table 13-2 Second Person Pronouns		
Case	**Singular**	**Plural**	**Case**	**Singular**	**Plural**
Nominative	*ego*	*nōs*	Nominative	*tū*	*vōs*
Genitive	*meī*	*nostrum/ nostrī*	Genitive	*tuī*	*vestrum/ vestrī*
Dative	*mihi*	*nōbīs*	Dative	*tibi*	*vōbīs*
Accusative	*mē*	*nōs*	Accusative	*tē*	*vōs*
Ablative	*mē*	*nōbīs*	Ablative	*tē*	*vōbīs*

Latin personal pronouns are used the same way as English personal pronouns are. There are, however, a couple of points to know about them.

First, thanks to personal endings on verbs, the nominative case form for the first and second person really isn't necessary. If a verb ends in –*m* or –*s* or –*mus* or –*tis*, then you automatically know that "I," "you," "we," or "you" is the subject. So why have it? Emphasis, that's all. When you want to emphasize a person in English, you simply raise your voice. "**I** want to go home!" For Latin, this approach is awkward. *Domum redīre volō!* Rather than yell an ending, Latin adds the nominative of the personal pronoun. ***Ego*** *domum redīre volō!* (The pronoun may then be yelled for added emphasis.)

The second point is that the genitive case form of first and second person personal pronouns (*meī, tuī, nostrī/nostrum, vestrī/vestrum*) are *never* used to show possession. To show possession (i.e., "my," "your," "our," "your"), you must use the possessive adjectives *meus, tuus, noster,* and *vester,* which agree in gender, case, and number with whatever noun they are modifying (e.g., *pater meus,* "my father"; *māter tua,* "your mother"; and so on). The genitive case forms of personal pronouns are used for any genitive use.

Why are there two different forms for the genitive plural? The first ones (*nostrum* and *vestrum*) tend to be used in a partitive sense, while the second ones (*nostrī* and *vestrī*) tend to be used objectively.

Partitive: *Nēmo nostrum rūs cessit.* (None of us went to the country.)
Objective: *Odium vestrī nōs retinuit.* (Hatred of you people kept us back.)

ALERT!

When a first or second person pronoun is used with the preposition *cum,* the pronoun becomes enclitic (like the conjunction *–que*); for example, *mēcum,* "with me"; *tēcum,* "with you"; *nōbīscum,* "with us"; *vōbīscum,* "with you."

Demonstrative Adjectives

A demonstrative adjective is a word that demonstrates (i.e., points out) which thing or person is being referred to. In English, there are only two demonstrative adjectives: "this" and "that." "This" points to something near the speaker; "that" points to something away from the speaker. They are relative words—"this dog" is near me, but for you across the room, it is "that dog."

Latin has four demonstrative adjectives, which, as substantives, are used as the personal pronouns for the third person (i.e., "he," "she," "it," and "they").

QUESTION?

What is a "substantive"?
Substantives are adjectives that are used like nouns. Their gender fills in for whatever they would otherwise agree with (e.g., *malae* are "evil women"). You know they're women because *–ae* is a feminine ending.

Hic, haec, hoc

Hic is basically Latin for "this." It is the demonstrative adjective that points to something near the speaker. Since grammatically the speaker is called the first person, you could think of *hic* as a sort of first person demonstrative adjective.

Hic has a very unusual declension, which you will have to memorize.

Table 13-3   Declension of the Demonstrative Adjective *hic, haec, hoc*

Case	Masculine	Feminine	Neuter
Singular			
Nominative	*hic*	*haec*	*hoc*
Genitive	*huius*	*huius*	*huius*
Dative	*huic*	*huic*	*huic*
Accusative	*hunc*	*hanc*	*hoc*
Ablative	*hōc*	*hāc*	*hōc*
Plural			
Nominative	*hī*	*hae*	*haec*
Genitive	*hōrum*	*hārum*	*hōrum*
Dative	*hīs*	*hīs*	*hīs*
Accusative	*hōs*	*hās*	*haec*
Ablative	*hīs*	*hīs*	*hīs*

If you study the declension of *hic* and try to ignore the occasional leading *hu–* or trailing *–c*, you will notice that you already know most of the endings.

Iste, ista, istud

Just as *hic* is a sort of first person demonstrative, *iste* is a sort of second person demonstative. Rather than being near the speaker, it refers to something near the person being spoken to. English doesn't have anything quite like this adjective. Instead, we have to say something along the lines of "that _____ by you" or "that _____ of yours."

		Table 13-4 Declension of the Demonstrative Adjective *iste, ista, istud*	
Case	**Masculine**	**Feminine**	**Neuter**
		Singular	
Nominative	*iste*	*ista*	*istud*
Genitive	*istīus*	*istīus*	*istīus*
Dative	*istī*	*istī*	*istī*
Accusative	*istum*	*istam*	*istud*
Ablative	*istō*	*istā*	*istō*
		Plural	
Nominative	*istī*	*istae*	*ista*
Genitive	*istōrum*	*istārum*	*istōrum*
Dative	*istīs*	*istīs*	*istīs*
Accusative	*istōs*	*istās*	*ista*
Ablative	*istīs*	*istīs*	*istīs*

Let's examine the peculiarities of the declension of *iste*.

- The nominative singular is unique and must be learned. This is not strange.
- The genitive singular is strange. *Hic* has *–ius* here, too.
- The dative singular in *–ī* is a normal third declension ending.
- What remains are regular first/second declension adjective endings!

FACT

By the time of the late Roman Republic (509–31 B.C.E.), the demonstrative *iste* had picked up a derogatory connotation. This bad spin may have come from the word's extensive use in the law courts, where opposing sides battled to brand each other as the evildoers.

Ille, illa, illud

The demonstrative *ille* is perhaps the adjective that most closely corresponds to the English "that." Before the adjective *iste* turned mean, *ille* referred to something neither near the speaker nor near the person being spoken to. After *iste* took on a life of its own, *ille* began to refer to anything that was **not** near the speaker.

Table 13-5   Declension of the Demonstrative Adjective *ille, illa, illud*

Case	Masculine	Feminine	Neuter
	Singular		
Nominative	*ille*	*illa*	*illud*
Genitive	*illīus*	*illīus*	*illīus*
Dative	*illī*	*illī*	*illī*
Accusative	*illum*	*illam*	*illud*
Ablative	*illō*	*illā*	*illō*
	Plural		
Nominative	*illī*	*illae*	*illa*
Genitive	*illōrum*	*illārum*	*illōrum*
Dative	*illīs*	*illīs*	*illīs*
Accusative	*illōs*	*illās*	*illa*
Ablative	*illīs*	*illīs*	*illīs*

The declension of *ille* is identical to that of *iste*.

Most Romance languages take their third person pronouns ("he" and "she") and definite article adjective (i.e., their word for "the") from *ille*. Spanish has *él, ella, el,* and *la* for "he," "she," "the" (masculine), and "the" (feminine). French: *il, elle, le, la.* Italian *lui, lei, il, la.*

Is, ea, id

If the demonstratives *hic, iste,* and *ille* cover first, second, and third person viewpoints, what could a fourth demonstrative refer to? The Latin demonstrative *is, ea, id* can be translated as "this" or "that." It doesn't matter which you chose because both are wrong. *Is* refers to something that was just mentioned, or something that is just about to be mentioned. Its reference point is conceptual, not spatial. Since *is* is so dependent on context, it is difficult to give a worthwhile example of it in action without a context. Where one sees *is* most often is as a pronoun. You will read about demonstratives as pronouns in the next section.

Table 13-6   Declension of the Demonstrative Adjective *is, ea, id*

Case	Masculine	Feminine	Neuter
Singular			
Nominative	*is*	*ea*	*id*
Genitive	*eius*	*eius*	*eius*
Dative	*eī*	*eī*	*eī*
Accusative	*eum*	*eam*	*id*
Ablative	*eō*	*eā*	*eō*
Plural			
Nominatve	*eī*	*eae*	*ea*
Genitive	*eōrum*	*eārum*	*eōrum*
Dative	*eīs*	*eīs*	*eīs*
Accusative	*eōs*	*eās*	*ea*
Ablative	*eīs*	*eīs*	*eīs*

Demonstratives As Pronouns

When demonstrative adjectives are used substantively, they become pronouns.

Bennie ate a dozen of those jelly doughnuts.
Bennie ate a dozen of those.

"Those" isn't a noun, but obviously it can stand in for one. Of course, you need context to know what "those" are. A pronoun always needs a referent, something it carries (*ferō*) back (*re–*) to. In Latin grammar, referents are usually called antecedents (*ante,* "before"; *cedō,* "go").

Latin has no devoted personal pronouns for the third person. That is because Latin uses demonstrative adjectives instead. This means that if Latin has four different demonstrative adjectives, Latin also has four different ways to say "he"—it depends on which "he" you are talking about!

"**He** went to Ponza to visit Postumus" could be translated:

1. *Hic Ponzam iit ut Postumum visitāret.*
2. *Iste Ponzam iit ut Postumum visitāret.*
3. *Ille Ponzam iit ut Postumum visitāret.*
4. *Is Ponzam iit ut Postumum visitāret.*

These sentences could all be translated the same way, but each means something a little different. Here is what the various "he's" are in the example:

1. "He" refers to this guy near me, the speaker.
2. "He" refers to that creep that the speaker cannot stand.
3. "He" refers to that guy over there.
4. "He" refers to the guy we are talking about at the moment.

If Latin has four words for "he," then there are also four words for "she" (*haec, ista, illa, ea*) and "it" (*hoc, istud, illud, id*). What is more, English has only "they" for a third person plural pronoun, but Latin also shows gender, so *eae* isn't just "they"; it specifically refers to a female/feminine group that is being discussed.

Reflexive Pronouns

Look in the mirror and what do you see? There are two answers to that question: your reflection and yourself. That is what reflexive pronouns are all about. Whenever something in a sentence refers back to the subject of the sentence, you need a reflexive pronoun. Unlike English, which uses a "–self"' word, Latin just uses the regular personal pronouns.

Tē videō. (I see you.)
Mē videō. (I see myself.)

Notice how Latin simply seems to say "I see me"? The reflexive pronouns in Latin—for the first and second person anyway—are identical to the personal pronouns. For the third person, however, as with the personal pronouns, something else is the case.

FACT

There are no nominative forms for the reflexive pronoun. The nominative case shows the subject and reflexives refer back to the subject. The subject can't help but refer to itself . . . it *is* itself!

There is a distinct form for third person reflexive pronouns. It has no nominative form, since the subject already *is* itself!

Table 13-7 The Third Person Reflexive Pronoun	
Nominative	——
Genitive	*suī*
Dative	*sibi*
Accusative	*sē*
Ablative	*sē*

*Marcus pecuniam **sibi** retinuit.* (Mark kept the money **for himself.**)
*Illī pecuniam **sibi** retinuērunt.* (Those guys kept the money **for themselves.**)

The difference in form between personal and reflexive pronouns for the third person can clear potential confusion in some instances where English can be vague, especially when possession is involved. As with personal pronouns, the genitive is never used to show possession. Instead there is a possessive adjective: *suus, –a, –um.* This adjective is good for both third person singular *and* plural. The genitive for *hic, iste, ille,* and *is,* on the other hand, can show possession.

> *Caesar copiās **suās** mīsit ut oppidum defenderent.* (Caesar sent **his** troops to defend the town [referring to Caesar's own troops].)
> *Caesar copiās **eius** mīsit ut oppidum defenderent.* (Caesar sent **his** troops to defend the town [referring to the troops of someone else].)

In the first example, the reflexive possessive adjective makes it clear that the subject of the clause is being referred to. In the second example, someone other than the subject is being referred to. Since *eius* is the genitive of the pronoun *is,* the reference must be to some other person, whom the context—if the example had one—would reveal.

Intensive Adjectives and Pronouns

In our earlier discussion of personal pronouns, you read that the nominative case forms of personal pronouns were redundant since the personal endings (for first and second person, anyway) were distinct. The function of the nominative case for personal pronouns, then, was to emphasize. Emphasis is the only role of intensive adjectives. Where demonstrative adjectives point a finger at something, intensive pronouns shake it. Like demonstrative adjectives, intensives can also be used as pronouns.

Ipse, ipsa, ipsum

In Latin, *ipse* is the most important intensive adjective used to show emphasis. In English, we can use tone, when speaking, or, when writing, use italics or underlining. There are also a couple of ways to phrase emphasis by adding words. Unfortunately, the words English uses to do what *ipse* does are usually used to show other things, so some awkwardness and confusion can occur.

One way is to use the word "very," as in "My grandfather used to live in this very house [as opposed to any other]." (*Avus meus in hāc domū ipsā habitābat.*) The other way is more confusing than awkward. It requires a "–self" word. The confusion arises in that English also uses –self words as reflexives, even though the two uses are extremely different. "I myself [as opposed to anyone else] used to live in this house, too." (*Et ego ipse in hāc domū habitābam.*)

As always, context will be your best guide.

Table 13-8   Declension of the Intensive Adjective *ipse, ipsa, ipsum*

Case	Masculine	Feminine	Neuter
	Singular		
Nominative	*ipse*	*ipsa*	*ipsum*
Genitive	*ipsīus*	*ipsīus*	*ipsīus*
Dative	*ipsī*	*ipsī*	*ipsī*
Accusative	*ipsum*	*ipsam*	*ipsum*
Ablative	*ipsō*	*ipsā*	*ipsō*
	Plural		
Nominative	*ipsī*	*ipsae*	*ipsa*
Genitive	*ipsōrum*	*ipsārum*	*ipsōrum*
Dative	*ipsīs*	*ipsīs*	*ipsīs*
Accusative	*ipsōs*	*ipsās*	*ipsa*
Ablative	*ipsīs*	*ipsīs*	*ipsīs*

After *iste* and *ille,* the declension of *ipse* should come as no surprise.

Īdem, eadem, idem

The intensive adjective *īdem* can be used the same way as *ipse,* but its true meaning lies closer to the English word "same." "My grandfather used to live in this same house [as opposed to any other]." (*Avus meus in hāc domū eādem habitābat.*)

This word has a peculiar declension.

Table 13-9	Declension of the Demonstrative Adjective *īdem, eadem, idem*		
Case	Masculine	Feminine	Neuter
Singular			
Nominative	*īdem*	*eadem*	*idem*
Genitive	*eiusdem*	*eiusdem*	*eiusdem*
Dative	*eīdem*	*eīdem*	*eīdem*
Accusative	*eundem*	*eandem*	*idem*
Ablative	*eōdem*	*eādem*	*eōdem*
Plural			
Nominative	*eīdem*	*eaedem*	*eadem*
Genitive	*eōrundem*	*eārundem*	*eōrundem*
Dative	*eīsdem*	*eīsdem*	*eīsdem*
Accusative	*eōsdem*	*eāsdem*	*eadem*
Ablative	*eīsdem*	*eīsdem*	*eīsdem*

You have, no doubt, already noticed what is peculiar about *īdem*—it declines on the *inside*! Or so it seems. The intensive adjective *īdem* is really *is* with the suffix *–dem* attached. The influence of the suffix creates a few changes in the forms of *is* that you should be aware of. First, the masculine nominative singular is missing the *s*. Second, for all forms of *is* that end with *m* (accusative singular and genitive plural), the *m* changes to *n*, so *eam + dem* gives you *eandem*. This occurs to make the word easier to say.

Relative Pronouns

Among the top three words in the Latin language judged by frequency of appearance is the relative pronoun *quī, quae, quod. Quī* is roughly the Latin word for "who," "which," "that" in English. It is used to begin relative clauses.

Before we delve into relative clauses, let's take a look at the forms.

Table 13-10   Declension of the Relative Pronoun *qui, quae, quod*

Case	Masculine	Feminine	Neuter
	Singular		
Nominative	*quī*	*quae*	*quod*
Genitive	*cuius*	*cuius*	*cuius*
Dative	*cui*	*cui*	*cui*
Accusative	*quem*	*quam*	*quod*
Ablative	*quō*	*quā*	*quō*
	Plural		
Nominative	*quī*	*quae*	*quae*
Genitive	*quōrum*	*quārum*	*quōrum*
Dative	*quibus*	*quibus*	*quibus*
Accusative	*quōs*	*quās*	*quae*
Ablative	*quibus*	*quibus*	*quibus*

The forms of *quī* are similar to those of the demonstratives and intensives you just learned. There are, however, some important departures from what you might expect. As usual, the nominative case is unto itself and must be learned—the feminine singular and neuter plural are especially strange. The really significant differences lie in the dative and ablative plural and the masculine accusative singular. They are third declension rather than first/second.

Relative Clauses

Relative clauses are essentially clause-long modifiers like adjectives and prepositional phrases. What distinguishes them is that they are a whole clause long! Here are three different ways to say the same thing using those three different types of modifiers.

Adjective: I saw a *three-legged* dog.
Prepositional Phrase: I saw a dog *with three legs.*
Relative Clause: I saw a dog *that had three legs.*

The relative clause example in Latin would be:

*Canem **quī tria crura habēbat** vīdī.*

The main clause is *canem vīdī* ("I saw a dog"). The relative clause tells what kind of dog I saw. As you know, for a clause to be a clause, it must have a subject and a predicate. For the main clause, that separation is obvious. For the relative clause, we'll have to look more closely.

The sense of our relative clause is that the dog had three legs. You could split the sentence in two:

Canem vīdī. (I saw a dog.)
Canis tria crura habēbat. (The dog had three legs.)

Both sentences include the word *canis*. In the first sentence, *canem* is accusative case because it is the direct object of *vīdī*. In the second sentence, *canis* is nominative case because it is the subject of *habēbat*. Since it is the job of pronouns to stand in place of nouns, you can link the two sentences by replacing one of the dogs with a pronoun. If you use a relative pronoun, you can change one of the sentences into a modifier—a relative clause.

If you want to make the *canem* of the first sentence modify the *canis* in the second one, you need to replace it with a relative pronoun. But which one? Well, *canem* is masculine accusative singular, so you need a masculine accusative singular form of *quī*, which is *quem*. Now the two sentences are:

quem vīdī   *Canis tria crura habēbat*

Since relative clauses are modifiers and in Latin modifiers tend to follow the words they modify, insert the relative clause after the word it's modifying in the second sentence. The result is: *Canis quem vīdī tria crura habēbat.* ("The dog that I saw had three legs.") That sentence tells which dog had three legs—the one I saw did.

If you substituted a relative pronoun for the dog in the other sentence, you'd follow the same procedure. Since *canis* is masculine nominative singular, you need the masculine nominative singular form of the relative pronoun, which is *quī*.

Canem vīdī   *quī tria crura habēbat*

Put them together and you get: *Canem quī tria crura habēbat vīdī.* (I saw a dog that had three legs.) This version tells what kind of dog I saw—one that had three legs.

The key points to keep in mind regarding relative clauses are:

- A relative pronoun takes its gender and number from its antecedent (the word it modifies).
- A relative pronoun takes its case from its own function in its own clause.

Since relative pronouns stand in for nouns, they can have any case and any case use a noun can have.

Nominative: *Canem **quī** tria crura habēbat vīdī.*
    (I saw a dog **that** had three legs.)
Genitive: *Dominus **cuius** servus effūgerat irātus erat.*
    (The master **whose** slave had run away was furious.)
Dative: *Servus **cui** pecuniam dedistī effūgit.*
    (The slave **to whom** you gave the money ran away.)
Accusative: *Canis **quem** vīdī tria crura habēbat.*
    (The dog **that** I saw had three legs.)
Ablative: *Oppidum in **quō** habitat parvum est.*
    (The town in **which** he lives is dinky.)

Relative Clauses of Purpose

You learned that Latin often shows the purpose of an action with *ut* followed by a subjunctive. You can also form a purpose clause with a form of *quī* followed by a subjunctive. The difference is that in the *ut* construction, you are showing the purpose behind the action of the main verb. With *quī*, you are showing the purpose of the pronoun's antecedent.

Caesar nuntium Romam mīsit ut auxilium peteret. (Caesar sent a
messenger to Rome to ask for help. [why he sent the messenger])
Caesar nuntium Roman mīsit quī auxilium peteret. (Caesar sent a
messenger to Rome to ask for help. [what the messenger was
supposed to do])

FACT

There is a related construction called a relative clause of
characteristic. It is used to make vague, general comments about
people or things. For example, *Sunt quī ova nōn ēssent* ("There
are people who don't eat eggs," *or* "Some people don't eat
eggs"). By using the subjunctive, the statement becomes less a
statement of fact as it is a hypothesis or opinion.

Special Declension Adjectives

There is a small group of adjectives in Latin that follow a special
declension. Their irregularities are very similar to the majority of new
forms presented here.

Table 13-11   Declension of the Special Adjective *tōtus, tōta, tōtum*

Case	Masculine	Feminine	Neuter
Singular			
Nominative	*tōtus*	*tōta*	*tōtum*
Genitive	*tōtīus*	*tōtīus*	*tōtīus*
Dative	*tōtī*	*tōtī*	*tōtī*
Accusative	*tōtum*	*tōtam*	*tōtum*
Ablative	*tōtō*	*tōtā*	*tōtō*
Plural			
Nominative	*tōtī*	*tōtae*	*tōta*
Genitive	*tōtōrum*	*tōtārum*	*tōtōrum*
Dative	*tōtīs*	*tōtīs*	*tōtīs*
Accusative	*tōtōs*	*tōtās*	*tōta*
Ablative	*tōtīs*	*tōtīs*	*tōtīs*

The most obvious difference from regular first/second declension adjectives (and most obvious similarity to the adjectives in this chapter) is in the genitive singular (–*īus*) and the dative singular (–*ī*).

The adjectives that fall into this category are:

ūllus, –a, –um (any)
nūllus, –a, –um (no, none)
uter, utra, utrum (either [of two])
uterque, utraque, utrumque (each [of two])
neuter, neutra, neutrum (neither [of two])
sōlus, –a, –um (only, alone)
tōtus, –a, –um (whole)
alius, –a, –um (another [of an infinite set])
alter, altera, alterum (the other [of two])

Numbers

Numbers are adjectives, and in Latin there are only four common ones that can be declined.

Unus, –a, –um (one) follows the pattern of special adjectives. There are no plural forms.

Duo, duae, duo (two) is an odd duck. It and only one other word, *ambō, ambae, ambō* ("both"), have kept the dual number forms.

Table 13-12   Declension of *duō, duae, duō*

Case	Masculine	Feminine	Neuter
Nominative	*duo*	*duae*	*duo*
Genitive	*duōrum*	*duārum*	*duōrum*
Dative	*duōbus*	*duābus*	*duōbus*
Accusative	*duōs*	*duās*	*duo*
Ablative	*duōbus*	*duābus*	*duōbus*

Trēs, tria (three) is a third declension adjective.

Mīlle (thousand) is a problem. In the singular, it is an indeclinable adjective. In the plural, however, it is a third declension *i*-stem neuter noun: *mīlia, mīlium, mīlibus, mīlia, mīlibus.*

Neither the Greeks nor the Romans used the zero either as a number or as a placeholder. For the Romans, tomorrow was two days from now. (Today is a day, so is tomorrow. That makes two.) Zero and the other Arabic numerals came to the West from India via the Arabs in the tenth century.

FACT

September got its name (as did October, November, and December) when March was the first month of the year. March is when we have the vernal equinox, so it's the beginning of spring. Makes sense, don't you think?

Table 13-13	Vocabulary
ūnus, –a, –um	one
duo, duae, duo	two
trēs, tria	three
quattuor	four
quīnque	five
sex	six
septem	seven
octō	eight
novem	nine
decem	ten
centum	hundred
mīlle	thousand
prīmus, –a, –um	first
secundus, –a, –um	second

continued on following page

Table 13-13	Vocabulary—*continued*
tertius, –a, –um	third
quārtus, –a, –um	fourth
quīntus, –a, –um	fifth
sextus, –a, –um	sixth
septimus, –a, –um	seventh
octāvus, –a, –um	eighth
nōnus, –a, –um	ninth
decimus, –a, –um	tenth
centēsimus, –a, –um	hundredth
mīllēsimus, –a, –um	thousandth

Latin-to-English Translations

Translate these Latin sentences into English.

1. *Accidit ut istud bellum effugere nōn possēmus.*

2. *Hī, quī anteā oppidōs suōs numquam relīquerant, trans mare transiērunt.*

3. *Mors Augustī, quī Romae imperātor prīmus erat, magna tristitiae causa erat.*

4. *Vīs tempestātis tanta erat ut milia nāvium frumentī, vinī, et servōrum plēnārum dēlēvit.*

5. *Ego mihi mortem servitūdine mālō.*

continued on following page

Latin-to-English Translations—*continued*

6. *Rēx illam, cuius filius eum servāvit, in matrimonium ducet.*

7. *Filia quīnta eius multō pulchrior quam cēterae est.*

8. *Domus, quae contrā sē dīvīsa est, stāre nōn potest.*

9. *Eō diē hominēs centum in mediō oppidō sē contulērunt.*

10. *Septimā diē post casum Pompēiīs, petere coepimus ullōs quī superfuerant.*

English-to-Latin Translations

Translate these English sentences into Latin.

1. Labiēnus was so skilled in (with respect to) the art of war that Caesar retained him. (*perītus*, "skilled")

2. The senate gave great honors to you alone.

3. Those brave (men whom we were just talking about) climbed this mountain in four days.

4. We brought the bodies of the men who had fallen back to the camp.

5. There were few who survived.

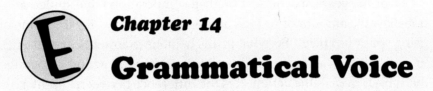

Chapter 14

Grammatical Voice

In grammar, the term "voice" refers to the relationship between the subject of a verb and the action of a verb. Ever since the beginning of this book, all the verb forms you have learned have been in the "active voice." This chapter covers the other voices that you will encounter in Latin.

What Is Grammatical Voice?

There are three types of grammatical voice in Latin: active, passive, and middle. In active voice, the subject, whether expressed by a word in the nominative case or simply by a personal ending, is the performer of the action.

Over the years, teachers of English composition have spilled an unbelievable amount of red ink across student essays for the crime of using "passive voice." So what is this heinous grammatical construction? In sum, while in active voice the subject *performs* an action, in passive voice the subject *receives* the action. It is the difference between "I sent a birthday card to my father" and "A birthday card was sent to my father by me."

If you read those two examples again out loud, you will be able to hear why English teachers reckon passive voice akin to nails scraping a chalkboard. It can be awkward and ugly. But the passive voice can help you elude more than just the grammar police! President Reagan provided a famous example of this during the Iran-Contra scandal. "Mistakes were made," he said. Congress was lied to, laws were broken, hostages were traded, arms were sold, terrorists supported . . . but by whom?

What makes passive voice so useful is that actions can be expressed without having to say who did them. In fact, it usually sounds better if you don't.

FACT

Since transitive verbs require direct objects, they convert easily to passive voice. Intransitive verbs, however, cannot have direct objects, so they cannot be turned around into passive voice quite so easily.

Let's return to our earlier passive voice birthday card example. We can make it sound far less awkward just by leaving the last two words off: "A birthday card was sent to my father." Who sent it? It really doesn't matter. What matters is the birthday card and the fact that he got one.

Rather than think of a subject as the doer of an action, it is more accurate to think of it as the topic of conversation. A subject is what is being talked about. The predicate (i.e., the rest of a sentence) is what is being said about the subject.

If what is being talked about happens to be who or what is performing an action, then active voice is needed. If, on the other hand, what is being talked about is just sitting there and is being acted upon, then passive voice is needed. In addition, if something happens and the agent (i.e., doer) truly *is* unknown, then passive voice becomes mandatory.

In sum, passive voice turns the table on active voice. What would be the direct object (accusative case) of a verb in active voice becomes the subject (nominative case) of a verb in passive voice.

Understanding Passive Voice

English forms the passive voice by pairing a form of the verb "to be" with the past participle of a verb; for example, "you were seen," "they will have been taken," et cetera. Latin's approach to forming passive voice is almost as easy.

There are two entirely different ways to form passive voice in Latin: one for the present system and one for the perfect system.

Passive Voice in the Present System

For the tenses of the present system (the present, imperfect, and future), a special set of personal endings is used. The endings you have learned were all for active voice. These passive personal endings appear in their place.

Table 14-1 Active and Passive Personal Endings

Person	Active	Passive
I	–m/–ō	–r/–or
you	–s	–ris
he	–t	–tur
we	–mus	–mur
you	–tis	–minī
they	–nt	–ntur

As you can see, they are quite distinctive and you should have no trouble recognizing them. While the *r* may quickly alert you to a verb being in passive voice, there are some alterations to stem vowels and tense indicators that occur.

ALERT!

There is an alternate form for the second person singular passive personal ending: *–re;* for example, *Cur patientiā meā abutere?* ("Why do you abuse my patience?") instead of *Cur patientiā meā abuteris?* The ending *–ris,* however, is far more common.

Table 14-2   Present Tense, Indicative Mood, Passive Voice Across the Conjugations

Person	*amō, amāre*	*habeō, habēre*	*agō, agere*
1st, sing.	amor	habeor	agor
2nd, sing.	amāris	habēris	ageris
3rd, sing.	amātur	habētur	agitur
1st, pl.	amāmur	habēmur	agimur
2nd, pl.	amāminī	habēminī	agiminī
3rd, pl.	amantur	habentur	aguntur

Person	*capiō, capere*	*audiō, audīre*
1st, sing.	capior	audior
2nd, sing.	caperis	audīris
3rd, sing.	capitur	audītur
1st, pl.	capimur	audīmur
2nd, pl.	capiminī	audīminī
3rd, pl.	capiuntur	audiuntur

The most striking oddity of conjugation in the present passive occurs in the second person singular. First and second conjugation verbs behave as you would expect, but in third conjugation you find an *–e–* where you would expect an *–i–*. Read down the paradigm for *agō,* and pay attention to the vowel pattern between the verb base (*ag–*) and the personal endings: *o, e, i, i, i, u.* You will see this vowel pattern again. This appearance of an *e* instead of *i* can be troublesome in that it makes the form look like future tense.

What is a paradigm?
Broadly speaking, a paradigm is the perfect example of a framework. In grammar, a paradigm is a chart showing a word in all its forms.

Table 14-3 Imperfect Tense, Indicative Mood, Passive Voice Across the Conjugations			
Person	***amō, amāre***	***habeō, habēre***	***agō, agere***
1st, sing.	*amābar*	*habēbar*	*agēbar*
2nd, sing.	*amābāris*	*habēbāris*	*agēbāris*
3rd, sing.	*amābātur*	*habēbātur*	*agēbātur*
1st, pl.	*amābāmur*	*habēbāmur*	*agēbāmur*
2nd, pl.	*amābāminī*	*habēbāminī*	*agēbāminī*
3rd, pl.	*amābantur*	*habēbantur*	*agēbantur*
Person	***capiō, capere***	***audiō, audīre***	
1st, sing.	*capiēbar*	*audiēbar*	
2nd, sing.	*capiēbāris*	*audiēbāris*	
3rd, sing.	*capiēbātur*	*audiēbātur*	
1st, pl.	*capiēbāmur*	*audiēbāmur*	
2nd, pl.	*capiēbāminī*	*audiēbāminī*	
3rd, pl.	*capiēbāntur*	*audiēbantur*	

Just as the imperfect tense offered regular, predictable forms for the active voice, it also does so in the passive voice.

The passive voice forms for the imperfect subjunctive are also predictable. Rather than have the infinitive with active voice personal endings, you have the infinitive with passive personal endings. So *agerem, agerēs, ageret,* et cetera, become *agerer, agerēris, agerētur,* and so forth.

Table 14-4 Future Tense, Indicative Mood, Passive Voice Across the Conjugations

Person	amō, amāre	habeō, habēre	agō, agere
1st, sing.	amābor	habēbor	agar
2nd, sing.	amāberis	habēberis	agēris
3rd, sing.	amābitur	habēbitur	agētur
1st, pl.	amābimur	habēbimur	agēmur
2nd, pl.	amābiminī	habēbiminī	agēminī
3rd, pl.	amābuntur	habēbuntur	agentur

Person	capiō, capere	audiō, audīre
1st, sing.	capiar	audiar
2nd, sing.	capiēris	audiēris
3rd, sing.	capiētur	audiētur
1st, pl.	capiēmur	audiēmur
2nd, pl.	capiēminī	audiēminī
3rd, pl.	capientur	audientur

As you recall, for active voice there are two different ways to form future tense, depending on the conjugation to which a verb belongs. First and second conjugation verbs follow a –bō, –bi–, –bu– pattern. Third and fourth conjugation verbs use "an *a* with five e's." These two different approaches to forming future tense are also present in passive voice. All the forms show the predictable exchange of passive for active personal endings with one exception. In the second person singular for first and second conjugation verbs, the tense indicator changes slightly—the active form –bis becomes –beris. Once again, read the paradigm for *amō* vertically and you will notice the same unusual vowel pattern you saw previously in the present tense of third conjugation verbs: *o, e, i, i, i, u.*

ESSENTIAL

Apart from *ferō, ferre*, all the irregular verbs you recently learned are intransitive, so you don't need to worry about passive voice forms for them. As for *ferō*, it is only irregular in the present tense: *ferō, **ferris, fertur,** ferimur, feriminī, feruntur.*

Passive Voice in the Perfect System

Passive voice in the perfect system is unlike anything you have seen Latin verbs do so far. In fact, Latin's approach to putting the perfect system tenses in passive voice is remarkably similar to English. Rather than relying on a special set of personal endings, Latin uses forms of the verb *sum*, not as endings, but in conjunction with a participle. Before examining the perfect, pluperfect, and future perfect tenses in passive voice, you need to know a little about participles. (Participles will be dealt with in Chapter 15 extensively.)

First and foremost, participles are verbal adjectives. They are verbal in that they are made from verbs and have tense and voice. They are adjectives in that they modify nouns. Take a look at these examples.

"The boy *broke* the window."

"Broke" is the past tense, active voice of the verb "to break."

"The window *was broken*."

"Was broken" is the past tense, passive voice of the verb "to break."

"A bird flew in the *broken* window."

"Broken" is an adjective simply describing the window.

The participle "broken" in the last example (Latin *fractus, –a, –um* from the fourth principal part of the verb *frangō, frangere, frēgī, fractum*) is perfect and passive. As a perfect participle, it shows something that happened before the main verb. (The bird couldn't have flown "in the *broken* window" unless the breaking had happened first!) As a passive participle, whatever word it modifies *passively* received the action; it didn't *actively* do anything.

In the second example sentence above, the passive verb "was broken" illustrates how English uses its past participle with a form of the verb "to be" to form passive voice. Latin uses the same approach. A translation of that second example sentence into Latin would be: *Fenestra fracta est.* You know that in Latin adjectives agree with their nouns in gender, case, and number. You shouldn't be surprised, then, to see that the perfect passive participle *fractus, –a, –um* is feminine nominative singular, since the word it modifies (*fenestra*) is feminine nominative singular.

As you may recall, all perfect system tenses are conjugated the same way regardless of their conjugation. This rule is also true in passive voice. That being the case, one passive voice example for each perfect system tense will suffice.

Table 14-5 Perfect Tense, Indicative Mood, Passive Voice of *agō, agere, ēgī, actum*	
Latin	**English**
actus (–a, –um) sum	I was driven
actus (–a, –um) es	you were driven
actus (–a, –um) est	he (she, it) was driven
actī (–ae, –a) sumus	we were driven
actī (–ae, –a) estis	you were driven
actī (–ae, –a) sunt	they were driven

The perfect passive is formed with the perfect passive participle and the present tense of the verb *sum*. Don't forget that participles are adjectives, and true to their adjectival nature agree with the subject in gender, case, and number. With *mulier* as the subject, you would see *acta est* for a verb because *mulier* is feminine singular. If it were more than one woman (*mulierēs*), the verb would be *actae sunt* (i.e., feminine plural).

ALERT!

Because the perfect passive uses the present tense of *sum* with a participle, you may be tempted to translate it as present tense. Remember, the perfect tense shows a single completed action in *past* time, so when you find *est*, for example, you should say "was."

Table 14-6 Pluperfect Tense, Indicative Mood, Passive Voice of *agō, agere, ēgī, actum*	
Latin	**English**
actus (–a, –um) eram	I had been driven
actus (–a, –um) erās	you had been driven
actus (–a, –um) erat	he (she, it) had been driven

continued on following page

Table 14-6 Pluperfect Tense, Indicative Mood, Passive Voice of *agō, agere, ēgī, actum—continued*	
actī (–ae, –a) erāmus	we had been driven
actī (–ae, –a) erātis	you had been driven
actī (–ae, –a) erant	they had been driven

The pluperfect passive is formed with the perfect passive participle of a verb plus the imperfect of *sum*. Just as all pluperfect active forms are always translated "had ____," so are pluperfect passive forms. If you had learned the tense indicator *–era–* to recognize the pluperfect active, you're in luck—here it is again!

FACT

The pluperfect subjunctive passive is made following the same rules. The only difference—and what makes it subjunctive—is that the imperfect subjunctive of *sum* (*essem, essēs, esset*, etc.) is used with the participle instead of the imperfect indicative.

Table 14-7 Future Perfect Tense, Indicative Mood, Passive Voice of *agō, agere, ēgī, actum*	
Latin	**English**
actus (–a, –um) erō	I will have been driven
actus (–a, –um) eris	you will have been driven
actus (–a, –um) erit	he (she, it) will have been driven
actī (–ae, –a) erimus	we will have been driven
actī (–ae, –a) eritis	you will have been driven
actī (—ae, –a) erunt	they will have been driven

The future perfect passive quite predictably uses the future tense of *sum* with the perfect passive participle.

The Present Infinitive Passive

You have known the second principal part of a verb as the infinitive for quite a while now. What you have not been told is that it is the present infinitive active. What this means, of course, is that there are other infinitives . . . other tenses, other voices. You will read about the other infinitive tenses in Chapter 17. For the moment, let's focus on voice.

English has passive infinitives as well; for example, "to break"/"to be broken," "to love"/"to be loved," "to write"/"to be written." Once again, English uses a past participle with a form of the verb "to be." Latin, on the other hand, has special endings for passive present infinitives.

Table 14-8	Active and Passive Present Infinitives	
Conjugation	**Active**	**Passive**
First	*amāre* (to love)	*amārī* (to be loved)
Second	*monēre* (to warn)	*monērī* (to be warned)
Third	*mittere* (to send)	*mittī* (to be sent)
Third *–iō*	*iacere* (to throw)	*iacī* (to be thrown)
Fourth	*sentīre* (to perceive)	*sentīrī* (to be perceived)

The basic pattern for changing active infinitives to passive voice is to change the short *e* at the end of the active ending to a long *ī*. The exception to this rule is for third conjugation verbs. For them, since the active infinitive is two short *e*'s (separated by an *r*), the entire ending is changed to a long *ī*. This is also one of the few instances when third conjugation *–iō* verbs behave like regular third conjugation verbs.

ALERT!

Because the present infinitive passive ending for third conjugation verbs is a long *ī*, it can be very easily confused with the first person singular perfect indicative active. For example, *capī* ("to be taken") versus *cēpī* ("I took"). The best way to tell them apart is by the verb stem. A present infinitive will have the present stem (*cap–*), and the perfect tense will have the perfect stem (*cēp–*).

Ablative of Agent

At the beginning of this chapter we discussed the potential usefulness and awkwardness of passive voice. While passive voice can be used to say something happened without having to say who did it, its true purpose is to allow a recipient of an action to become the subject of a sentence. The whodunit is optional.

In English, if you do want to include the agent of a passive verb, you have two methods. First, if a thing is responsible for the act, you use the preposition "with." If a person is responsible, you say "by."

The window was broken **with** a rock.
The window was broken **by** the boy.

In Latin there are also two different ways based on the same criteria.

Fenestra saxō fracta est.
Fenestra ā puerō fracta est.

In the first example, since the doer is a thing, you use the ablative of means (which doesn't take a preposition). In the second example, since the doer is a person, you use the ablative of agent.

The ablative use called the ablative of agent requires the preposition *ā*, a people word, and a passive verb. If you see all three of these items in a clause, odds are that you have an ablative of agent, in which case you translate the *ā* "by" rather than "away" or "from."

The Middle Voice

In active voice, the subject performs an action. In passive voice the subject receives an action. It's hard to imagine what could possibly lie in the middle! If we take a quick review of a few things, middle voice might be easier.

- Grammatical voice is the relationship of a subject and its verb.
- Passive voice essentially turns a sentence around, making the direct object (accusative) the subject (nominative).

- The basic idea behind the dative case is to show someone with an interest in an action.
- When an action is reflexive, the subject is performing an action on itself.

Pull all these ideas together and you have a grammatical voice in which a subject performs an action in his own interest, on himself, or is otherwise personally involved. Here are some examples using the verb *lavō, lavāre, lāvī, lautum* to illustrate the sense of middle voice:

Active: *canem lavat* (he is washing the dog)
Reflexive: *sē lavat* (he is washing himself)
Passive: *lavātur* (he is being washed)
Middle: *lavātur* (he is bathing)

The active and reflexive examples are easy enough. The passive is rather simple as well. "He" is getting cleaner, but at someone else's hands. The example for middle voice might be a little harder to see because the distinction is so subtle. Setting our canine friend aside, the last three examples all bring us to the same result in the end. Of those three examples, only the reflexive and the middle have the same person doing the scrubbing. Now think very carefully about the subtle difference between washing yourself and bathing. "Bathing" is more personally involved, more intimate even, don't you think? The difference in meaning between active and middle voice is quite delicate and usually lost entirely in translation.

Look at the examples again and you'll see that middle voice and passive voice forms are the same. This is a problem, especially since the thought behind middle voice is far more akin to active voice than to passive voice.

Deponent Verbs

The solution to the middle voice conundrum is simpler than you might expect. There is a group of verbs that were used so often in middle voice and so rarely in active or passive voice that they abandoned their active forms and passive uses, keeping only their middle voice forms and middle voice sense. These verbs are called deponents.

When you learn your vocabulary, or run across deponents in your dictionary, they will be immediately obvious. Their principal parts all appear passive in form, but they still give you all the information you need to be able to conjugate them fully. For example:

morior, morī, mortuus sum (to die)

The first principal part, *morior*, is the first person present tense. It tells you if the verb is an *–iō* verb, which *morior* is. The second principal part, *morī*, is the present infinitive. It tells you the conjugation of the verb. In this case, the ending *–ī* suggests third conjugation. The third principal part of a deponent verb does the work of the third and fourth principal parts of regular verbs. It is the first person singular perfect tense. Being a passive form, it includes the perfect passive participle.

The only trouble deponent verbs are likely to give you is if you forget that they are deponent. Their passive-looking forms and active-sounding meanings can be quite deceiving.

FACT

Deponents are not the only instances of middle voice in Latin. Any verb can appear in middle voice, but it isn't very common that they do, and when they do, context usually gives them away.

Semideponent Verbs

In addition to fully deponent verbs, there is a small group of semideponent verbs. As their name suggests, they are only half deponent. Their present system is regular, but their perfect system is deponent. They, too, can be recognized by their principal parts. For example:

audeō, audēre, ausus sum (to dare)

The most common deponent and semideponent verbs are included in the vocabulary list in **TABLE 14-9**.

Table 14-9	Vocabulary
audeō, audēre, ausus sum	to dare
*coepī, coepisse, coeptum**	to begin
debeō, –ēre, –uī, –itum	to owe, ought, should, must
gaudeō, gaudēre, gāvīsus sum	to be happy, rejoice
gens, gentis, f.	family (as in clan)
gradior, gradī, grassus sum	to walk, step, go
familia, ae, f.	family (as in household, including slaves)
fiō, fierī, factus sum	to be made, be done, happen, become, be
*inquam***	I say
irascor, irascī, irātus sum	to become angry
iubeō, –ēre, iussī, iussum	to order
loquor, loquī, locūtus sum	to speak, talk
mīror, mīrārī, mīrātus sum	to wonder, be amazed, stare at
morior, morī, mortuus sum	to die
nascor, nascī, nātus sum	to be born
nātus, –ī, m.	child, offspring
oculus, –ī, m.	eye
orior, orīrī, ortus sum	to rise, attack
parens, parentis, c.	parent
patior, patī, passus sum	to suffer, endure
pectus, pectoris, n.	chest, breast, heart
potis, –e	able, powerful
proprius, –a, –um	one's own, peculiar
sequor, sequī, secūtus sum	to follow
sōl, –is, m.	sun
*soleō, solēre, solitus sum****	to be in the habit of, to be accustomed
studium, –ī, n.	eagerness, enthusiasm
usque, adv.	thoroughly, continuously, all the way
*ūtor, ūtī, ūsus sum*****	to use (takes an ablative object)

* **Coepī** is a defective verb. (A defective verb is one that is lacking forms.) *Coepī* only has perfect system forms.

** **Inquam** is also a defective verb with only scattered, third conjugation forms. It is used to introduce direct quotations.

*** **Soleō** is most often seen with a complementary infinitive. It is best translated "usually" with its person, number, tense, mood, and voice transferred to its accompanying infinitive: *Rus aestāte īre solitī sumus.* ("We usually went to the country in the summer.")

**** **Ūtor** actually means "to benefit oneself." The ablative that it uses as its object is an ablative of means.

The Irregular Verb *fiō, fiērī, factus sum*

The only irregular verb left for you to learn is *fiō*. It was saved for this chapter because it serves as the passive of *faciō, facere, fēcī, factum*. It is also somewhat semideponent in appearance. Like most other irregular verbs, *fiō* has irregular forms in the present tense, then its imperfect and future tense forms are the same as those of a third conjugation *–iō* verb.

Table 14-10 Present, Imperfect, and Future Tense of *fiō, fiērī, factus sum*			
Person	**Present**	**Imperfect**	**Future**
1st, sing.	*fiō*	*fiēbam*	*fiam*
2nd, sing.	*fīs*	*fiēbās*	*fiēs*
3rd, sing.	*fit*	*fiēbat*	*fiet*
1st, pl.	*fīmus*	*fiēbāmus*	*fiēmus*
2nd, pl.	*fītis*	*fiēbātis*	*fiētis*
3rd, pl.	*fiunt*	*fiēbant*	*fient*

The perfect system has entirely regular passive forms (e.g., *factus sum*, et cetera).

What is even more distinctive about *fiō* than its forms is its meaning. In addition to serving as the passive for *faciō*, *fiō* can be used as a verb meaning "to be." The sense of being that *fiō* conveys is not the same as that of *sum, esse*. *Sum* points to being in terms of existence. *Fiō* refers more to coming into being, becoming, or being temporarily. The best example of *fiō* in action is from the Bible: *fiat lux*, "let there be light." (The form *fiat* is present subjunctive, which we haven't covered yet.)

Latin-to-English Translations

Translate these Latin sentences into English.

1. *Cum gens Iuliī Caesaris pauper esset, ille tamen nōtus dīvesque factus est.*

---

2. *Familia propria cuique cara esse debet.*

---

3. *Omnia quae mihi monstrābās mīrābar nam tibi nōn credidī.*

---

4. *Tam irātus est ut tōtum exercitum oppidum orīrī iubēret.*

---

5. *Deinde nova quae tam diū exspectābantur Athēnīs lāta sunt et gāvīsī sunt.*

English-to-Latin Translations

Translate these English sentences into Latin.

1. If you (plural) follow us, you (plural) will be safe. (*tūtus, –a, –um*—safe)

---

2. You (singular) will always be loved by me with all my heart.

---

3. We were amazed at the carnage of the first day. (*caedēs, caedis,* f.—carnage)

---

4. Your brother used my advice.

---

5. The old men of this town dared to speak with great enthusiasm in the senate at Rome. (*Cūria, –ae,* f.—Senate)

Chapter 15

Participles

Participles are forms of verbs used as adjectives. Latin has four different participles, which are used extensively because of their ability to convey much meaning in little space. English usually needs an entire clause to say what a Latin participle can in one word.

Introducing Participles

Participles are verbal adjectives. As adjectives they must agree with the noun they modify in gender, case, and number. They can also be used as substantives and even as comparatives!

The verbal features of participles are tense and voice. You learned about voice in Chapter 14. Latin has two active participles (present and future) and two passive participles (perfect and future). English has only two participles, present active (e.g., "chewing") and past participle, which is passive (e.g., "chewed").

The tenses assigned to participles are not the same as for regular verb forms. The tenses of a participle are relative.

- **Present** participles show action happening at the **same time** as the main verb.
- **Perfect** participles show action that happened **before** the main verb.
- **Future** participles show action that will happen **after** the main verb.

Present Active Participles

The present active participle in Latin roughly corresponds to the present participle in English (i.e., the "–ing" form of a verb), which is also active voice. There is no present passive participle in either language.

In form, Latin's present active participle is a third declension adjective of one termination. It uses the present stem as a base and adds *–ns*, which declines to *–ntis*.

First conjugation: *amō, amāre* becomes *amāns, amantis*
Second conjugation: *doceō, docēre* becomes *docēns, docentis*
Third conjugation: *agō, agere* becomes *agēns, agentis*
Third conjugation *–iō*: *faciō, facere* becomes *faciēns, facientis*
Fourth conjugation: *sentiō, sentīre* becomes *sentiēns, sentientis*

FACT

Deponent verbs do keep their present participles, even if they are active; for example, *mīrāns, verēns, loquēns, patiēns, oriēns*.

Table 15-1   Present Participle Declension

Case	Masculine	Feminine	Neuter
		Singular	
Nominative	*agēns*	*agēns*	*agēns*
Genitive	*agentis*	*agentis*	*agentis*
Dative	*agentī*	*agentī*	*agentī*
Accusative	*agentem*	*agentem*	*agentem*
Ablative	*agentī/e*	*agentī/e*	*agentī/e*
		Plural	
Nominative	*agentēs*	*agentēs*	*agentia*
Genitive	*agentium*	*agentium*	*agentium*
Dative	*agentibus*	*agentibus*	*agentibus*
Accusative	*agentēs*	*agentēs*	*agentia*
Ablative	*agentibus*	*agentibus*	*agentibus*

Always remember that the present active participle refers to an action happening at *the same time* as the main verb. Whatever the tense of the main verb, the present active participle is concurrent.

Mātrēs flentēs consolārī nōn poterāmus.
(We were not able to console the weeping mothers.)

The "weeping" and the inability to console were simultaneous.

The most common substantive use of a present active participle is to show a person who performs the action, much like the suffix *–or* does when attached to the stem of the fourth principal part of a verb. Both *amāns* and *amātor*, therefore, mean "lover." Latin, however, uses participles as substantives quite freely, where English does not. Sometimes you need to get the sense of the Latin; then, rather than "translate," consider how English would express the same thought.

Flentēs consolārī nōn poterāmus.
(We were not able to console the weepers.)

Perhaps "weeping women" would sound better. Of course, the form *flentēs* could be masculine as well as feminine, so "weeping men" is also possible. If this sentence were in context, you would know which meaning would be best.

ALERT!

When a present active participle is being used like a noun (i.e., a substantive), its ablative singular form is like that of a third declension noun. So instead of *agentī* you will find *agende*.

Perfect Passive Participles

The perfect passive participle is a first/second declension adjective. There are no tricks or exceptions to this rule. It is formed by replacing the *–um* of the supine of a verb with regular first/second declension endings *–us, –a, –um*, et cetera. (Supines are covered later in this chapter.) The supine of a verb can usually be found as the fourth principal part of a verb. Not all verbs have supines, though.

timeō, timēre, timuī, ——	none
*ferō, ferre, tulī, **lātum***	supine
videō, vidēre, vīdī, vīsum	supine
*sum, esse, fuī, **futūrus***	future active participle

Some verbs have no fourth principal part at all. Most verbs have the supine. A few verbs have no supine or perfect passive participle, but they do have a future active participle and it is used as the fourth principle part.

You can distinguish supines or perfect passive participles from future active participles by examining the ending. Future active participles add *–ūrus* to the supine stem of a verb, or to what the supine stem would be if it had a supine. The supine/perfect passive participle will end in *–tum/–tus*. Sometimes you see *–sum/–sus* because when a dental stop is added to a dental stop, the result is an *s*. The supine/perfect passive participle is made by adding *–tus* to the base of a verb.

teneō, –ēre, tenuī, tentum   ten + **tum** ➡ tentum
videō, –ēre, vīdī, vīsum   vid + **tum** ➡ vīsum
mittō, –ere, mīsī, missum   mitt + **tum** ➡ missum

QUESTION?

What is a dental stop?

The sounds represented by the letters *t* and *d* are dental stops. In linguistics, a stop is a sound made by blocking the air in your mouth, then suddenly releasing it. "Dental" is when you block the air by pressing your tongue against your upper teeth.

There are two key points to remember when you encounter perfect passive participles. First, they always refer to something that occurred *before* the main verb. Second, they are passive, so whatever they refer to received the action rather than performed it.

Perfect passive participles—especially when used as substantives— allow Latin to express in a single word what would require a phrase in English. The first sentence below is easy to understand and translate; the second is not:

> ***Vulnerātī*** *cum diligentiā curābantur.*
> (**The wounded** were carefully tended to.)
> ***Collāta*** *in castrīs tenēbantur.*
> (**The brought together things** were kept in the camp.)

We'll discuss strategies for understanding and translating situations like this last example later in this chapter.

Future Active Participles

English has present active and perfect passive participles as does Latin. English does *not,* however, have any future participles. As you might expect, the tense value of future participles is relative to the main verb. In the case of future participles, the reference is to an action that happens *after* the main verb.

Future active participles are easy to form and recognize. They are first/second declension adjectives (no tricks!) formed by adding –*ūrus* to the stem of the supine. They are easy to spot if you remember –*ūrus*— future. Also, future active participles are all made the same way regardless of conjugation.

timeō, timēre, timuī, ——— (no supine)	no future active participle
ferō, ferre, tulī, **lātum** (supine stem *lāt*–)	*lātūrus, –a, –um*
videō, vidēre, vīdī, vīsum (supine stem *vīs*–)	*vīsūrus, –a, –um*
sum, esse, fuī, **futūrus** (no supine)	*futūrus, –a, –um*

The future active participle usually bears an idea of intention, or that something is just about to happen (*after* the main verb, of course). It is most often seen in a construction called the active periphrastic. This construction consists of the future active participle plus a form of the verb *sum*.

> *In forum itūrī erāmus, cum . . .*
>> We were *about to go* to the marketplace, when . . .
>> We were *going to go* to the marketplace, when . . .
>> *We intended to go* to the marketplace, when . . .

Using Participial Phrases

Remember that participles are *verbal* adjectives. As verbs, the active participles can have direct objects (e.g., *servus omnia parāns* ["the slave getting everything ready"]; *servus omnia parātūrus* ["the slave about to get everything ready"]). The passive participles can have ablatives of means or agent to show who or what was responsible for the deed (e.g., *mīles sagittā vulnerātus* ["the soldier wounded by an arrow"]). These are examples of participial phrases.

A participial phrase is a construction consisting of a noun (called a head noun), sometimes a complement (i.e., an object or prepositional phrase), then a participle. In Latin, participial phrases almost always take the form of a sandwich, with the head noun and participle as the bread, and whatever else you need—if anything—for the filler.

Even though a participial phrase expresses a thought that could, if rewritten, be expressed as a complete sentence, you need to recognize it as a discrete unit because it is only a phrase. Here is an example that illustrates what is meant by a "discrete unit."

SUBJECT	PREDICATE
Mīles	*in campō totam noctem iacēbat.*
The soldier	lay in the field for the entire night.
Mīles vulnerātus	*in campō totam noctem iacēbat.*
The wounded soldier	lay in the field for the entire night.
Mīles sagittā vulnerātus	*in campō totam noctem iacēbat.*
The soldier, wounded by an arrow,	lay in the field for the entire night.
Mīles fortis sagittā vulnerātus	*in campō totam noctem iacēbat.*
The brave soldier, wounded by an arrow,	lay in the field for the entire night.

In this example, the participial phrase acts as the subject, so the head noun is in the nominative case, as is the participle that must agree with it. Participial phrases, however, can function in any case, not just the nominative. In the following example, our soldier is the direct object.

> *Mīlitem fortem sagittā vulneratum ex campō mane trahent.*
> (The brave soldier, wounded by an arrow, they will pull from the field in the morning.)

The whole phrase functions as the direct object of the main verb *trahent* and sits apart as a discrete unit. Also, since the whole phrase functions as the direct object, the head noun and participle are in the accusative, while the filler words are in whatever case they need to be in to do their job: *fortem* is masculine accusative singular to agree with its noun *mīlitem*; *sagittā* is ablative (without a preposition) to show the means by which he was *vulnerātum*.

The translation isn't much more mellifluous (*mel*, "honey"; *fluō*, "to flow") when the participial phrase is inserted elsewhere: "They will pull the brave soldier, wounded by an arrow, from the field in the morning."

Reading Participial Phrases

Treating a participle as a simple adjective is one approach. All too often, however, that approach leads to awkward, stilted phrasing, as in this last example. A remedy for this is to remove the Latin participial phrase and expand it into a whole clause in English. There are five different types of clauses you can use. Each type suggests a certain relationship between a participial phrase and the main clause that it is a part of. As usual, context is your best guide.

The simple adjective approach plus the five different types of clauses give us six possible ways to read or translate a sentence containing a participial phrase. Here is a fresh example for us to work with. You are probably familiar with it—it is the traditional greeting gladiators used to give to the sponsor of games before the games began: *Nōs moritūrī tē salutāmus.*

- Simple adjective: We, *about to die,* salute you.
- Relative clause: We, **who** *are about to die*, salute you.
- Temporal clause: **As/When** *we are about to die*, we salute you.
- Causal clause: **Since/Because** *we are about to die*, we salute you.
- Coordinate clause: *We are about to die* **and** we salute you.
- Concessive clause: **Even though** *we are about to die*, we salute you (anyway).

In these translations, the words that represent the participial phrase are in italics. The words in boldface are the keywords—usually conjunctions—that make a clause the type that it is.

When you read a participial phrase in a temporal (*tempus, temporis,* "time") sense, be mindful of the relative time value of the tenses of participles.

> Present (same time): *Nōs morientēs tē salutāmus.*
> (**While** we are dying, we salute you.)
> Perfect (time before): *Nōs mortuī tē salutāre nōn poterimus.*
> (**After** we die, we won't be able to salute you.)
> Future (time after): *Nōs moritūrī tē salutāmus.*
> (**Before** we die, we salute you.)

Also noteworthy is that with concessive clauses, you will almost always find the word *tamen* ("anyway") in the main clause. Remember that this was also true for concessive *cum* clauses.

It is *very* important to remember that since a participial phrase serves a function in the main clause, its removal cannot be complete. That is to say, you have to put a pronoun in the main clause to take its place. If you look closely at the sample translations above, you will notice that there is a "we" in the main clause standing in for the *nōs moritūrī* that had been removed to make a new clause.

ALERT!

Single word participles used as substantives are not phrases. They are both nouns and participles at the same time. Earlier you read the awkward example: ***Collāta** in castrīs tenēbantur.* (**The brought together things** were kept in the camp.) It would be much better to expand the Latin word into an English clause: **When the things had been brought together, they** were kept in the camp.

Ablatives Absolute

There is an amazing use of the ablative case in Latin called the "ablative absolute" that is the very picture of the economy of the language. It can compress an entire story into only a couple of words. It is a type of participial phrase complete with head noun and participle, both in the ablative. What distinguishes it from the participial phrases that you just read about is that it sits independently of the main clause it goes with.

Here are two examples to examine:

Hostēs captōs occidimus.
   (After **the enemies** had been captured, we killed **them.**)
Hostibus captīs, castra mōvimus.
   (After **the enemies** were captured, we broke camp.)

In the first example, "the enemies" appears twice. Since they are both head noun in a participial phrase and at the same time direct objects of the main verb, they need to be represented twice: once in the expanded participial phrase, then again in the main clause. Rather than repeat "the enemies" twice, it sounds better to replace one occurrence with a pronoun.

In the second example, there are also two actions, killing and breaking, but the enemies are only involved with one of the verbs, namely the killing. Since the enemies have—at least grammatically—nothing to do with the main clause, they are absolute (*ab*, "away"; *solūtus* from *solvō*, "to turn loose"). That is why the head noun, *hostibus*, and the participle pertaining only to them, *captīs*, are in the ablative and set off from the rest of the sentence.

An ablative absolute phrase can be translated *nearly* the same way as ordinary participial phrases. The simple adjective and relative clause approaches are awkward, stilted, or make no sense.

- Simple adjective: *The enemies having been captured,* we broke camp.
- Relative clause: *The enemies **who** had been captured,* we broke camp.
- Temporal clause: ***After** the enemies had been captured,* we broke camp.
- Causal clause: ***Since** the enemies had been captured,* we broke camp.
- Coordinate clause: *The enemies were captured, **and** we broke camp.*
- Concessive clause: ***Although** the enemies had been captured,* we broke camp.

Rēs ipsa loquitur. ("The matter speaks for itself.")

Gerunds

Gerunds (and gerundives, covered in the next section) are not participles *per sē* ("by themselves"), but as you will soon see, there is no better place to put them. English does have gerunds, but it doesn't have gerundives. Gerundives are *suī generis* ("of their own kind").

Gerunds are verbal nouns. In English they take the form of "–ing" words (e.g., "*reading* is fundamental"), which makes them identical in appearance to English present participles. Latin gerunds also resemble Latin present participles, but with some important distinctions (like spelling and declension) that will help you recognize and distinguish them without a problem.

The Latin gerund is a second declension neuter noun made from the present stem with the suffix *–nd–* plus an ending.

Table 15-2   Gerund Declension

Case	First Conj.	Second Conj.	
Nominative	———	———	
Genitive	*amandī*	*docendī*	
Dative	*amandō*	*docendō*	
Accusative	*amandum*	*docendum*	
Ablative	*amandō*	*docendō*	
Case	**Third Conj.**	**Third Conj. *–iō***	**Fourth Conj.**
Nominative	———	———	———
Genitive	*agendī*	*faciendī*	*sentiendī*
Dative	*agendō*	*faciendō*	*sentiendō*
Accusative	*agendum*	*faciendum*	*sentiendum*
Ablative	*agendō*	*faciendō*	*sentiendō*

Apart from the fact that gerunds have no nominative form, the remaining cases still function with the same uses as they do for any other noun; for example, *modus operandī* ("way of working"). (If you want a verb to be the subject of another verb, you have to use an infinitive. More on this in Chapter 17.)

Gerunds have a special use. In the accusative preceded by *ad,* or in the genitive followed by *causā* or *gratiā,* they can show purpose much like *ut*/*nē* with the subjunctive "can."

> *Vēiīs ēgressī sunt ut Romae habitārent.*
> (They left Veii to live in Rome.)
> *Vēiīs ēgressī sunt ad Romae habitandum.*
> (They left Veii to live in Rome.)
> *Vēiīs ēgressī sunt Romae habitandī causā.*
> (They left Veii to live in Rome.)
> *Vēiīs ēgressī sunt Romae habitandī gratiā.*
> (They left Veii to live in Rome.)

As *verbal* nouns, gerunds can take objects. When this happens, though, gerundives come into play . . .

FACT

The verb *sum, esse, fuī, futūrus* has only one participle: *futūrus.* It has no gerunds or gerundives either. If you ever find a sentence that is lacking a verb, assume that the missing verb is the appropriate form of *sum.* For instance, the ablative absolute phrase *Caesar duce* has no participle but still works: "Since Caesar was the leader . . ."

Gerundives

Gerundives are verbal adjectives that have a sense of duty, obligation, and necessity. In form they look like gerunds (i.e., *–nd–* plus first/second declension adjective endings), but gerundives have all genders, cases, and numbers.

Gerundives have two main uses. One is in conjunction with gerunds. The other is in passive periphrastic conjugation.

Case	Masc.	Fem.	Neut.
Table 15-3 Gerundive Declension			
		Singular	
Nominative	*dandus*	*danda*	*dandum*
Genitive	*dandī*	*dandae*	*dandī*
Dative	*dandō*	*dandae*	*dandō*
Accusative	*dandum*	*dandam*	*dandum*
Ablative	*dandō*	*dandā*	*dandō*
		Plural	
Nominative	*dandī*	*dandae*	*danda*
Genitive	*dandōrum*	*dandārum*	*dandōrum*
Dative	*dandīs*	*dandīs*	*dandīs*
Accusative	*dandōs*	*dandās*	*danda*
Ablative	*dandīs*	*dandīs*	*dandīs*

Gerunds and Objects

When gerunds take objects, a curious transformation usually occurs within the phrase. The object of the gerund takes the gerund's case, and a gerundive takes the gerund's place, changing its form to agree with the newly changed object. Are you confused about this presto-chango? Sometimes we do the same thing in English.

Ebrius fimus vinum bibendō becomes *Ebrius fimus vinō bibendō.*
"We get drunk by drinking wine" becomes "We get drunk by wine
    drinking."

Both are acceptable constructions in each language. Latin prefers *vinō bibendō,* "by wine drinking"; English prefers "by drinking wine" (*vinum bibendō*).
    Dē gustibus nōn est disputandum. ("[Matters] concerning tastes shouldn't be argued about"; i.e., "taste is not to be disputed.")

Passive Periphrastic

When used with a form of *sum,* the gerundive—which is passive—denotes necessity or obligation, as in the phrase *dē gustibus nōn est disputandum.* A passive periphrastic construction merely points to existence of a need or obligation.

Omnia haec facienda sunt. (All these things have to be done.)

Since gerundives are passive, there is no need to say whose problem it is. If you *do* want to make a reference to the person who needs to attend to the matter, you use the case that shows interest in something—the dative.

Omnia haec tibi facienda sunt.
      (All these things have to be done by you.)

A better translation would be "You have to do all these things." That translation, however, is blunt and loses the indirect, beating-around-the-bush flavor of the original Latin. The Latin actually says something more akin to "As for you, all these things need to be done. (And just *what* are you going to do about it, eh?)"

This use of the dative case is called the dative of agent.

FACT

Some Latin gerundives have made their way into everyday English. The neuter plural of the gerundive of *agō,* for example, is *agenda,* "things which must be done." Another good example is *memorandum,* "a thing that must be remembered."

The Supine Form

You have been hearing the term "supine" since the beginning of this book. It is finally time to reveal its mystery. The supine's most important job is to be the fourth principal part of a verb, from which the perfect passive and future active participles are made.

The supine is another verbal noun, but with very limited forms and even more restricted use. It is a fourth declension noun only found in the accusative and ablative singular.

In the accusative—which is the form presented as the fourth principal part of a verb—it shows purpose when with a verb of motion.

Vēiīs ēgressī sunt Romae habitātum. (They left Veii to live in Rome.)

In the ablative, its use is restricted to an ablative of respect with adjectives.

Marcus est pulcher vīsū. (Mark is handsome to see.
[Literally, "handsome with respect to seeing"])

Table 15-4 Vocabulary	
adversus, –a, –um	opposite, against
aurum, –ī, n.	gold
cīvitās, –tātis, f.	city, state, citizenry
colō, –ere, cōluī, cultum	to tend to, nurture, cultivate, worship
condō, –ere, condidī, condītum	to found, establish, put together
dexter, dextra, dextrum	right (as opposed to *sinister, –tra, –trum* left)
dīligō, –ere, dīlexī, dīlectum	to love
dux, ducis, c.	leader
fātum, –ī, n.	fate
fidēs, –eī, f.	respect for fulfillment of obligations, faith
fortūna, –ae, f.	luck, destiny
grātus, –a, um	pleasing, grateful
haud, adv.	not (emphatic)
honos, honōris, m.	honor, public office
iaceō, –ēre, iacuī, ——	to lie (be in a horizontal position)
iaciō, –ere, iēcī, iactum	to throw
item, adv.	likewise

continued on following page

Table 15-4	Vocabulary—*continued*
laus, laudis, f.	praise
lēx, lēgis, f.	law
littera, –ae, f.	letter (of the alphabet)
litterae, –ārum, f. pl.	letter (*epistula*), literature
mūnus, mūneris, n.	duty, a gift, a sponsored event
niger, nigra, nigrum	glossy black
orbis, orbis, m.	circle, anything round (*orbis terrārum*—the world)
patria, –ae, f.	country, fatherland
pereō, perīre, periī, peritum	to die, perish
perveniō, –īre, –vēnī, –ventum	to arrive
premō, –ere, pressī, pressum	to press, push
procul, adv.	far, at a distance
recipiō, –ere, recēpī, receptum	to take (back), receive
regnum, –ī, n.	royal power, kingdom
reliquus, –a, –um	remaining, leftover
reperiō, –īre, repperī, repertum	to find, learn
servō, –āre, –āvī, -ātum	to save, keep, guard, protect
trahō, –ere, traxī, tractum	to pull, drag
umquam, adv.	ever
vehō, –ere, vexī, vectum	to carry
vehor, vehī, vectus sum (with the abl.)	to ride
vertō, –ere, vertī, versum	to turn

Latin-to-English Translations

Translate these Latin sentences into English.

1. *Dulce et decorum est prō patriā morī.*

2. *Aliī ad theatrum vīsum veniēbant, aliī ut vīsī essent.*

3. *Librō scriptō, gāvīsī sunt.*

4. *Nōbis Romā profectūrīs, pluere coepit.* (*proficiscor,* "to depart"; *pluere,* "to rain")

5. *Hospitibus ad ianuam pervenientibus, canēs latrābant.*

6. *Caesar inquit, "Alea iacienda est."* (*alea, –ae,* f., "a die")

7. *Mīlitēs mortuōs ē campō tractōs diē sequentī sepelīvērunt.*

8. *Agrīs colentibus, aurum invēnit agricola.*

9. *Vīta beāta fautīs ā Fortunā reperitur.* (*faveō, –ēre, fāvī, fautum,* "to favor")

10. *Vīta beāta ā Fortunā fautīs reperitur.*

English-to-Latin Translations

Translate these English sentences into Latin.

1. The boy saw his father dying.

2. The boy saw his father dead.

3. The boy saw his father on the verge of dying.

4. I intended to send that letter to you tomorrow (*cras*).

5. If Fortune stays nearby (not far off), we will be saved.

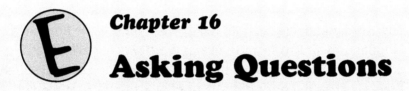

Chapter 16

Asking Questions

One of the first grammatical structures to come from a baby's mouth—of the mouth of anyone learning a language—is the question. What makes this remarkable is that questions are among the most sophisticated linguistic constructions. Some questions beg for adjectives, some for nouns, some for verbs, and some even for adverbs. Others simply want confirmation.

True or False?

The Romans had no word for "yes" or "no." They did, however, have three ways to ask a yes or no question! Lacking a simple yes or no, gestures, head bobs, or head shakes were used (not *all* language is verbal!). One could also repeat whatever was in question with or without negation.

FACT

The word you may associate most with "yes" in the Romance languages is *si. Si* is from the Latin word *sīc,* "just like that." English also has a ghost of the old Latin *sīc.* You see it in square brackets after the quotation of an obvious gaffe that a news reporter doesn't want to take blame for (e.g., "Bush said not to misunderestimate [*sic*] him").

You have already learned the enclitic *–que.* It means "and" (in a special way), and, as an enclitic, cannot stand on its own. It is a syllable that needs to be attached to the end of another word. The enclitic *–ne* works in a similar fashion. You can attach *–ne* to the end of the first word of a sentence and instantly convert it to a yes/no question. Shifting word order shifts emphasis.

> *Tū mē amās.* (You love me.)
> *Tūne mē amās?* (Do **you** love me?)
> *Mēne amās?* (Do you love **me**?)
> *Amāsne mē?* (Do you **love** me?)

The interrogative adverb *nōnne* also poses a yes/no question, but it baits the answerer for a yes.

> *Nōnne mē amās?* (You love me, don't you?)

If you pull *nōnne* apart you will see that it is actually just *nōn* with *–ne* on the end. It essentially makes *nōn* into a question. "You love me. No?"

The adverb *num* does the opposite. It expects a "no" answer.

Num mē amās? (You don't love me, do you?)

The word *num* is most often seen in the sense of the English word "whether." "Whether" suggests a sort of conditional situation where the outcome is doubtful. Latin takes this dubious situation to a more pessimistic end: "(I don't know) whether you love me (you don't, do you)?"

QUESTION?

What is the origin of the question mark?
The Romans did not use punctuation. Using dots and squiggles to tell you how to read did not occur until the Middle Ages. The question mark is an elongated Q, standing for the Latin word *quaestiō* ("question") set on top of a period.

What Are They Asking?

Some questions ask for confirmation or rejection of a statement, but most questions are in pursuit of specific information. The sort of information requested determines the interrogative (i.e., question word) employed. For example, "why?" looks for "because," "which?" wants an adjective, and so on. Latin is rich in question words. Here is a table of them along with the types of responses you can expect:

Table 16-1   Questions and Responses

Interrogative	Response
cur? (why?)	*quod* or *quia* (because) or a *cum* clause, or a participial phrase
quare? (with respect to what? why?)	*quod* or *quia* (because) or a *cum* clause, or a participial phrase
quot? (how many?)	*tot* (so many) or a number
quomodo? (by what method? how?)	an infinite number of ways to respond
ubi? (where?)	*ibi* (there) or *hīc* (here), or a place in the ablative with preposition, or in the locative

continued on following page

Table 16-1 Questions and Responses—*continued*	
unde? (from where?)	*inde* (from there) or *hunc* (from here), or a place in the ablative (with or without preposition)
quō? (where to?)	*eō* (to that place), *hūc* (to this place), or a place in the accusative (with or without preposition)
quandō? (when?)	a time or date
qualis, –e?* (what kind?)	*talis, –e* (such a kind) or an adjective
quantus, –a, –um? (how much/big?)	*tantus, –a, –um* (so much/big) or an adjective
quantī, –ae, –a? (how many?)	*tantī, –ae, –a* (so many) or a number, or an adjective
quotus, –a, –um? (which? [in number])	*prīmus* (first), *secundus* (second), etc.
quotiens (how often? how many times?)	*totiens* (so often, so many times)
quis, quid (who? what?)**	a noun
quī, quae, quod _____ ?** (which _____?)	an adjective (with or without the repetition of that noun)

* N.B. (*Nota bene*): *qualis/talis, quantus/tantus,* and *quantī/tantī* are adjectives, which is why they seek adjectives in response.
** N.B.: *quis* and *quī* require separate consideration.

The English question words "whither" ("to what place?"), "whence" ("from what place?"), and "where" ("in what place") have corresponding answers, too. From the speaker's vantage point, motion toward him is "hither," and motion toward a place distant from him is "thither." Likewise, "hence" shows motion away from the speaker, and "thence" is motion away from a place not near him. Only the words "where," "here," and "there" (i.e., place where) survive. To get the ideas of motion toward or motion away from in modern English, the prepositions "to" and "from" are added to "where."

Asking Who and What

The Latin interrogative pronouns *quis, quid* ask for nouns. Their declension is one that you should immediately recognize. The only real differences in form between the interrogative pronoun and the relative pronoun are in the singular—the same forms serve for both the masculine and the feminine. In the plural, the forms are identical.

Table 16-2	Declension of the Interrogative *quis, quid*		
Case	Masc.	Fem.	Neuter
Singular			
Nominitive	*quis*	*quis*	*quid*
Genitive	*cuius*	*cuius*	*cuius*
Dative	*cui*	*cui*	*cui*
Accusative	*quem*	*quem*	*quid*
Ablative	*quō*	*quō*	*quō*
Plural			
Nominative	*quī*	*quae*	*quae*
Genitive	*quōrum*	*quārum*	*quōrum*
Dative	*quibus*	*quibus*	*quibus*
Accusative	*quōs*	*quās*	*quae*
Ablative	*quibus*	*quibus*	*quibus*

The case of the pronoun heading a question anticipates the case of the answer. The number anticipates the answer to be singular or plural.

Nominative: *Quis puerōs cūrābit?* (Who will take care of the boys?)
Antōnia. (Antonia.)

Genitive: *Cuius filius es?* (Whose son are you?)
Marcī. (Mark's.)

Dative: *Cui pecuniam dedērunt?* (To whom did they give the money?)
Iuliae. (To Julia.)

Accusative: *Quōs vīdistī?* (Whom did you see?)
Multōs servōs. (Many slaves.)

Ablative: *Quō occisus est?* (By what was he killed?)
Sagittā. (By an arrow.)

Ablative: *A quō occisus est?* (By whom was he killed?)
A Hermanō. (By Herman.)

Asking Which

The forms of the interrogative adjective are identical to those of the relative pronoun. Since it is an adjective, it agrees with a noun. And since it is an *interrogative* adjective, it asks for another adjective.

> *Quōs honorēs accēpit?* (What/which honors did he receive?)
> *Honorēs mīlitārēs.* (Military honors.)

Indefinite Adjectives and Pronouns

Related to the interrogative adjectives and pronouns is another group of words called indefinite adjectives and pronouns. They are similar in form to the interrogatives, and like the interrogatives they stand in for unknown or unexpressed persons or things. The most common words of this class are:

- *quīdam, quaedam, quoddam* (someone, something, a certain)
- *quisque, quidque* (each)
- *quisquis, quidquid* (whoever, whatever; *quisquis* is almost always seen in the nominative)
- *aliquis, aliquid* (anyone, anything)

In form, the words *quīdam* and *quisque* are simply *quī* and *quis* with the suffixes *–dam* and *–que*. In the cases where the forms of *quī* and *quis* end with the letter *m* (i.e., accusative singular and the genitive plural), the *m* changes to an *n*. For example, if you add *–dam* to *quem* the result is *quendam*.

There is an old rhyme that says "After *sī, nisi, num,* and *nē* all the *ali*–'s fall away." This means that when *aliquis* follows any of the words in that little list, you will see only forms of *quis* (e.g., *sī quis advēnit*, "if anyone came").

The Present and Perfect Subjunctive

At long last, here are the only verb forms that remain for you to learn. They are the least frequently seen of all the verb tenses. Once you have mastered these two tenses, you will have mastered all the verb tenses. There are a few more stray forms, but they are nothing to worry about.

The Present Subjunctive

No tense of the subjunctive mood has forms that are difficult to make or recognize. The present subjunctive is the most complicated because it varies from conjugation to conjugation just as the present indicative forms do. For the present subjunctive, however, there is a quick way to take care of them.

This sounds silly, but the easiest way to learn the present subjunctive is to think of a verb having a "vowel movement." Where you expect to see an *a* on the present stem, you find an *e*. Where there would be an *e* on the stem, you find an *a*. A shortcut is to change the *ō* of the first principal part of a verb to the other vowel, then apply active or passive personal endings.

Table 16-3   The Present Subjunctive Active

Person	*amō, amāre*	*habeō, habēre*	*dūcō, ducere*
1st, sing.	amem	habeam	dūcam
2nd, sing.	amēs	habeās	dūcās
3rd, sing.	amet	habeat	dūcat
1st, pl.	amēmus	habeāmus	dūcāmus
2nd, pl.	amētis	habeātis	dūcātis
3rd, pl.	ament	habeant	dūcant
Person	*iaciō, iacere*	*audiō, audīre*	
1st, sing.	iaciam	audiam	
2nd, sing.	iaciās	audiās	
3rd, sing.	iaciat	audiat	
1st, pl.	iaciāmus	audiāmus	
2nd, pl.	iaciātis	audiātis	
3rd, pl.	iaciant	audiant	

Unfortunately, it cannot be said that all the irregular verbs fall into line with these rules. Most do, but *sum* and *volō* do not.

Table 16-4   The Present Subjunctive of *sum* and *volō*

Person	*sum, esse*	*possum, posse*	
1st, sing.	sim	possim	
2nd, sing.	sīs	possīs	
3rd, sing.	sit	possit	
1st, pl.	sīmus	possīmus	
2nd, pl.	sītis	possītis	
3rd, pl.	sint	possint	
Person	***volō, velle***	***nōlō, nōlle***	***malō, malle***
1st, sing.	velim	nōlim	mālim
2nd, sing.	velīs	nōlīs	mālīs
3rd, sing.	velit	nōlit	mālit
1st, pl.	velīmus	nōlīmus	mālīmus
2nd, pl.	velītis	nōlītis	mālītis
3rd, pl.	velint	nōlint	mālint

The Perfect Subjunctive

The least common of all verb tenses in Latin is the perfect subjunctive. You will find that you basically already know the active voice for the perfect subjunctive and could have predicted the passive voice.

Since all verbs make their perfect system tenses the same way regardless of conjugation or irregularity, one verb will suffice for an example.

Table 16-5   The Perfect Subjunctive Active *ferō, ferre, tulī, lātum*

Person	Singular	Plural
1st	tulerim	tulerimus
2nd	tuleris	tuleritis
3rd	tulerit	tulerint

Table 16-6   The Perfect Subjunctive Passive of *ferō, ferre, tulī, lātum*

Person	Singular	Plural
1st	*lātus (—a, –um) sim*	*lātī (–ae, –a) sīmus*
2nd	*lātus (–a, –um) sīs*	*lātī (–ae, –a) sītis*
3rd	*lātus (–a, –um) sit*	*lātī (–ae, –a) sint*

The perfect subjunctive active is virtually identical to the future perfect indicative active. The only difference occurs in the first person singular, where you find *–erim* instead of *–erō*.

The perfect subjunctive passive is entirely logical. As you recall, for the indicative mood, the perfect passive is formed with the perfect passive participle (from the fourth principal part) and the present indicative of *sum*. Here, for the perfect subjunctive passive, you also use the perfect passive participle, but with the present subjunctive of *sum*.

Conditions

For those of you familiar with computer programming, you already know that a "condition" is an IF/THEN statement. Guess where programming got that term? In grammar, however, there are six different kinds of conditions. These six types of conditions are distinguished by time (present, past, and future) and by whether they concern factual or hypothetical situations.

Each kind of condition has a formal name and employs a verb in a certain tense and mood. Concrete things are in the indicative mood. Fuzzy things go in the subjunctive.

There are, of course, no "facts" in the future. This is where it becomes important to remember that grammatical mood reflects the way the speaker *is treating* an action—as a fact or as an idea or wish. The actual veracity of the statement is beside the point.

- **Simple Fact Present:** Use the present indicative.
  Sī hoc facit, in perīculō sumus.
  (If he is [in fact] doing this, then we are [in fact] in danger.)

- **Simple Fact Past:** Use the perfect or imperfect indicative.
  Sī hoc fēcit, in perīculō erāmus.
  (If he did [in fact] do this, then we were [in fact] in danger.)

- **Future "More Vivid":** Use the future indicative.
  Sī hoc faciet, in perīculō erimus.
  (If he does [in fact] do this [in the future], then we will [in fact] be in danger.)

- **Future "Less Vivid":** Use the present subjunctive.
  Sī hoc faciat, in perīculō sīmus.
  (If he were to do this [later, but maybe he won't], then we would be in danger.)

- **Present Contrary to Fact:** Use the imperfect subjunctive.
  Sī hoc faceret, in perīculō essēmus.
  (If he were doing this [right now, which he isn't], then we'd be in danger [but we're not].)

- **Past Contrary to Fact:** Use the pluperfect subjunctive.
  Sī hoc fēcisset, in perīculō fuissēmus.
  (If he had done this [but he didn't], then we would have been in danger [but we were not].)

FACT

Contrary to fact conditions are one of the very few places where English still uses the subjunctive mood. "If I were you (which I am not), I wouldn't wear that (so I won't)." Many people incorrectly say "If I was . . .," but "was" is indicative, which, as you know, treats an action as a fact. This is a good example of the tendency of analytical languages to move away from using forms to convey meaning.

Table 16-7	**Vocabulary**

accēdō, –ere, accessī, accessum	to approach, go toward
aetās, –tātis, f.	age, a lifespan
*āiō**	to say (yes), affirm
aliquis, aliquid, pron.	anyone, someone, anything, something
aperiō, –īre, aperuī, apertum	to open, uncover
auferō, auferre, abstulī, ablātum	to carry away, remove, steal
bis, adv.	twice
cernō, –ere, crēvī, crētum	to distinguish, decide
contingō, –ere, contigī, contactum	to touch, happen
cupiō, –ere, cupīvī, cupītum	to desire
dīves, dīvitis	wealthy
ēligō, –ere, ēlēgī, ēlectum	to pick out, choose
etsī, conj.	even if
fīnis, fīnis, m.	end, edge, boundary (*fīnēs*, pl.—territory)
incipiō, –ere, incēpī, inceptum	to begin
ingenium, –ī, n.	talent, character, disposition
ingēns, ingentis	huge
iustus, –a, –um	just, fair
iuvō, iuvāre, iūvī, iūtum	to help, please
mīrus, –a, um	amazing, wonderful
nimius, –a, –um	very great, very much
nisi, conj.	unless, if not
ostendō, –ere, ostendī, ostentum	to show, point out
permittō, –ere, permīisī, permissus	to let go, send through, allow
praestō, –āre, praestitī, praestitum	to be outstanding
quamvīs, adv.	although, however much
quī, quae, quod, interrogative adj.	which
quīcumque, quaecumque, quodcumque, adj.	whoever, whichever, whatever
quīdam, quaedam, quoddam, adj.	a certain, a particular
quis, quid, interrogative pron.	who, what
quisquam, quaequam, quidquam, pron.	anybody, anyone, anything

continued on following page

Table 16-7	Vocabulary—*continued*
quisque, quidque, adj.	each
quisquis, quaequae, quidquid, pron.	whoever, whichever, whatever
quoniam, conj.	since, because
ratiō, rationis, f.	account, transaction, theory, reason
regō, –ere, rexī, rectum	to guide, rule, direct
rogō, –āre, –āvī, –ātum	to ask
saevus, –a, –um	savage, wild
sedeō, –ēre, sēdī, sessum	to sit
semel, adv.	once
signum, –ī, n.	sign, signal
ter, adv.	three times
velut, adv.	as, just as, for instance

* Defective verb chiefly seen in the present and imperfect tenses.

Latin-to-English Translations

Translate these Latin sentences into English.

1. *Quare tālia mala Quintum, virum tantō ingeniō, contingunt?*

2. *Nisi senatorēs in Forō sēdissent, barbarīs Rōmam invadentibus, tam saevē interfectī nōn essent.*

3. *Signō datō, incipientne ludī?*

4. *Unde venit ille sonus?*

5. *Sī id bellum iustum esset, spēs fīeret libertātī.*

continued on following page

Latin-to-English Translations—*continued*

6. *Sī captivōs hodie permittet, statim in aciēs hostium redībunt.*

7. *Librōs iam semel lectōs amicīs dare solēmus.*

8. *Etsi librōs nōn cupiunt, libenter eōs accipiunt.*

9. *Quis, velut Cicerō vel Dēmosthenēs, in oratiōne sīc praestat ut cunctīs persuadēre potest?*

10. *Sī illa arbor ingens cadat, domus vestra quidem deleātur.*

English-to-Latin Translations

Translate these English sentences into Latin.

1. If the army has attacked the Germans (*Germānī*) twice, why have they not been conquered?

2. You will help me, won't you?

3. You won't help me, will you?

4. Will you help me?

5. If anyone approaches the door, should he be allowed in (i.e., "sent through")?

Chapter 17

Infinitives

As you recall, verbs have five characteristics: person, number, tense, mood, and voice. The first two characteristics (person and number) are revealed solely by personal endings. Take apart the word "infinitive," and you will find the prefix "in-" meaning "not" and the base "fin" from *fīnīs* ("end"). An infinitive, then, is a verb form that doesn't have personal endings, but it *does* have tense and voice.

The Form of Infinitives

So far you have been exposed to two infinitives (the present active and present passive) and one infinitive use (complementary). There are, in fact, six infinitives and four infinitive uses. Don't worry. Once again you will see that this is mostly stuff you already know, but didn't know you knew!

The six infinitives comprise three tenses and two voices. The tenses are present, perfect, and future; the voices are, of course, active and passive. This matrix should sound familiar. Participles are organized the same way. Infinitives, however, don't leave any blank spaces in their chart.

Table 17-1 Infinitives			
Voice	**Present**	**Perfect**	**Future**
Active	*amāre*	*amāvisse*	*amātūrus esse*
Passive	*amārī*	*amātus esse*	*amātum īrī*
Active	*habēre*	*habuisse*	*habitūrus esse*
Passive	*habērī*	*habitus esse*	*habitum īrī*
Active	*dūcere*	*duxisse*	*ductūrus esse*
Passive	*dūcī*	*ductus esse*	*ductum īrī*
Active	*iacere*	*iēcisse*	*iactūrus esse*
Passive	*iacī*	*iactus esse*	*iactum īrī*
Active	*sentīre*	*sensisse*	*sensūrus esse*
Passive	*sentīrī*	*sensus esse*	*sensum īrī*

Take a good look at the forms on this chart and examine the tenses that you have learned.

- Present active: the second principle part of a verb
- Present passive: short *e* changes to an *ī*
- Perfect active: pluperfect subjunctive active without personal endings (perfect active stem plus *–isse*)
- Perfect passive: pluperfect subjunctive passive without personal endings (perfect passive participle with *esse*)

- Future active: future active participle with *esse*
- Future passive: supine with *īrī* (*īrī* being the only new form for you to learn in this chapter!)

ALERT!

The future active infinitive usually appears without the *esse*. It is also important to know that the future active infinitive of *sum*, *futūrus esse*, quite often appears as *fore*. Furthermore, *fore* is also sometimes used in place of *esse*, especially in forming the imperfect subjunctive of *sum*; for example, *forem* for *essem*, et cetera.

The Subjective Infinitive

In English, we use infinitives for a host of different things. In Latin, there are only four uses, one of which you have already learned, namely, the complementary infinitive. The other three are the subjective infinitive, the objective infinitive, and the main verb in a construction called indirect statement.

The tense value of infinitives, like participles, is relative to the tense of the main verb. A present infinitive *always* shows something happening at the *same time* as the main verb, the perfect *before*, and the future *after*.

As its name suggests, the *subjec*tive infinitive acts as the *subject* of the main verb. Since infinitives have no personal endings, they are ideally suited as subjects for so-called impersonal verbs.

The term "impersonal" uses the word "person" in the grammatical sense. In English, we see impersonal verbs very often in expressions relating to the weather. For example, "it is snowing." What does the "it" refer to? If the answer is "the sky," why not just say so? Furthermore, pronouns are used to stand for things that have already been mentioned (i.e., antecedents). With impersonal verbs in English, the antecedent is not expressed. In other expressions, such as "it is crucial . . . ," the "it" is a place-marker for something that hasn't been expressed yet. In the sentence "It is crucial that you submit everything on time," "that you submit everything on time" is actually the subject—it is the "it" that is crucial.

Latin, like English, uses impersonal verbs to describe the weather (e.g., *ningit* ["it is snowing"]), and it also has impersonal expressions such as *necesse est*. In Latin, however, an infinitive phrase is usually used to express the subject of this impersonal expression. *Necesse est canibus cibum dare.* ("It is necessary to give food to the dogs.") What is *necesse*? The infinitive phrase *canibus cibum dare* is what is necessary. Since this phrase—with its infinitive—is the subject, this infinitive use is called "subjective."

These impersonal verbs take dative objects:

libet: (it pleases)	*Tē vidēre mihi libet.* (It pleases me to see you; i.e., I am happy . . .)
placet: (it pleases)	*Venī mēcum sī tibi placet.* (Come with me if it pleases you; i.e., . . . if you like.)
licet: (it is allowed)	*Tibi mēcum venīre licet.* (It is allowed for you to come with me; i.e., You may . . .)
opus est: (there is need)	*Tibi mēcum venīre opus est.* (There is need that you come with me; i.e., you need to . . .)
necesse est: (it is necessary)	*Tibi mēcum venīre necesse est.* (It is necessary that you come with me; i.e., you must . . .)

These impersonal verbs take accusative objects:

oportet: (one should):	*Tē mēcum venīre oportet.* (You ought to come with me.)
decet: (it is proper)	*Tē mēcum venīre decet.* (It is proper that you come with me.)
iuvat: (it is pleasing)	*Ōlim et haec meminisse iuvabit.* (Someday even this will be pleasing to remember.)

Latin also has impersonal verbs to express certain emotional situations. For this special set of verbs, there are some unusual grammatical constructions that need to be memorized. Translating them literally would make absolutely no sense. They can use subjective infinitives or infinitive phrases for their subjects, though they can also use nouns.

FACT

Despite the Romans' reputation for frankness and stolid constitution, the linguistic convention of impersonal verbs offers a glimpse into the true mind and heart of the Roman people. They were not especially shy, but they did possess a reserved attitude toward certain things. Concepts of duty, shame, boredom, sluggishness, and urgency were more comfortably shoved off to an impersonal agent that thrust unhappy situations on unwitting victims.

The following impersonals are found with a genitive showing the source of the feeling and an accusative for the person affected:

miseret (it causes pity): *Tuī mē miseret.* (I pity you.)
paenitet (to cause regret): *Frāris tuī mē paenitet.* (I'm sorry about your brother.)
piget (it disgusts): *Istius mē piget.* (That man disgusts me.)
pudet (it causes shame): *Tuī mē pudet.* (I am ashamed of you.)
taedet (it tires): *Sermōnis mē taedet.* (The conversation bores me.)

The Objective Infinitive

Earlier, you were presented with one infinitive use, namely the complementary infinitive. The use is called *comple*mentary because the infinitive *comple*tes the idea of the main verb.

Gaius Rōmam īre vult. (Gaius wants **to go** to Rome.)

The most significant thing about this infinitive use is that both the infinitive and the main verb go back to the same person. In this example, Gaius is the one who wants, and Gaius is the one who goes.

The objective infinitive works very much like this. As you might have guessed, rather than go back to the subject of the main verb, the *objective* infinitive goes back to the *object* of the main verb.

*Gaius **tē** Rōmam **īre** vult.* (Gaius wants **you to go** to Rome.)

In this example, *Gaius* is the subject, *vult* is the main verb, and *tē Rōmam īre*—the whole infinitive phrase!—is the object. The pronoun *tē* simultaneously serves as both the accusative direct object of *vult* and the accusative subject of the infinitive *īre*.

FACT

English also uses accusative subjects for infinitives. Which sounds better to you: "I told **he to be** here by noon" or "I told **him to be** here by noon"?

Indirect Discourse

Pay attention the next time you are reading or hear someone speaking. You will be amazed at how much of what is communicated is really just the *reporting* of what someone else—sometimes even the speaker himself!—is saying, thinking, feeling, or asking. "He was saying that . . .," "We knew that it . . .," "I hear that she . . .," "They wondered why I. . . ." This type of reporting is called indirect discourse. In this chapter you will be introduced to two types of indirect discourse, namely indirect statement and indirect question.

Constructing an Indirect Statement

Indirect statement is the most common infinitive use in Latin. It is also the grammatical construction that is least like the construction English uses to express the same thing. In fact, if you try to translate the Latin literally, you get a hopeless garble of words. Let's take a look at how English reports things first.

Direct Statement: Caesar has a powerful army.
Indirect Statement: I hear that Caesar has a strong army.

English takes the original, direct subject-verb-object statement ("Caesar"–"has"–"a strong army"), and uses the conjunction "that" to link it to a main, subject-verb clause ("I"–"hear"). On the whole, the resulting sentence is actually just a normal subject-verb-object sentence. What differentiates a normal English sentence from one with an indirect statement is that English uses an *entire clause* as a direct object instead of a simple noun (or noun phrase).

It will come as no surprise that Latin is entirely logical about this construction. If the construction needs a direct object, Latin says that a direct object it shall have.

Direct Statement: *Caesar exercitum potentem habet.*
Indirect Statement: *Ego Caesarem exercitum potentem habēre audiō.*

All indirect statements are introduced by a verb of saying, thinking, knowing, or perceiving; for example, "I told you that . . .," "I believe that . . .," "I understand that . . .," "I see that . . .," and so on. The indirect statement itself consists of an accusative subject, a complement, and an infinitive. So here we have:

ego	*Caesarem exercitum potentem habēre*	*audiō*
subject	object	main verb (of saying, thinking, etc.)

If we take a closer look at the infinitive phrase that is serving as the object of *audiō*, a little "subclause" of predictable word order appears:

Caesarem	*exercitum potentem*	*habēre*
subject	object	main verb

- *Caesarem* is accusative because it is the subject of the infinitive *habēre*, and subjects of infinitives are always in the accusative case.
- *Exercitum* is accusative because it is the direct object of the infinitive *habēre* and direct objects of transitive verbs are always in the accusative case.

- *Potentem* is accusative because it is an adjective modifying *exercitum* and adjectives agree with their nouns in gender, case, and number.
- *Habēre* is an infinitive because infinitives are used as main verbs for indirect statement.

Tenses

As noted earlier, the three tenses of infinitives show time relative to the main verb. The relationships are the same as for participles. The present infinitive shows something happening at the same time as the main verb, the perfect infinitive shows time before, and the future infinitive time after.

*Caesarem exercitum potentem **habēre** audiō.* (present infinitive)
I hear that Caesar **has** a powerful army. (same time)

*Caesarem exercitum potentem **habuisse** audiō.* (perfect infinitive)
I hear that Caesar **had** a powerful army. (time before)

*Caesarem exercitum potentem **habitūrum** audiō.* (future infinitive)
I hear that Caesar **will have** a powerful army. (time after)

QUESTION?

Shouldn't the future infinitive of *habeō* be *habitūrum esse*?
Strictly speaking, yes. Future infinitives, however, are quite frequently found without the *esse*. You can tell the infinitive from the participle by the construction. In indirect statement, for example, an infinitive would be called for.

These during, before, and after relationships are all relative to the tense of the main verb, whatever that tense happens to be. In the above examples, the main verb (*audiō*) is present tense. If we change it to the perfect, for instance, the meanings (i.e., translations) will shift as well.

*Caesarem exercitum potentem **habēre** audīvī.* (present infinitive)
I heard that Caesar **had** a powerful army. (same time)

*Caesarem exercitum potentem **habuisse** audīvī.* (perfect infinitive)
I heard that Caesar **had had** a powerful army. (time before)

*Caesarem exercitum potentem **habitūrum** audīvī.* (future infinitive)
I heard that Caesar **was going to have** a powerful army. (time after)

Constructing an Indirect Question

Indirect statement can be challenging because its construction is very different from that of English. The construction of indirect question in Latin, on the other hand, is virtually identical to that in English. The only real, notable difference is that Latin uses a subjunctive.

Direct question: Where is Caesar's army?
Indirect question: I wonder where Caesar's army is.

Direct question: *Ubi est exercitus Casaeris?*
Indirect question: *Mīror ubi exercitus Caesaris sit.*

As you can see, the Latin construction parallels the English beautifully. The only exception is in the mood of the verb in the clause expressing the indirect question.

You can usually expect some type of indirect discourse if the main verb of a sentence pertains to saying, thinking, knowing, or perceiving. Use those types of verbs as signposts. With an accusative, you can expect an infinitive (indirect statement). With a question word, you can expect a subjunctive (indirect question).

Tenses

The relative nature of infinitive tense in indirect statement finds some similarity with the tenses of the subjunctive in indirect question. In indirect question, however, verbal aspect also plays an important role. If a main verb is in a present or future tense, you can expect to find a present subjunctive if the action in the subjunctive clause happens at the same time or after, and a perfect subjunctive if it is the time before. This is called primary sequence. If the main verb is in a past tense, then the imperfect is used for same time or after actions, and a pluperfect for time before. This is called secondary sequence.

- Primary sequence: *Mīror ubi exercitus Caesaris sit.*
  (I wonder where Caesar's army is [or will be].)
    Mīror ubi exercitus Caesaris fuerit.
    (I wonder where Caesar's army was [or has been].)
- Secondary sequence: *Mīrābar ubi exercitus Caesaris esset.*
  (I wondered where Caesar's army was.)
    Mīrābar ubi exercitus Caesaris fuisset.
    (I wondered where Caesar's army had been.)

When there is a subordinate clause within an indirect statement or question, its verb goes in the subjunctive, even though it would ordinarily go in the indicative. *Putō Caesarem legiōnem **quae modo advēnerit** trāns Alpēs mox ductūrum esse.* ("I think that Caesar will soon take across the Alps the legion **that just arrived**.")

Table 17-2 Vocabulary	
albus, –a, –um	white (dull, flat white)
anima, –ae, f.	soul, breath (of life)
candidus, –a, –um	white (bright, shiny white)
citus, –a, –um	fast, quick
cōgō, –ere, coēgī, coactum	to drive together, force, compel
constō, constāre, consititī, constātum	to stand together, depend on, stand still (*constat*, impersonal, it is agreed, certain, sure)
cor, cordis, n.	heart
cras, adv.	tomorrow
dīvīnus, –a, –um	holy, divine
foedus, –a, –um	foul, nasty, stinky

continued on following page

Table 17-2   Vocabulary—*continued*

foris, adv.	outside
herī, adv.	yesterday
hodiē, adv.	today
interim, adv.	meanwhile
licet, licēre, licuit, licitum, impersonal	it is allowed
lūmen, lūminis, n.	light, eyes
magister, –trī, m.	master, chief
modo, adv.	just, just now, recently
mollis, –e	soft, flexible
mundus, –a, –um	neat, clean
mundus, –ī, m.	world, universe
negō, –āre, –āvī, –ātum	to deny, say no
nesciō, –īre, –īvī, –ītum	not to know
nondum, adv.	not yet
num, adv.	whether
ordō, ordinis, m.	row, order, rank
placeō, placēre, placuī, placitum	to please (*placet,* it is pleasing)
pūrus, –a, –um	pure, clean
putō, –āre, –āvī, –ātum	to think
quaerō, –ere, quaesīvī, quaesītum	to look for, miss, ask
quondam, adv.	former, at a certain time
rogō, –āre, –āvī, –ātum	to ask
rursus, adv.	back, again, in return
sciō, –īre, –īvī, –ītum	to know
sentiō, –īre, sensī, sensum	to perceive, feel
somnus, –ī, m.	sleep
tamquam, adv.	like, as
tūtus, –a, –um	safe
utrum . . . an	whether . . . or
uxor, –is, f.	wife
venus, veneris, f.	charm, grace, beauty (*Venus, Veneris,* f., Venus)

Latin-to-English Translations

Translate these Latin sentences into English.

1. *Troiā relictā, Aenēas ā Venere, deā mātreque suā, Hesperiam petere coactus est.*

2. *Titus Livius scripsit Hersiliam uxōrem Rōmulī esse.*

3. *Dīcitur cor istius virī foedum fuisse et minimē mundum.*

4. *Negāvit iterum iterumque sē ubi aurum celātum esset scīre.*

5. *Mulierēs inter sē colloquentēs nondum nesciēbant sē spectārī.*

English-to-Latin Translations

Translate these English sentences into Latin.

1. We felt that we would be safer at home.

2. They kept asking whether we had seen the god himself.

3. The senator said that Caesar was sending a messenger to Rome. (*nuntius, –ī,* m."messenger")

4. The senator said that Caesar would send a messenger to Rome.

5. The senator said that Caesar had sent a messenger to Rome.

Chapter 18

 Getting Attention and Giving Commands

The Romans have a reputation for having been bossy people and not being very nice about it. While that may be true, we do our fair share of telling people what to do—and reporting what we were told to do. In this chapter you will learn how to call names, bark orders, and get things done in gentler ways as well.

Interjections

Before you can tell anyone what to do, you need to get their attention first. There are many ways to call someone's attention, either to yourself or to something else. You can perform an outrageous act and wind up in the newspaper, of course, but looks, gestures, and words are by far more frequent.

The only part of speech that has thus far not been addressed is the interjection. While they were surely common in the everyday speech of the average Roman, they do not find their way into literature very often. Interjections are those little, often nonsense-sounding words yelled to call attention (e.g., "Hey!"). They do more, however, than merely call attention—a simple scream could do that! They bear meaning, calling attention and expressing a speaker's emotions at the same time. Consider the range of meanings these English interjections represent: "Ouch!" "Yea!" "Uh-oh!" "Wow!" "Damn!" Like all words, interjections come and go, either changing over time (like "halloa!" to "hello!") or being completely abandoned and replaced. For example, the nineteenth-century cheer "huzzah!" was exchanged for "hurrah!" then "hooray!" and now, at the time of this writing, we hear "woo-hoo!"

Here are some of the more common interjections in Latin. Since interjections tend to be colloquial, there are probably many more—especially the "colorful" ones—that we will never know.

- *Ēn! ecce!* (Look!)
- *Ehem! eīa! ō! vāh!* (surprise)
- *Pol! edepol! mēherclē! pro di*! (surprise with religious reference)
- *Heu! ēheu! vae!* (pain or anger)
- *Papae! iō! euge! eugepae!* (happiness)
- *Eho! ehodum! heus! ho! st!* (calling attention)

The Vocative Case

The least common noun case to find but easiest to learn is the vocative. The name "vocative" is from the Latin verb *vocō, vocāre* meaning "to call."

And that's exactly what the vocative case does—it turns nouns, usually names, into interjections (e.g., "Jeff!").

It is the easiest of the cases to learn because the forms are identical to the nominative case with only two exceptions: the second declension masculine nominative ending *–us* changes to *–e*, and *–ius* changes to *–ī*. If you were to call Marcus, for example, you would shout *"Marce!"* If you needed Publius's attention, you would yell *"Publī!"* On the other hand, if you wanted Vipsania to notice you, the form would be *"Vipsānia!"* (i.e., just like the nominative).

Giving Commands

As you recall, mood shows how a speaker treats an action. The indicative mood treats an action as a fact. The subjunctive mood treats action as a wish or idea. The imperative mood treats action as a command. There are other ways of seeing that a job gets done, though, than simply issuing orders.

FACT

The English words "imperative" and "emperor" are related by the base *imperā–*, meaning "command." "Emperor" comes from the Latin *imperātor*, which is a military rank roughly equivalent to our "general." You may think of ancient Rome as always having been led by emperors, but, in fact, emperors didn't head the Roman government until 68 C.E., when the army began choosing and installing their leaders as virtual dictators. The *first three-quarters* of Roman history saw a few other forms of government!

Imperative Mood

Giving direct commands is essentially a second person phenomenon—someone tells you to do something. In English, imperative mood is the infinitive without the usual "to." Also, the form doesn't vary between giving an order to one person or to many. To make the command negative, you just add "don't" in front.

Affirmative Singular: Knock it off, kid!
Affirmative Plural: Knock it off, you guys!
Negative Singular: Don't take candy from strangers, Bobby.
Negative Plural: Don't take candy from strangers, boys.

Latin makes the imperative mood by a process similar to the English one, though it isn't quite as easy. In Latin, you also begin by trimming the present infinitive, specifically the final –*re*. To form the plural, the ending –*te* is added to the stem. Third conjugation verbs experience a predictable stem vowel change.

Table 18-1	**The Imperative Active**		
Person	*portō, portāre*	*videō, vidēre*	*premō, premere*
2nd, sing.	*portā*	*vidē*	*preme*
2nd, pl.	*portāte*	*vidēte*	*premite*
Person	*capiō, capere*	*veniō, venīre*	
2nd, sing.	*cape*	*venī*	
2nd, pl.	*capite*	*venīte*	

Just as English adds "don't" to the imperative to make it negative, Latin adds a word to the infinitive. The word Latin uses to express a negative command is *nōlī*, or *nōlīte*, which is actually the imperative of the verb *nōlō, nōlle*. Since *nōlō* means "to be unwilling," negative commands in Latin are rather quaint. *Nōlī mē occidere!* ("Don't kill me!") actually orders the would-be murderer not to want to do the deed. (Be unwilling to kill me!)

ALERT!

The verbs *dīcō, dūcō, faciō,* and *ferō* have slightly irregular imperatives. Due to the fact that these verbs were so common in everyday use, they were clipped down to one-syllable words, namely: *dīc, dūc, fac,* and *fer*. Their plurals are fairly predictable (*dīcite, dūcite, facite,* and *ferte*), and the negative command follows normal rules (*nōlī dīcere*, "don't tell," etc., . . .).

In addition to active voice forms for the imperative mood, there are also passive voice forms. While any verb that can take passive voice forms can appear in the imperative passive, usually only deponent verbs are found in Latin literature.

Table 18-2   The Imperative Passive

Person	*portō, portāre*	*videō, vidēre*	*sequor, sequī*
2nd, sing.	*portāre*	*vidēre*	*sequere*
2nd, pl.	*portāminī*	*vidēminī*	*sequiminī*

Person	*morior, morī*	*inveniō, invenīre*
2nd, sing.	*morere*	*invenīre*
2nd, pl.	*moriminī*	*invenīminī*

The imperative passive forms, in the singular, employ the alternate personal ending for the second person singular passive. That is to say, it uses *–re* instead of *–ris*. The result is a singular imperative passive that is identical to the present infinitive active. In the case of deponents, of course, the form resembles what the present infinitive active would have looked like had they had any active infinitives.

In the plural, imperative passive forms are the same as the second person plural, present indicative passive. There you will find the regular personal ending *–minī*.

Indirect Commands

Indirect questions in English and Latin share construction similar to what you learned for indirect discourse. First there is a main verb of saying, thinking, knowing, or perceiving, then a question word leading off a clause with a verb in the subjunctive mood.

Commands can also be reported indirectly. In this type of indirect discourse, a third construction comes into play.

Caesar mīlitibus imperāvit **ut flūmen transīrent.**
   (Caesar ordered the soldiers **to cross the river.**)
Ego identidem monitus sum **nē ūllum fidem istī habērem.**
   (I was warned repeatedly **not to place any trust in that creep.**)

This construction should look quite familiar. It is the exact same thing used in purpose clauses! So, if both constructions begin with the subordinating conjunctions *ut* or *nē* followed by a verb in the subjunctive, how are you supposed to be able to tell them apart? There is the usual reply to this question—context—but there are also a couple of other things that might tip you off.

First, consider the real spirit of the meanings embedded in these two constructions (i.e., purpose and indirect command). Using our examples again, the purpose of Caesar's order was to get his men over to the other side of the river. You can also imagine the original command: *Mīlitēs, flūmen transīte!* So, with respect to sense, they are really one and the same idea.

Second, the easiest way to spot this construction is by the sort of verb that introduces it. This kind of indirect discourse starts off like the other two types, namely with a verb of saying, thinking, knowing, or perceiving. In the case of indirect command, however, there is a short list of verbs that involves notions of getting someone else to do something that often introduces indirect commands.

- *imperāre alicui ut* . . . . (to order someone to . . .)
- *persuādēre alicui ut* . . . . (to persuade someone to . . .)
- *hortārī aliquem ut* . . . . (to encourage someone to . . .)
- *monēre aliquem ut* . . . . (to warn or advise someone to . . .)
- *ōrāre aliquem ut* . . . . (to beg someone to . . .)
- *rogō aliquem ut* . . . . (to ask someone to . . .)
- *petere ab aliquō ut* . . . . (to ask someone to . . .)
- *precārī ab aliquō ut* . . . . (to pray or beg someone to . . .)
- *quaerere ab aliquō ut* . . . . (to ask someone to . . .)

Note that some of the verbs take dative objects, some take accusative objects, and others use a prepositional phrase, namely *ā* plus the ablative.

ALERT!

A main verb of saying, thinking, knowing, or perceiving does not necessarily have to begin any form of indirect discourse. It is just as possible to hear a bird chirping, as it is to hear that Lucius Cornelius Sulla is marching on Rome.

The Hortatory and Jussive Subjunctives

All the uses for the subjunctive mood that you have been presented with so far have been dependent or subordinate: They depend on being introduced by a subordinating conjunction and cannot stand alone as clauses.

There are also a few subjunctive uses referred to as independent because they do not require a subordinating conjunction to introduce them. Now is a good time to learn the most common of them since they also, in varying degrees, involve getting someone else to do something.

The imperative prompts movement to action in a direct, not-so-subtle way. You can take advantage of the subjunctive mood's treatment of actions as ideas or wishes to get a ball rolling in a gentle, nudging way.

The term "hortatory" comes from the verb *hortor, hortārī, hortātus sum,* which means "to urge" or "to encourage." The hortatory subjunctive is an independent use of the subjunctive that, in the present tense, can be used to rouse a group, to ask permission for oneself, or to give permission to someone else to do something. If the encouragement is negative, *nē* is used.

> *Gaudeāmus igitur, iuvenēs dum sumus.*
> (So let's party while we are still young.)
> *Potiōnem habeam et omnia vobīs narrābō.*
> (Let me have a drink and I will tell you everything.)
> *Caveat emptor.* (Let the buyer beware.)
> *Nē intrant!* (Let them not enter! i.e., Don't let them in!)

When used in the imperfect or pluperfect tense, the hortatory subjunctive shows something that should have happened in the past, but didn't. The only difference between the imperfect and pluperfect tenses for this subjunctive use is that the pluperfect is more emphatic about the time being in the past.

> *Tam bonus, tam venūstus erat Marcus. Nē morerētur.*
> (Marcus was so good, so charming. He shouldn't have died.)
> *Cum vinī tē pigēret, alium poposcissēs.*
> (Since you really didn't like the wine, you should have asked for a different one.)

What is the difference between "hortatory" and "jussive"?
In practice, there really isn't any. Some grammatical traditions reserve the term "hortatory" for first person forms only. The others they refer to as "jussive," from the verb *iubeō, iubēre, iussī, iussum* meaning "to order."

Clauses after Verbs of Fearing

This subject—clauses after verbs of fearing—may seem to be a very odd thing to bring up in the middle of this discussion. It is, however, extremely relevant. In Latin, if whatever is feared is not a noun (e.g., *lupum metuērunt puerī* ["The boys were afraid of the wolf"]), but is a verb, then a hortatory (jussive) clause follows the verb of fearing. This can cause great confusion because the words that introduce the clause are the exact *opposite* of what you would have expected. When you see *nē,* you think negative; when you see *ut,* positive. Compare the subordinating conjunctions in the following examples.

> *Timuimus **nē** lupus puerōs comederet.*
>   (We were afraid that the wolf **would** gobble the boys up.)
> *Timuimus **ut** puerī lupum effugerent.*
>   (We were afraid that the boys **wouldn't** escape from the wolf.)

For English speakers, these sentences seem to say the exact opposite of what is intended since *nē* usually negates a verb. To the Roman mind, however, these sentences say this:

> *Timuimus **nē** lupus puerōs comederet.*
>   (We were afraid. **Don't let** the wolf gobble the boys up!)
> *Timuimus **ut** puerī lupum effugerent.*
>   (We were afraid. **Let** the boys escape from the wolf!)

Instead of *ut* to introduce a negative clause, *nē . . . nōn* is sometimes found.

Wishing in the Subjunctive

The optative subjunctive is all about wishing. This use of the subjunctive mood is extremely sensitive to tense. The present subjunctive suggests that the wish is still possible. The imperfect tense, however, also refers to the present, but it notes that the wish is, as of yet, unaccomplished. In the pluperfect subjunctive, the wish was not fulfilled in the past. To negate these uses of the subjunctive, the word to use is *nē*. In addition, you may sometimes see the word *utinam* preceding an optative subjunctive, though it isn't required.

> *Diūtius vīvam ut filiōs meōs in plēnam virtūtem crescere vidērem.*
>> (I hope I live longer so that I can see my boys grow into full manhood.)
> *Utinam nē id quod factum erat vīdissem.*
>> (I wish that I hadn't seen that which [i.e., what] had happened.)

The Potential Subjunctive

The potential subjunctive is an independent use of the subjunctive that goes back to the original function of the mood, before it merged with the optative. It is used to express an idea as a possibility without suggesting that it is wished for.

> *Aliquis **dīcat** tē stultum esse.*
>> (Someone **could** [**might**] **say** that you are a fool.)

In this example, the speaker is merely suggesting the possibility of someone saying this. There is no hint that the speaker actually wants someone to do this.

The Deliberative Subjunctive

The fuzziest of the subjunctive uses is the deliberative subjunctive. It is a perfect blend of the original subjunctive and optative moods. With it, the speaker asks himself a question, pondering out loud whether an action is possible or even desired. You make a deliberative subjunctive question negative with the adverb *nōn*.

> *Quid faciāmus?* (What can we do? What are we supposed to do?)
> *Nōnne adessem?* (Shouldn't I have been there?)

Table 18-3 Vocabulary	
aciēs, –ēī, f.	sharp edge, battle line, insight
arbor, –is, f.	tree
cantō, –āre, –āvī, –ātum	to sing, play (a musical instrument)
cōpia, –ae, f.	supply, abundance
cōpiae, –ārum, f. pl.	troops
dēserō, –ere, –uī, dēsertum	to abandon, leave, break ties with
dolor, dolōris, m.	pain, grief
eques, –itis, m.	horseman, cavalry, knight (a social order between plebs and patricians)
exercitus, –ūs, m.	army, training
fāma, –ae, f.	rumor, reputation
flamma, –ae, f.	flame
flōs, flōris, m.	flower
flūmen, flūminis, n.	river
glōria, –ae, f.	glory, fame
imperium, –ī, n.	power, command
Iuppiter, Iovis, m.	Jupiter
iūs, iūris, n.	right, law
lacrima, –ae, f.	tear
lingua, –ae, f.	tongue, language

continued on following page

Table 18-3   Vocabulary—*continued*

lūx, lūcis, f.	light (daylight)
namque, conj.	emphatic form of *nam* (because)
numerus, –ī, m.	number
opēs, opum, f. pl.	resources
ops, opis, f.	wealth
postquam, conj.	after
princeps, principis, c.	leader, chief
proelium, –ī, n.	battle
quīn, conj.	*(with indicative)* why not?, rather; *(with subjunctive)* who/that not, but that
saeculum, –ī, n.	a generation, a life span, an age
sanguis, sanguinis, m.	blood
sermō, sermōnis, m.	conversation, talk
sīdus, sīderis, n.	star, constellation
silva, –ae, f.	forest
sive (seu), conj.	or if *(sīve . . . sīve—whether . . . or)*
spēs, –eī, f.	hope
umbra, –ae, f.	shadow, shade, ghost
unda, –ae, f.	wave, water
ventus, –ī, m.	wind
versus, –ūs, m.	verse, row, line, a turning
virgō, virginis, f.	a young woman
vōtum, –ī, n.	a vow
vultus, –ūs, m.	face, expression on the face

Latin-to-English Translations

Translate these Latin sentences into English.

1. *Latrōnem capite, canēs, nē effugiat!*

2. *Canibus imperāvī ipse ut latrōnem capiant nē effugiat.*

3. *Latrōnem capiant canēs. Ita nōn effugiat.*

4. *Metuō nē latrō effugiat.*

5. *Vereor ut canēs latrōnem capiant.*

6. *Utinam canēs latrōnem capiant!*

7. *Nisi canēs latrōnem cēpissent, effūgisset.*

8. *Nesciō utrum canēs latrōnem capiant an effugiat.*

9. *Canibus veteribus, nesciō quīn effugiat latrō.*

10. *Cum canēs latrōnem cēpissent, ille tamen effūgit.*

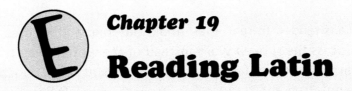

Chapter 19

Reading Latin

T he day comes for all who study foreign languages when formal grammar
ends and the first dip into reading the au-
thentic begins. Whatever language you
have prepared for, that first exposure is
shocking. You may even wonder what language you had just "learned"!

The Reading Process

Reading, like speaking, is something that is easy to take for granted. Your eyes skip along a page without thinking about what you are really doing, and what you are really doing is quite amazing! Let's slow down the process and see what actually takes place.

FACT

The Romans tended to read their books out loud and let their minds process the *spoken* word instead of the written one. It might have been easier for them, since in ancient times punctuation was not used and frequently no spaces were left between words (canyouimaginealwaysreadinglikethis).

To shove along through that parenthetical sentence you probably had to slow down and sound it out. For the Romans, that process was easier since every letter represented only one sound.

Setting punctuation aside, the smallest unit in writing is a letter of the alphabet. Odds are, though, that when you read you don't scrutinize each individual letter and produce the sound it represents. Even if the word is very long or new to you, you probably sound it out by syllables or by familiar clusters of syllables. When most readers read, they see words, and those words are actually little more than shapes. People who read quickly can also misread words of similar shapes, leading to some bizarre sentences that cause double takes.

Column A	Column B
Lincoln said	Lincoln said
that that	that that politician
politician was	was so corrupt
so corrupt	that the only thing
that the	he wouldn't steal
only thing	is a red hot stove.
he wouldn't	
steal is	
a red	
hot stove.	

Still, reading is more than seeing a series of words. Words cluster into phrases, much like syllables group into words, and the phrases cluster into clauses. Reading, then, is a process of seeing and digesting discrete linguistic chunks, and we chunk as we read naturally, without conscious reflection. Try reading down Column A of the chart out loud, giving a slight pause before starting each new line. Then read Column B, also pausing briefly between lines.

Column B probably sounded better—smoother, more natural, and, frankly, more intelligible. The chunks find themselves by their own logic, not by any mathmatical formula!

The same is true when reading Latin. Your temptation will be to go word by word like a child, and that's okay at first. You must remember, however, that Latin is an *inflected* language, not an *analytical* one. In English, syntax (i.e., the way words show their relationship to each other) is governed by word order. Because of a word's position in a sentence, you know whether it is acting as a subject or an object, and words are free to bear virtually nothing more than a meaning. In Latin, things are very different. Word order doesn't matter much at all. The syntax information lies encoded in the endings. The upshot of this is that when reading Latin words, you have to take into consideration the endings *as well as* the meanings!

The downfall of many a novice to Latin is tripping along a sentence, taking in only the meanings of words as if they were in English. When this is done, the result is a jumbled mass of meanings. The real danger— not to mention frustration and disappointment—comes if you start wandering around in a sentence looking for meanings that sound nice together. The original Latin is usually abandoned at this point, as you arrange and rearrange words like so many Scrabble tiles. This is not a good approach. Translation and understanding by this method are doomed to miss the mark.

In the Beginning

For your first foray into "real" Latin—that is to say Latin that was written while the Roman Empire was still a force to be reckoned with—here is a passage that you might recognize. (Have your dictionary handy!) If you do recognize the passage, you might be surprised that it doesn't say quite what you thought it did.

In principiō creāvit Deus caelum et terram.

Terra autem erat inānis et vacua, et tenebrae erant super faciem abyssī, et Spīritus Deī ferēbātur super aquās.

Dixitque Deus: Fīat lux. Et facta est lux. Et vīdit Deus lūcem quod esset bona: et dīvīsit lūcem ā tenebrīs. Appellāvitque lūcem Diem, et tenebrās Noctem: factumque est vespere et māne, diēs ūnus.

Dixit quoque Deus: Fīat firmāmentum in mediō aquārum: et dīvidat aquās ab aquīs. Et fēcit Deus firmāmentum, dīvīsitque aquās, quae erant sub firmāmentō, ab hīs, quae erant super firmāmentum. Et factum est ita. Vocāvitque Deus firmāmentum, Caelum: et factum est vespere et māne, diēs secundus.

Did you recognize it? It is from the *Editiō Vulgāta* by Jerome. Familiarity with the text should help you focus on the grammar. Still, it is possible that it just looked like some strange words floating in a foreign sea. Here is the same passage broken into chunks.

In principiō	In the beginning
creāvit Deus	God created
caelum et terram.	sky and land.
Terra autem	And the land
erat inānis et vacua,	was empty and hollow,
et tenebrae erant	and there was darkness
super faciem abyssī,	over the face of the bottomless pit,
et Spīritus Deī	and the Breath/Spirit of God
ferēbātur super aquās.	was carried over the waters.
Dixitque Deus:	And God said:
Fīat lux.	Let light be made.
Et facta est lux.	And light was made.
Et vīdit Deus lūcem	And God saw the light
quod esset bona:	that/because it was (supposed to be) good:
et dīvīsit lūcem	and he divided the light
ā tenebrīs	from the darkness.
Appellāvitque lūcem Diem,	And he called the light Day,

et tenebrās Noctem:	and the darkness Night:
factumque est.	and it was done
vespere et māne, ...	with respect to evening and morning,
diēs ūnus.	day one.
Dixit quoque Deus:	God also said:
Fīat firmāmentum	Let the vault of the sky be made
in mediō aquārum:	in the middle of the waters:
et dīvidat aquās ab aquīs.	and let it divide the waters from the waters.
Et fēcit Deus firmāmentum, ...	And God made the vault of the sky,
dīvīsitque aquās, ...	and he divided the waters,
quae erant sub firmāmentō, ...	which were under the vault of the sky,
ab hīs, ...	from these,
quae erant super firmāmentum.	which were over the vault of the sky.
Et factum est ita.	And it was made like this.
Vocāvitque Deus	And God called
firmāmentum, Caelum:	the vault of the sky, Heaven:
et factum est	and it was done
vespere et māne, ...	with respect to evening and morning,
diēs secundus.	the second day.

If you compare the text written as a paragraph with the text broken into chunks, you will see that the word order was not changed to make it readable. Look back over it and you will notice that the chunks are not made randomly. They are grammatical units. Some are subject phrases, some are predicates. There are some prepositional phrases, and a few are whole clauses.

The more practice and exposure to Latin you receive, the more comfortable you will become with it. Read and reread this passage, either in the paragraph or chunk style. Read it slowly out loud with the translation hidden, and try to understand the Latin as it goes by without translating it. Examine each form and see if you can describe the forms and explain their function. You might even like to go back and review Chapters 3 and 5 (the overviews of Latin's verb and noun system).

Understanding Taxis

In linguistics, the term "taxis" (pronounced like the English word "taxes") is a loan word from Greek and means "arrangement" or "order." The specific arrangement or order referred to is that of clauses. The last passage was made a little easier to read because its style is "paratactic." "Parataxis" refers to the act of placing clauses one after another like railroad cars. Parataxis is contrasted with "hypotaxis." In hypotaxis, clauses are tucked one inside another resulting in a structure that resembles an onion more than a train.

> **Parataxis:** *The puppy wandered into the garden* and it was chased away.
> **Hypotaxis:** The puppy, *which wandered into the garden*, was chased away.

In the first (train) example, one clause is linked to the next clause with a conjunction. In the second (onion) example, the same clause is converted into a relative clause and nested within the other clause. This nesting is called subordination.

Parataxis is a simple, almost childlike way of writing (e.g., *Dick and Jane*). Hypotaxis is more sophisticated. As you might suspect, the language of most literature is hypotactic. When reading, then, you have to remember that sometimes chunks are within chunks, in which case you have to pick up a clause from where you left off when starting a new, subordinated clause.

ALERT!

In the next passage, watch out for a trick known as "parallel structure." In parallel structure, a clause can appear to be missing a crucial element (like a verb). What you do in this situation is understand what that missing word might be *based on context*. For example, the sentence "I prefer apricots, and Scott mangoes" is not one clause expressing my preference for two things. There are two clauses and the verb "prefer" is understood in the second.

Reading Caesar

Traditionally, the first Latin literature that someone who is fresh from grammar is introduced to is Julius Caesar's *Commentaries on the Gallic War*. His style offers a good mix between paratactic and hypotactic sentences. Read through this passage and you will see that it is not quite as simple as Jerome's boxcars. Don't worry about understanding everything as it goes by on this first pass. Just move through it slowly, noticing groups of words that seem to belong together, and getting a feel for the structure of the passage as a whole.

> Gallia est omnis dīvisa in partēs trēs, quārum ūnam incolunt Belgae, aliam Aquītānī, tertiam quī ipsōrum linguā Celtae, nostrā Gallī appellantur. Hī omnēs linguā, institūtīs, lēgibus inter sē differunt. Gallōs ab Aquītānīs Garumna flūmen, ā Belgīs Mātrona et Sēquana dīvidit. Hōrum omnium fortissimī sunt Belgae, proptereā quod ā cultū atque hūmānitāte prōvinciae longissimē absunt, minimēque ad eōs mercātōrēs saepe commeant atque ea quae ad effēminandōs animōs pertinent important, proximīque sunt Germānīs, quī trans Rhēnum incolunt, quibuscum continenter bellum gerunt.

If you felt intimidated by that passage, don't. True, it is only four sentences (if you count the periods *we moderns* have put in), but you must remember that reading happens in chunks, not sentences. The longer the sentence, the more chunks there are.

If you look at those sentences as being one long one after another, you might surrender unto Caesar. If you slow down and read the chunks, you will be able to see the clauses with no difficulty.

Whatever the case, take your time when reading and always mind the chunks!

The smoothest English translation would be:

> As a whole, Gaul is divided into three parts, one of which the Belgians inhabit, another, the Aquitanians, and the third is occupied by a people who by their own language are called Celts, but in our language are called Gauls. All these peoples differ amongst themselves in language, customs, and laws. The Garonne river separates the Gauls from the Aquitanians, and the Marne and the Seine separate them from the Belgians. Of all these peoples, the Belgians are the most courageous, largely because they are the farthest away from the refinement and civilization of Province, and because merchants only rarely meet with them and, as a consequence bring them those things that tend to enervate brave souls. They also live closest to the Germans, who live across the Rhine, and with whom they constantly wage war.

Tradition

After reading Caesar, novice Latin students traditionally read Cicero, his *First Oration Against Catiline* in particular. Cicero's style is extremely hypotactic. He is able to nest an amazing number of clauses within one another. Apart from speeches, he also has some philosophical essays and letters extant (i.e., that have survived). You might consider approaching his essay *Dē Amicitiā* ("On Friendship") or *Dē Senectūte* ("On Old Age"). His letters provide an interesting, personal take on the breakdown of the Roman republic in the mid–first century B.C.E. And they are not so hypotactic!

After Cicero traditionally comes Vergil's *Aeneid*. While the basic linguistic concepts of parataxis and hypotaxis apply, poetry in Latin is a whole other story. Latin poetry is not based on a rhyming scheme. Instead, it is governed by meter, which involves rules for the arrangement of long and short syllables (i.e., vowels). The meters of Latin poetry assure a steady rhythmic quality that is very beautiful. In addition, poetry also can take full advantage of Latin's being an inflected rather than analytical language. Free from the strictures of word order, an incredible new world of word play and imagery is possible. Ⓔ

Chapter 20

Quae cum ita sint . . .

"Since that's the way things are . . .," this chapter looks at some of the long-term benefits of knowing Latin. Ancient Rome is a long-ago and faraway place, but the influence of that city and her people lives on today in ways the ancient Romans themselves would have never imagined.

A Foundation for the Romance Languages

One of the immediate benefits of knowing Latin is that it provides a foundation for understanding the other Romance languages—if your intellectual curiosity ever steers you in that direction. As noted earlier in the book, the primary Romance languages are French, Italian, Portuguese, Romanian, and Spanish. They ultimately represent the way local peoples (mostly those whom the Romans conquered) changed Latin as they incorporated it into their everyday speech.

The idea of the Romans' "conquering" foreign peoples is probably not exactly what you may think. By force or by request, the Romans set up military bases all over the Mediterranean (*pax Rōmāna*), not too unlike the way the United States has military bases all over Western Europe (*pax Americāna*), ostensibly for "protection." The peoples under Rome's watchful eye were free to maintain whatever form of government, customs, religion, or language they wished. If, however, you wanted to rise in the world or do business with the Romans, you needed to know Latin. Over time Latin merged with and to varying degrees replaced the native languages.

Not only does Latin provide a grammatical foothold for understanding the Romance languages (although none is as inflected as Latin), it also provides a large set of common vocabulary stems. Look at how similar these words are:

Table 20-1   Latin and the Romance Languages

Latin	French	Italian	Portuguese	Romanian	Spanish
caballus	cheval	cavallo	cavalo	cal	caballo
māter	mère	madre	mae	mama	madre
niger	noir	nero	negro	negru	negro
viridis	vert	verde	verde	verde	verde

See any patterns? Admittedly, Latin isn't exactly a decoder ring, but knowing it certainly gives you a tremendous advantage when and if you decide to tackle a Romance language, as the chart above indicates.

A Deeper Understanding of English

Another consequence of knowing Latin is that it will help you better understand and appreciate English. A common complaint at this point might take the form of a question: If you want to learn about English, then why not examine English instead of Latin? Fair enough. You can certainly gain insights into English if you study its grammar and vocabulary.

There is, however, another way to look at this question. If you have ever been in an airplane, or at the top of a tall building, or even on the roof of a house, one of the first things you notice is how different things look, even things with which you might be familiar. The reason they look different is because your perspective has changed. Most of the time, our knowledge of something increases when we view it from a different perspective. The same is true of any language. With regard to Latin and English, you'll probably notice that your knowledge of Latin grammar has made you more aware of English grammar. It's also likely that you'll be more sensitive to the number of words you have to use in English in order to express even simple thoughts—and this sentence is a good example of that assertion! And while it's too much to claim that your knowledge of Latin will improve your writing style in English, it might inspire you to omit needless words, something most stylists advocate.

FACT

There are many artificial rules imposed on English because of Latin. The reason you were taught not to use double negatives or to split infinitives is due to Latin's influence. Ironically—as you now know—double negatives do occur in Latin, and you couldn't split a Latin infinitive even if you wanted to. So much for trying to make one language look and act like another one!

In addition to enhancing your appreciation of English, knowing Latin will assist you in expanding your vocabulary. You saw in the chapter that introduced prefixes and suffixes how knowledge of these "particles" (along with stems) can greatly help you figure out the meaning of a word you don't recognize. Since a whole range of standardized tests (such as the SAT) include uncommon words, students often enroll in Latin classes as a way to prepare for such tests.

Latin and the Law

Latin will also enable you to cut through the thicket of alien vocabulary used by the legal and medical professions. Initially, Latin was used in both fields because, for hundreds of years, the universal language (the *lingua franca*) of learning and scholarship in Western Europe was—you guessed it!—Latin. Even after Latin stopped serving this function, much of the terminology used by lawyers and physicians had already been established. Of course, more cynical observers might argue that those two professions continue to use Latin in order to keep ordinary people mystified. Your newly gained knowledge will allow you to escape from this state of mystification. For example, you can now probably figure out the following legal terms/phrases:

- *Amicus curiae* (friend of the court)
- *Ex post factō* (from after the fact)
- *Habeās corpus* (you may have the body)
- *In locō parentis* (in the place of a parent)
- *Nōlō contendere* (I don't want to fight)
- *Nōn compos mentis* (not having full control of the mind)

Having some context would help you decipher the exact meanings of the terms above, but you can certainly get their gist.

Uses in Medicine

Medical terms are a little trickier. The Latin itself isn't any trickier, it's just that a fair number of medical terms come from Greek words. This is partly due to the fact that scientists have borrowed equally from Greek and Latin when coining new words. Even still, your study of Latin should enable you to determine the general meaning of the following medical terms:

- *Ante cibōs* (before foods; i.e., meals)
- *Bis in diē* (twice in a day)
- *Horā somnī* (at the hour of sleep)
- *Rigor mortis* (stiffness of death)
- *Sī opus sit* (if there is need)

As a few of these words attest, the difficulty in reading a physician's prescription sometimes has nothing to do with sloppy handwriting. It is caused more by the fact that most physicians still write their prescriptions in Latin. And, to return to our comment about mystification, wouldn't you agree that "subcutaneous" sounds far more impressive than "under the skin"?!

Learning History

So far, we've discussed only how Latin has added to your knowledge of grammar and vocabulary. Latin has also given you a glimpse into the institutions and traditions of ancient Rome. That's significant for a number of reasons. Rome created the largest empire the world has ever known, which was no small military or administrative accomplishment. Its customs, including its political system, form the basis of many of our own cultural beliefs and practices (even the names of our months bear witness to Roman influence). And at least two Roman inventions— bureaucracy and concrete—affect our lives on a daily basis. Since all languages tell us something about the societies that use them, your knowledge of Latin has given you a peek into an ancient world that, for better or worse, continues to affect our modern lives. Reflect on that the next time you hear someone say that Latin is a dead language!

Influences on the Church

After the Roman Empire collapsed in the fifth century C.E., Latin continued to play an important role in an institution that remains part of the western cultural heritage: the Christian Church. As noted in a previous chapter, both the Old and New Testaments of the Bible had been translated into Latin by the fourth century C.E. And, until the Protestant Reformation in the sixteenth century, Christian church services (known as masses) were in Latin. Virtually none of the laity knew Latin, so this was another example of where Latin was used to keep the common people in awe (recall the earlier remarks about the medical and legal fields). In fact, until the 1960s, Catholic churches continued to conduct masses in Latin. Even though some Catholic churches still have Latin masses, the "official" language of the pope (i.e., the language of papal documents such as encyclicals and bulls) remains Latin. The phrase *ex cathedrā* ("from the chair") owes much of its continued use to its adoption by the Papacy in the nineteenth century. Thus, whether or not you are a Christian, your knowledge of Latin will help you understand this particular religious faith.

FACT

While Latin was the language of influence in the western Mediterranean, Greek was (and for a long time had been) the common language in the East. After the Western Empire fell in 476, the Eastern Empire continued to flourish (and speak Greek!) for a very long time afterward. It then came to be known as the Byzantine Empire.

Maintaining Proficiency

Unlike the case with many other languages, you cannot travel anywhere to speak, hear, or read Latin. There are no menus, bus schedules, or phrase books written in Latin. So, where do you go in order to find Latin? Well, almost all of the real Latin—as opposed to the exercises in this book— exists in the works of ancient Roman authors. Appendix B includes a list of some sources of Latin writing that you can use to challenge yourself and further your understanding of the Latin language.

What can you do, besides reading "real" Latin, to keep your skills sharp? Now that you've had a basic introduction, one thing you can do is get a more advanced, "traditional" Latin textbook, then work through it from beginning to end. You'll be impressed at how much you understand, though being exposed to a different perspective will also add to your knowledge of Latin.

Another thing you might do is to get in the habit of stopping occasionally to analyze an English word for its Latin elements. (This is often more convenient than pulling out of stack of vocabulary flash cards, although flash cards have their place!) Finally, if you are reading something in Latin, you can always translate sample sentences into good English; then, translate those sentences back into Latin, comparing your result with the original text. This sort of exercise will assist you more than you might think in refreshing your knowledge of certain grammatical points.

Finally, congratulations are in order. For approximately 2,000 years, Latin has been part of the West's educational system, and you are now a part of that tradition. You won't receive any medals or prizes, but you should feel enormous satisfaction at having acquired a solid understanding of Latin, as well as a greater appreciation for the beauty and complexity of the language itself. You are now fully prepared to continue your exploration of Latin and the people who spoke it. Ⓔ

Appendices

Appendix A
Latin-English Vocabulary

Appendix B
Latin Literature

Appendix C
Answer Key to Exercises

Appendix A

Latin-English Vocabulary

The following is a list of the most commonly found words in Latin literature. Not all the variant forms for each word are presented, nor are all the possible uses for a word. Here are the most common forms and the most common uses. Frequently appearing proper nouns and adjectives with obvious meaning (e.g., *Rōma* or *Rōmānus*) have been left out as well. For more information, consult your dictionary.

ā, ab   prep.+ abl., from, away from; by

abeō, abīre, abiī, abitum   to go away

absum, abesse, āfuī, āfutūrus   to be away

ac   See *atque*

accēdō, –ere, accessī, accessum   to approach, go near

accidō, –ere, accidī   to happen, fall down, ask for help

accipiō, –ere, accēpī, acceptum   to welcome, receive

ācer, ācris, ācre   fierce, sharp, painful

aciēs, –ēī, f.   battle line, edge

ad   prep. + acc., to, toward, near

addō, –ere, addidī, additum   to add, give to

adeō   adv., still, so far, up to this point; so much, so

adeō, adīre, adiī, aditum   to go to, approach

adhūc   adv., still, up to this point in time, even

adsum, adesse, adfuī   to be present, be nearby

adversus (adversum)   adv. and adj. + acc., against, opposite

aeger, aegra, aegrum   sick, ill, poor

aequor, –ōris, n.   the sea, a plain, any flat surface

aequus, –a, –um   level, flat, even, fair

aes, aeris, n.   copper, bronze, money

aetās, aetātis, f.   age, lifetime

aeternus, –a, –um   eternal

aether, –is, m.   (acc. *aethera*), heaven, the upper air

aevum, –ī, n.   age, lifetime, a period of time

afferō, affere, attulī, allatum   to bring, bring to

ager, agrī, m.   field, land

agitō, –āre   to agitate, think about, get *something* going

agmen, agminis, n.   marching column, train

agō, –ere, ēgī, āctum   to do, drive, lead, be busy

āiō   defective; to say, say yes (opposite of *negō*)

āla, –ae, f.   wing

albus, –a, –um   white, dull white

āles, ālitis   winged, having wings

aliēnus, –a, –um   someone else's, foreign (often with bad connotation)

aliquandō   sometimes, at some time

aliquis, aliquid, pron.   someone, something, anyone, anything

alius, –a, –um   another, different; *aliī . . . aliī* "some . . . others"

alter, –a, –um   the other (of two); *alter . . . alter,* "the one . . . the other"

altus, –a, –um   high, deep (an extreme vertical distance)

amicitia, –ae, f.   friendship

amicus, –a, –um   friendly

āmittō, –ere, āmīsī, āmissum   to send away, let go, lose

amnis, amnis, m.   stream, river

amō, –āre, –āvī, –ātum   to like, love

amor, amōris, m.   love

amplus, –a, –um   spacious, large (on the inside)

an   conj., or, whether

anima, –ae, f.   soul, breath, breeze

animal, animālis, n.   animal

animus, –ī, m.   mind, spirit, courage

annus, –ī, m.   year

ante   prep. + acc., before, in front of

antīquus, –a, –um   old, old fashioned, ancient

aperiō, –īre, –uī, apertum   to open, uncover

Apollo, Apollinis, *or* **Apollōnis**, m.   Apollo

appareō, –ēre, –uī, –itum   to appear

appellō, –āre, –āvī, –ātum   to call (often by name)

aptus, –a, –um   suitable, fit, fitted to/for

apud   prep. + acc., among, in the presence of, near, at the home of

aqua, –ae, f.   water

arbor, –is, f.   tree

ārdeō, –ēre, ārsī   to burn, be on fire

argentum, –ī, n.   silver, money

arma, –ōrum, n. pl.   weapons, arms

armō, –āre, –āvī, –ātum   to equip with weapons

ars, artis, f.   art, skill, method

arvum, –ī, n.   land, arable land, a plowed field

arx, arcis, f.   fortress, citadel

ascendō, –ere, ascendī, ascēnsum   to climb, go up

aspiciō, –ere, aspexī, aspēctum   to look at

astrum, –ī, n.   star

at, conj.   but, moreover

atque, (ac)   conj., and, and so, and even

auctor, auctōris, m.   originator, founder, author

audāx, audācis   bold, daring, rash

audeō, –ēre, ausus sum   to dare

audiō, –īre, –īvī, –ītum   to hear, listen

auferō, auferre, abstulī, ablātum   to carry away

augeō, –ēre, auxī, auctum   to increase, enlarge

Augustus, –ī, m.   Augustus

aura, –ae, f.   air

aureus, –a, –um   golden, made of gold

auris, auris, f.   ear

aurum, –ī, n.   gold, money

aut   conj., or (a choice between mutually exclusive things); **aut . . . aut** "either . . . or"

autem   conj., moreover, however

auxilium, –ī, n.   help

avis, avis, f.   bird

——

Bacchus, –ī, m.   Bacchus, Dionysus

beātus, –a, –um   blessed, happy

bellum, –ī, n.   war

bene   adv., well

benedīcō, –dīcere, –dixī, –dictum   to speak well of, bless

bibō, –ere, bibī, bibitum   to drink

blandus, –a, –um   flattering, enticing

bonus, –a, –um   good

brevis, –e   short

——

cadō, –ere, cecidī, cāsum   to fall

caecus, –a, –um   blind

caedēs, –is, f.   slaughter, gore

caelestis, –e   heavenly, pertaining to the sky

caelum, –ī, n.   sky, heaven

campus, –ī, m.   field

candidus, –a, –um   white, bright white

canis, canis, c.   dog

canō, –ere, cecinī, cantum   to sing, play (an instrument)

cantō, –āre, –āvī, –ātum   to sing, play (an instrument)

cantus, –ūs, m.   a song, a music session

capiō, –ere, cēpī, captum   to take, catch

caput, capitis, n.   head

careō, –ēre, –uī, –itūrus   to lack, be without (uses an ablative object)

carmen, –minis, n.   song, poem

cārus, –a, –um   dear, expensive

castra, –ōrum, n. pl.   camp

castus, –a, –um   clean, chaste, pure

cāsus, –ūs, m.   a fall, accident, disaster

causa, –ae, f.   cause, reason, lawsuit

caveō, –ēre, cāvī, cautum   to beware, be on guard

cēdō, –ere, cessī, cessum   to go, withdraw, yield

celebrō, –āre, –āvī, –ātum   to visit often, make well known

celer, celeris, celere   quick, fast

centum   hundred

cernō, –ere, crēvī, crētum   to separate, distinguish, pick out

certō, –āre, –āvī, –ātum   to struggle, decide by contest

certus, –a, –um   certain, sure, reliable

cessō, –āre, –āvī, –ātum   to do nothing, slack off

cēterus, –a, –um   the rest, the other

chorus, –ī, m.   chorus, a dance

cibus, –ī, m.   food

cingō, –ere, cinxī, cinctum   to surround, wrap

cinis, cineris, m.   ash

circā   adv. and prep. + acc., around, near

citus, –a, –um   quick, fast

cīvis, cīvis, c.   citizen

cīvitās, –tātis, f.   state, city, citizenship

clāmor, –is, m.   shouting, ruckus

clārus, –a, –um   clear, bright, famous

claudō, –ere, clausī, clausum   to close, conclude

coepī, coepisse, coeptum   defective, to have begun

cōgitō, –āre, –āvī, –ātum   to think, ponder

cognōscō, –ere, cognōvī, cognitum   to learn; in the perfect system, to know

cōgō, –ere, coēgī, coāctum   to compel, gather, drive, force

cohors, cohortis, f.   a company, retinue

colligō, –ere, collēgī, collectum   to gather, collect

colō, –ere, coluī, cultum   to pay attention to, nurture, cultivate

color, –is, m.   color

coma, –ae, f.   hair (on the head)

comedō, –ere, –ēdī, –ēsum, or –estum   to eat up

comes, comitis, c.   companion

committō, –ere, –mīsī, –missum   to connect, combine; entrust

commūnis, –e   common, approachable

comparō, –āre, –āvī, –ātum   to prepare, buy, furnish

complector, –plectī, –plexus sum   to hug, embrace

compōnō, –ere, –posuī, –positum   to put, put together, arrange

concēdō, –ere, –cessī, –cessum   to go away, withdraw, yield

condō, –ere, –didī, –ditum   to found, build; put in safe keeping, hide

cōnferō, conferre, contulī, collātum   to bring together, compare, engage

cōnficiō, –ere, –fēcī, –fectum   to finish

confiteor, confitērī, confessus sum   to confess, admit

coniunx, coniugis, c.   spouse

cōnor, –ārī, –ātus sum   to try

cōnsequor, –ī, cōnsecūtus sum   to follow, pursue, obtain

cōnsilium, –ī, n.   plan, advice, consultation, an assembly

cōnstituō, –stituere, –stituī, –stitūtum   to stand or set something up, decide

cōnstō, –āre, –stitī, –stātum   to stand together, stand still, stop

cōnsul, –is, m.   consul (chief magistrate)

cōnsulō, –ere, consuluī, consultum   to consult

contemnō, –ere, –tempsī, –temptum   to despise

contineō, –ēre, –tinuī, –temptum   to hold together, contain

contingō, –ere, –tigī, –tactum   to touch, affect; happen

contrā adv. and prep. + acc., against, opposite

conveniō, –īre, –vēnī, –ventum to come together, meet, be fitting, agree

convertō, –ere, –vertī, –versum to turn around

convīvium, –ī, n. feast, party

cōpia, –ae, f. abundance; f. pl. supplies, troops

cor, cordis, n. heart

cōram adv., openly

cornū, –ūs, n. horn, wing (of a battle line)

corpus, corporis, n. body

crēdō, –ere, crēdidī, crēditum to trust, rely on, believe (usually with the dative)

creō, creāre, –āvī, –ātum, to create, elect

crēscō, –ere, crēvī, crētum to grow

crīmen, crīminis, n. accusation, guilt, alleged crime

culpa, –ae, f. guilt, blame, fault

cum conj., when, since, because, although

cum prep. + abl., with

cunctus, –a, –um all (as a group)

cupīdo, cupīdinis, f. desire, ambition

cupiō, –ere, –īvī, –ītum to desire, long for

cūr adv., why

cūra, –ae, f. care, attention, concern, anxiety

cūria, –ae, f. the senate house

cūrō, –āre, –āvī, –ātum to take care of

currō, –ere, cucurrī, cursum to run

cursus, –ūs, m. course, route, direction

custōdia, –ae, f. guardianship, care, custody

custōs, custōdis, m. guard, guardian

——

damnum, –ī, n. loss, damage

dē prep. + abl., down from, from, concerning, about

dea, –ae, f. goddess

dēbeō, –ēre, –uī, –itum to owe; to be bound

decet, –ēre, –uit impersonal; it is right, fitting, proper

dēcipiō, –ere, –cēpī, –ceptum to deceive, cheat

decus, decoris, n. honor, distinction

dēdūcō, –ere, –dūxī, –ductum to lead down or away

dēfendō, –ere, defendī, dēfensum to defend, drive off

dēferō, dēferre, dētulī, dēlātum to bring down, report

dēficiō, –ere, –fēcī, –fectum to fall short, fail, desert, rebel

deinde adv., from that place, then, next

dēnique adv., finally, at last

densus, –a, –um thick, dense

dēscendō, –ere, –scendī, –scensum to climb down

dēserō, dēserere, dēseruī, dēsertum to desert, abandon, break off from

dēsum, dēesse, dēfuī, dēfutūrus to be down, fail, fall short

deus, –ī, *m.* god

dexter, –tra, –trum right

dextra, –ae, f. right hand

dīcō, –ere, dīxī, dictum to tell, say

diēs, diēī, m. day

digitus, –ī, m. finger, toe

dignitās, –tātis, f. reputation, dignity, honor, worth

dignus, –a, –um worthy, fitting

dīligēns, –ntis careful, attentive

dīligō, –ere, –lexī, –lectum to love, esteem, pick out

dīmittō, –ere, –mīsī, –missum to send away, abandon

dīrigō, –ere, –rexī, –rectum to direct, arrange

discēdō, –ere, –cessī, –cessum to leave, separate

discō, –ere, didicī to learn

diū adv., for a long time

dīversus, –a, –um different, turned in different directions

dīves, dīvitis wealthy

dīvidō, –ere, dīvīsī, dīvīsum to divide

dīvīnus, –a, –um divine

dīvitiae, –ārum, f. pl.   riches

dīvus, –a, –um   divine, deified

dō, dare, dedī, datum   to give

doceō, –ēre, –uī, doctum   to teach

doleō, –ēre, –uī, dolitīrus   to feel pain, to cause pain

dolor, –is, m.   pain, grief

dominus, –ī, m.   master

domus, –ūs, f.   house, home

dōnec, conj.   until, while

donō, –āre, –āvī, –ātum   to give (as a gift)

donum, –ī, n.   gift

dormiō, –īre, –īvī, –ītum   to sleep

dubius, –a, –um   doubtful

dūcō, –ere, dūxī, ductum   to take someone someplace, lead

dulcis, –e   sweet

dum, conj.   while

duo, duae, duo   two

dūrus, –a, –um   hard, tough

dux, ducis, m.   leader

———

ē, ex   prep. + abl., out (of), from

ecce   interj., look!

ecclesia, –ae, f.   assembly

ēdo, ēsse *or* **edere, ēdī, ēsum**   to eat

efficiō, –ere, effēcī, effectum   to do, effect, bring it about that

ego   pron., I

ēgredior, –ī, ēgressus sum   to leave, go out

ēligō, –ere, ēlēgī, ēlectum   to pick out, choose

enim   conj., because, since, "you see" (used to introduce an explanation of something just said that may have been unclear)

eō, īre, iī, itum   to go

eques, equitis, m.   horseman, a member of the Roman social class between patricians and plebeians

equus, –ī, m.   horse

ergō   adv., so, thus, therefore

ēripiō, –ere, –uī, ēreptum   to grab, to take out violently

errō, –āre, –āvī, –ātum   to wander, be wrong

et   conj., and, also, even, too

etiam   conj., still, yet, even

ēvādō, –ere, ēvāsī, ēvāsum   to go out, escape

ēveniō, –īre, –vēnī, ēventum   to come out, result

excipiō, –ere, –cēpī, –ceptum   to take out, take up, catch, receive

exemplum, –ī, n.   example, precedent

exeō, –īre, –iī, –itum   to go out, end

exerceō, –ēre, –uī, –itum   to make strong, train, harass

exercitus, –ūs, m.   army

existimō, –āre, –āvī, –ātum   to think, judge, evaluate

experior, experīrī, expertus sum   to try, test, prove

exspectō, –āre, –āvī, –ātum   to wait for

extremus, –a, –um   outermost

———

fābula, –ae, f.   story

faciēs, –ēī, f.   face, image

facilis, –e   easy

faciō, –ere, fēcī, factum   to make, do

fallō, –ere, fefellī, falsum   to deceive

falsus, –a, –um   wrong, false

fāma, –ae, f.   rumor, reputation

fames, –is, f.   hunger

famulus, –a, –um   servile

fātum, –ī, n.   fate, destiny, misfortune

fax, facis, f.   torch

fēlix, fēlīcis   lucky, fertile

femina, –ae, f.   woman, a female

ferē   adv., nearly, almost

ferō, ferre, tulī, lātum   to carry, bring, bear, endure

ferrum, –ī, n.   iron, sword

ferus, –a, –um   wild

fessus, –a, –um   tired

fēstus, –a, –um pertaining to a holiday
fidēlis, –e trustworthy, loyal
fidēs, –eī, f. trust
fīgō, –ere, fixī, fictum to fasten, affix
fīlia, –ae, f. daughter
fīlius, –ī, m. son
fīnēs, fīnium, m. pl. territory
fingō, –ere, finxī, fictum to shape, form
fīnis, fīnis, m. end, boundary
fīō, fierī, factus sum to be made, be done, be, become, happen, (used for passive of **faciō**)
flamma, –ae, f. flame, fire
fleō, –ēre, flēvī, flētum to weep
flōs, flōris, m. flower
flūmen, flūminis, n. river
fluō, –ere, fluxī, fluctum to flow
foedus, –a, –um foul, horrible
fons, fontis, m. a spring, fountain
fore future infinitive and used for imperfect subjunctive of **sum**
foris adv., outside, outdoors
forma, –ae, f. shape, image
forsitan adv., perhaps, maybe
fortis, –e strong, brave
fortūna, –ae, f. luck, chance, fortune
frangō, –ere, frēgī, fractum to break
frāter, frātris, m. brother
frequens, –ntis crowded, "often"
frons, –ntis forehead, front
fructus, –ūs, m. profit, fruit, enjoyment
frustrā, adv. in vain
fuga, –ae, f. flight, escape
fugiō, –ere, fūgī, fugitum to run away, flee
fundō, –ere, fūdī, fusum to pour
fūnus, fūneris, n. funeral
fūr, fūris, c. thief

———

Gallia, –ae, f. Gaul
Gallus, –a, –um Gallic
gaudeō, –ēre, gāvīsus sum to rejoice, be happy
gaudium, gaudiī, n. joy, happiness

gens, gentis, f. family, clan, nation, race
genus, generis, n. birth, origin, type, kind
gerō, –ere, gessī, gestum to carry, wage, accomplish
gignō, –ere, genuī, genitum to give birth, cause
gladius, –ī, m. sword
glōria, –ae, f. glory, fame
Graecus, –a, –um Greek
grātia, –ae, f. charm, thanks
grātus, –a, –um pleasing
gravis, –e heavy, serious

———

habeō, –ēre, –uī, –itum to have, hold, consider, regard
habitō, –āre, –āvī, –ātum to, live, dwell, inhabit
haud adv., not
herba, –ae, f. grass, a plant
heu interj., oh no!, alas!
hic, haec, hoc this, the latter
hiems, hiemis, f. winter
hinc adv., from here
historia, –ae, f. inquiry, history
homō, hominis, m. person, a human being
honos, honōris, m. honor, political office
hōra, –ae, f. hour, time
hortus, –ī, m. garden, a park
hospes, hospitis, c. host, guest, stranger
hostēs, hostium, c. pl. the enemy
hostis, hostis, c. an enemy
hūc adv., to this place
hūmānus, –a, –um human, kind
humus, –ī, f. the ground, soil

———

iaceō, –ēre, iacuī to recline, lie
iaciō, –ere, iēcī, iactum to throw
iam adv., now, already, at this point in time
ibi adv., there
idem pron., the same
ideō adv., for that reason

igitur adv., therefore

ignis, ignis, m. fire

ignōrō, –āre, –āvī, –ātum not to know

ignōtus, –a, –um unknown

ille, illa, illud that, the former

illīc adv., there

imāgō, imāginis, m. portrait, image

imber, imbris, m. rainstorm

imitor, –ārī, –ātus sum to copy

immensus, –a, –um vast, unmeasurable

imperātor, –is, m. a military general, emperor

imperium, –ī, n. power, command

imperō, –āre, –āvī, –ātum to give an order (with dative object)

impleō, –ēre, implēvī, implētum to fill up

impōnō, –ere, imposuī, impositum to put upon

improbus, –a, –um substandard, naughty

in prep. + acc., in, into, onto, against; + abl., in, on

inānis, –e empty

incipiō, –ere, incēpī, inceptum to begin

inde adv., from that place, then

indicō, –āre, –āvī, indicātum to make known, betray

induō, –ere, induī, indūtum to put on, dress

inferō, inferre, intulī, inlātum to bring in, introduce

inferus, –a, –um lower

ingenium, –ī, n. talent, disposition, nature, character

ingēns, ingentis huge

ingredior, ingredī, ingressus sum to step in, begin

inimicus, –a, –um unfriendly

inquam, inquis, inquit, etc. say (defective verb denoting a direct quotation)

insignis, –e outstanding, distinguished

instituō, –ere, instituī, institūtum to set up, instruct, decide

instruō, –ere, instruxī, instructum to build, equip

integer, integra, integrum whole, intact, pure

intellegō, –ere, intellexī, intellectum to understand, be aware of, appreciate

intendō, –ere, intendī, intentum to stretch, intend, aim at

inter prep. + acc., between

interficiō, –ere, interfēcī, interfectum kill

interrogō, –āre, –āvī, –ātum to ask

intrā prep. + acc., within

intrō, –āre, –āvī, –ātum to enter

inveniō, –īre, invēnī, inventum to come upon, find

invideō, –ēre, invīdī, invīsum to cast the evil eye, envy

ipse, ipsa, ipsum intensive pron., –self

īra, –ae, f. anger

īrascor, –ī, irātus sum to become angry

is, ea, id demonstrative pron., this, that (referring to something recently stated)

iste, ista, istud demonstrative pron., that (often used with contempt)

ita adv., like this, in this way, thus

itaque adv., and so, therefore

item adv., likewise

iter, itineris, n. route, journey, way

iterum adv., again

iubeō, –ēre, iūssī, iūssum to order

iūcundus, –a, –um content, happy

iūdex, iūdicis, m. judge

iūdicium, –ī, n. judgement, a trial

iugum, –ī, n. yoke, mountain ridge, anything that joins

iungō, –ere, iunxī, iunctum to join, connect

Iuppiter, Iovis, m. Jupiter

iūrō, –āre, –āvī, –ātum to swear

iūs, iūris, n. a right, law

iustus, –a, –um just, lawful, suitable

iuvenis, –is, c. a young person

iuvō, iuvāre, iūvī, iūtum   to help, please
iuxtā   prep. + acc., very near

———

labor, –is, m.   work, effort, suffering
lābor, lābī, lāpsus sum   to slip
labōrō, –āre, –āvī, –ātum   to work, suffer
lacrima, –ae, f.   tear
lacus, –ūs, m.   lake
laetus, –a, –um   happy, fat
lapis, lapidis, m.   stone
lateō, –ēre   to lie hidden
lātus, –a, –um   wide
laudō, –āre, –āvī, –ātum   to praise
laus, laudis, f.   praise
legio, legiōnis, f.   legion
legō, –ere, lēgī, lectum   to choose, pick, gather, read
leo, leōnis, m.   lion
levis, –e   light, gentle
lex, lēgis, f.   law
libens, libentis   glad, willing
liber, librī, m.   book
līber, –a, –um   free
līberō, –āre, –āvī, –ātum   to set free
licet, licēre, licuit or **licitum est**   impersonal verb, it is allowed, okay
lignum, –ī, n.   wood
līmen, līminis, n.   threshold
lingua, –ae, f.   tongue, language
linquō, –ere, līuī   to abandon, leave
littera, –ae, f.   letter (of the alphabet)
litterae, –ārum, f. pl.   a letter (epistula), literature
lītus, lītoris, n.   shore
locus, –ī, n.   place
loca, –ōrum, n. pl.   places (somehow connected)
locī, –ōrum, m. pl.   individual places, passages of literature
longus, –a, –um   long, tall
loquor, loquī, locūtus sum   to talk, speak
lūdō, –ere, lūsī, lūsum   to play, deceive

lūmen, lūminis, n.   light, lamp, eye
lūna, –ae, f.   moon
lux, lūcis, f.   light, daylight, eye

———

maestus, –a, –um   sad, gloomy
magis   adv., more
magister, –trī, m.   master, director, teacher, captain
magnitūdō, –tudinis, f.   greatness, size
magus, –a, –m   magical
mālō, mālle, mālui   to want more, prefer
malus, –a, –um   bad
mandō, –āre, –āvī, –ātum   to entrust, order
māne   (indeclinable n.), morning
maneō, –ēre, mansī, mansum   to stay
manus, –ūs, f.   hand, group
mare, maris, n.   the sea
Mars, Martis, m.   Mars
māter, mātris, f.   mother
māteria, –ae, f.   raw material, lumber
mecum   with me
medeor, –ērī   to heal (with a dative)
medius, –a, –um   the middle (of)
membrum, –ī, n.   limb, body part
meminī, meminisse   (defective, + gen.), to be mindful, remember
memor, memōris   mindful
memoria, –ae, f.   memory
memorō, –āre, –āvī, –ātum   to remind, mention
mēns, mentis, f.   mind
mensa, –ae, f.   table
mēnsis, mēnsis, m.   month
mereō, –ēre, –uī, –itum   to deserve, earn
metuō, –ere, –uī, –ūtum   to fear
metus, –ūs, m.   fear
meus, –a, –um   my
mīles, mīlitis, c.   soldier
mille   (indeclinable adj.), thousand
milia, milium, n. pl.   (indeclinable adj. in the singular; neuter noun in the plural), thousands
minister, –trī, m.   helper, subordinate

minus adv., less

mīror, –ārī, –ātus sum to marvel at, wonder, be amazed

mīrus, –a, –um amazing, wonderful

misceō, –ēre, miscuī, mixtum to mix

miser, misera, miserum poor, wretched

mitis, –e soft, mild

mittō, –ere, mīsī, missum to send, release, throw, to make something go away under its own power

modus, –ī way, method, measure

moenia, moenium, n. pl. fortifications

mollis, –e soft, smooth, flexible

moneō, –ēre, –uī, –itum to warn, advise

mōns, montis, m. mountain

mora, –ae, f. a delay, a pause

morior, morī, mortuus (fut. part. moritūrus) to die

mors, mortis, f. death

mortālis, –e mortal, destined to die

mortuus, –a, –um dead

mōs, mōris, m. characteristic, custom

mōrēs, mōrum, m. pl. character, morals

moveō, –ēre, mōvī, mōtum to move

mox adv., soon

mulier, –is, f. woman

multitūdō, –tūdinis, f. a large number

multus, –a, –um much, many

mundus, –ī, m. the world

mundus, –a, –um elegant, refined

mūnus, mūneris, n. gift, duty, an office

mūrus, –ī, m. wall (an outer wall)

mutō, –āre, –āvī, –ātum to change, move

———

nam conj., because, for

namque conj., an emphatic form of **nam**

narrō, –āre, –āvī, –ātum to tell (in story form)

nascor, nascī, nātus sum to be born

nātūra, –ae, f. nature

nātus, –ī, m. son, child

nāvis, nāvis, f. ship

nē, conj. not

–ne enclitic conj., attached to the end of a first word of a statement to convert it to a yes/no question

nec See *neque*

necessārius, –a, –um unavoidable

necessārius, –ī, m. a close relative or friend

necessitās, –tātis, f. necessity

neglegō, –ere, –lexī, lectum to neglect

negō, –āre, –āvī, –ātum to deny, say no

negotium, –ī, n. business

nēmō, nēminis, c. no one

nemus, nemoris, n. a grove

neque (nec) conj., and . . . not; **neque . . . neque,** neither . . . nor

nesciō, –īre, –īvī, –ītum not to know

niger, nigra, nigrum black

nihil (nīl), n. indeclinable; nothing

nimis adv., too much, very much, excessively

nimius, –a, –um very great, very much

nisi conj., if not, unless

nix, nivis, f. snow

nōbilis, –e well known, noble

noceō, –ēre to harm, be harmful (with the dative)

nocturnus, –a, –um nocturnal, at night

nōlō, nōlle, nōluī irreg., not to want, to be unwilling

nōmen, nominis, n. name

nōminō, –āre, –āvī, –ātum to name, mention

nōn adv., not

nōndum adv., not yet

nōs pron., we

noscō, –ere, nōvī, nōtus to learn; in perfect system, to know, recognize

noster, nostra, nostrum our

nōtus, –a, –um known

novus, –a, –um new, young, strange

nox, noctis, f. night

nūdus, –a, –um naked

nullus, –a, –um no, none

nūmen, nūminis, n.   divine will, a nod, deity

numerus, –ī, m.   number

numquam, adv.   never

nunc adv., now

nuntius, –ī messenger

ō interj., oh!

ob prep. + acc., on account of, in front of, in exchange for

obvius, –a, –um in the way, on hand

occīdō, –ere, occīdī, occīsum to kill

oculus, –ī, m.   eye

offerō, offerre, obtulī, oblātum to offer

officium, –ī, n.   duty, respect

ōlim adv., once upon a time, at that time

omnis, –e all, every, whole

oportet, oportēre, oportuit someone should, ought

ops, opis, f.   abundance

opēs, opum, f. pl.   wealth, resources

optimus, –a, –um very good, excellent, best

optō, –āre, –āvī, –ātum to choose

opus, operis, n.   a work; **opus est,** there is need

ōrātiō, ōrātiōnis, f.   a speech, speech, eloquence

orbis, orbis, m.   a circle

ordō, ordinis, m.   row, rank, (social) class

orior, orīrī, ortus sum to rise

ornō, –āre, –āvī, –ātum to decorate

ōrō, –āre, –āvī, –ātum to beg, ask, speak, pray

ōs, ōris, n.   mouth, face

os, ossis, n.   bone

ostendō, –ere, ostendī, ostentum to show

ōtium, –ī free time, leisure

ovis, ovis, f.   sheep

---

paene adv., almost

pandō, –ere, pandī, pansum to open up, stretch

pānis, pānis, m.   bread

pār, paris equal

parcō, –ere, pepercī, parsum to spare, be sparing (with the dative)

parens, parentis, c.   a parent

pariō, –ere, peperī, partum to give birth, produce

parō, –āre, –āvī, –ātum to get ready, obtain

pars, partis, f.   part, direction

parum, adv.   not enough, too little

parvus, –a, –um little

pateō, –ēre, patuī to lie open, exposed

pater, patris, m.   father

patior, patī, passus sum to suffer, experience

patria, –ae, f.   fatherland, (one's) country

paucī, –ae, a few

paulus, –a, –um little

pauper, pauperis poor

pax, pacis, f.   peace

peccō, –āre, –āvī, –ātum to make a mistake, sin

pectus, pectoris, n.   chest, heart

pecūnia, –ae, f.   money, property

pelagus, –ī, n.   the sea

pendō, –ere, pependī, pensum to hang, weigh, pay

per prep. + acc., through, by, on account of

percutiō, –ere, percussī, percussum to hit, strike

perdō, –ere, perdidī, perditum to lose, destroy, waste

pereō, –īre, periī, peritum to die, go through, be lost

perficiō, –ere, –fēcī, –fectum to complete

pergō, –ere, perrexī, perrectum to continue

perīculum, –ī, n.   danger

permittō, –ere, –mīsī, –missum to allow, send through, throw

perpetuus, –a, –um continuous

perveniō, –īre, –vēnī, –ventum to arrive

pēs, pedis, m.   foot

petō, –ere, petīvī, petītum to look for, ask, attack (go somewhere for a strong reason)

philosophus, –a, –um philosophical

pietās, –tātis, f.   duty, devotion (especially to gods or country)

piscis, piscis, m.   fish

pius, –a, –um   dutiful

placeō, –ēre, –uī, –itum   to please

placidus, –a, –um   peaceful, quiet

plēnus, –a, –um   full

plērīque, plēraeque, plēraque   very many

plūrimus, –a, –um   very much; pl., very many

plūs, plūris, indeclinable n. sing.   more

plūrēs, plūra   adj. in pl. many

poena, –ae, f.   penalty, punishment

poeta, –ae, m.   poet

pondus, ponderis, n.   weight

pōnō, –ere, posuī, positum   to put, lay

pontus, –ī, n.   the sea

populus, –ī, m.   a people

porta, –ae, f.   gate

portō, –āre, –āvī, –ātum   to carry, bring

possum, posse, potuī   to be able

post   prep. + acc., after, behind

posteā   adv., afterwards

postquam   conj., after

postulō, –āre, –āvī, –ātum   to demand

potens, potentis   powerful, capable

potestās, –tātis, f.   power, ability

potis, pote   able

prae   prep. + abl., in front, before

praebeō, –ēre, –uī, –itum   to offer

praecipiō, –ere, –cēpī, –ceptum   to teach, take ahead of time

praecipuus, –a, –um   special

praedīcō, –ere, –dixī, –dictum   to predict, warn

praemium, –ī, n.   reward

praesens, –entis   present, ready

praestō, –āre, –stitī, –stitum   to surpass

praeter   prep. + acc., except, beyond

praetereō, –īre, –iī, –itum   to go past

precor, –ārī, –ātus sum   to pray, beg

premō, –ere, pressī, pressum   to press, push

pretium, –ī, n.   price, worth

prex, precis, f.   prayer, request

prīmus, –a, –um   first

princeps, principis, c.   leader, chief

principium, –ī, n.   beginning

prior, prius   former

prius   adv., earlier, first

prīvō, –āre, –āvī, –ātum   to deprive

prōcēdō, –ere, –cessī, –cessum   to go ahead

procul   adv., far away

proelium, –ī, n.   battle

promittō, –ere, –mīsī, –missum   to promise, send ahead

prope   prep. + acc., near

properō, –āre, –āvī, –ātum   to hurry

prōpōnō, –ere, –posuī, –positum   to put forward, tell

proprius, –a, –um   one's own, peculiar

propter   prep. + acc., on account of, near

prōsum, prōdesse, prōfuī, prōfutūrus   to benefit, be useful

prōtinus   adv., immediately

proximus, –a, –um   next, closest

publicus, –a, –um   public

pudor, pudōris, m.   shame, modesty

puella, –ae, f.   girl

puer, –ī, m.   boy, child

pugna, –ae, f.   fight

pugnō, –āre, –āvī, –ātum   to fight

pulcher, pulchra, pulchrum   beautiful, handsome

pulsō, –āre, –āvī, –ātum   to hit, knock

pūrus, –a, –um   pure, clean, simple

putō, –āre, –āvī, –ātum   to think, value

---

quaerō, –ere, quaesīvī, quaesītum   to look for, ask

quālis, –e   what kind of

quam   adv., how, as, than

quamquam   conj., although

quamvīs   adv., however much, to one's heart's content

quandō adv., when

quantus, –a, –um how great, how much

quārē adv., how, why, for what reason

quasi adv., as if

–que enclitic conj., and; **–que . . . –que,** both . . . and

queror, –ī, questus sum to complain

quī, quae, quod pron. and adj., who, which, that

quia conj., because

quicumque, quaecumque, quodcumque pron., whoever, whichever, whatever

quīdam, quaedam, quoddam adj. and pron., a certain (person or thing)

quidem adv., of course, indeed; **nē . . . quidem,** not even . . .

quiescō, –ere, quiēvī, quiētum to rest

quīlibet, quaelibet, quodlibet pron. and adj., anyone, anything

quīn conj., why not, but

quis, quid pron., who, what

quisquam, quidquam pron., anyone, anything

quisque, quaeque, quodque pron. and adj., each, every

quisquis, quidquid pron., whoever, whatever

quō adv., to what place

quod conj., because, that

quōmodō adv., how

quondam adv., former, at some point (in time)

quoniam adv., since, because

quoque adv., also

quot adv., how many

---

rapiō, –ere, rapuī, raptum to take (forcefully)

rārus, –a, –um scattered, rare

ratiō, ratiōnis, f. reason, account, business

recēdō, –ere, –cessī, –cessum to go back

recipiō, –ere, –cēpī, –ceptum to accept, take back

rectus, –a, –um straight, correct

reddō, –ere, reddidī, redditum to give back, surrender, repeat

redeō, –īre, –iī, –itum to go back

referō, referre, rettuli, relātum to bring back, reply

rēgīna, –ae, f. queen

regiō, regiōnis, f. region, line, direction

rēgius, –a, –um royal

regnō, –āre, –āvī, –ātum to rule

regnum, –ī, n. royal power, kingdom

regō, –ere, rexī, rectum to rule, guide

religiō, religiōnis, f. superstition, scruples

relinquō, –ere, relīquī, relictum to abandon, leave

reliquus, –a, –um left behind, remaining

reperiō, –īre, repperī, repertum to find

requīrō, –ere, –quīsīvī, –quīsītum to demand, ask, miss

rēs, reī, f. thing, matter, affair

respiciō, –ere, –spexī, –spectum to look back

respondeō, –ēre, respondī, respōnsum to answer, correspond

retineō, –ēre, –uī, –tentum to hold back, keep

revertō, –ere, –vertī, –versum to turn back

revocō, –āre, –āvī, –ātum to call back

rēx, rēgis, m. king

rīdeō, –ēre, rīsi, rīsum to laugh, smile

rīpa, –ae, f. riverbank

rogō, –āre, –āvī, –ātum to ask

rogus, –ī, m. funeral pyre

rosa, –ae, f. rose

rumpō, –ere, rūpī, ruptum to break, burst

rursus adv., back, backward

rūs, rūris, n. the country, countryside

rūsticus, –a, –um rural

---

sacer, sacra, sacrum sacred, holy

sacerdōs, –dōtis, c. priest, priestess

saeculum, –ī, n. a generation, lifetime, an age

saepe adv., often

saevus, –a, –um fierce, savage

salus, salūtis, f.   health

sanctus, –a, –um   holy, sacred, inviolable

sanguis, sanguinis, m.   blood

sapiens, sapientis   wise

sapientia, –ae, f.   wisdom

satis   adv., enough

saxum, –ī, n.   a rock

scelus, sceleris, n.   crime, evil deed

scientia, –ae, f.   knowledge, skill

scilicet   adv., of course, apparently

sciō, –īre, scīvī, scītum   to know

scrībo, –ere, scrīpsī, scrīptum   to write, draw

sēcum   with him, her, etc. (ablative of reflexive pronoun with enclitic **–cum**)

secundus, –a, –um   second, following, favorable

sēcūrus, –a, –um   carefree, safe

sed   conj., but, rather

sedeō, –ēre, sēdī, sessum   to sit, stay put

sēdēs, sēdis, f.   a seat, chair, home

semel   adv., once, one time

semper   adv., always

senex, senis   old

sensus, –ūs, m.   feeling, sense

sententia, –ae, f.   opinion, thought, meaning

sentiō, –īre, sēnsī, sēnsum   to perceive, experience, realize

sepeliō, –īre, –īvī, sepultum   to bury

sepulcrum, –ī, n.   grave, tomb

sequor, sequī, secūtus sum   to follow

sermō, sermōnis, m.   conversation, talk

serviō, –īre, –īvī, –ītum   (with dative), to be a slave, serve

servō, –āre, –āvī, –ātum   to save, keep, guard, protect

servus, –ī, m.   slave

seu   conj., see *sīve*

sī   conj., if

sīc   adv., like this, in this way

sīcut   adv., as, like

sīdus, sīderis, n.   star, constellation

signum, –ī, n.   sign, signal, seal

silentium, –ī, n.   silence

silva, –ae, f.   forest

similis, –e   similar, like

simul   adv., at the same time

sine   prep. + abl, without

singulus, –a, –um   single

sinus, –ūs, m.   curve, fold, bay

sīve (seu)   conj., or if; **sīve . . . sīve,** whether . . . or

sōl, sōlis, m.   sun

soleō, –ēre, solitus sum   to be in the habit of doing something, usually do something

sollicitus, –a, –um   upset, anxious

sōlus, –a, –um   alone, only

solvō, –ere, solvī, solūtum   to loosen, untie, pay

somnus, –ī, m.   sleep

sonō, –āre, –āvī, –ātum   to make a sound

soror, sorōris, f.   sister

sors, sortis, f.   prophecy, fate, share, lot

spargō, –ere, sparsī, sparsum   to scatter, sprinkle

spatium, –ī, n.   space, period, pause

speciēs, –ēī, f.   sight, appearance

spērō, –āre, –āvī, –ātum   to expect, hope

spēs, speī, f.   expectation, hope

spīritus, –ūs, m.   breath, life, spirit

statim   adv., immediately

stella, –ae, f.   star

sternō, –ere, strāvī, stratum   to spread, stretch

stō, stāre, stetī, statum   to stand, stay

studeō, –ēre, –uī   to be eager, be busy with

studium, –ī, n.   eagerness, fondness

sub   prep., under, at the foot of (+ acc. for motion toward; + abl. for place where)

subeō, –īre, –iī, –itum   to go under, approach

subitō   adv., suddenly

sublīmis, –e   high

sum, esse, fuī, futūrus   to be, exist

summus, –a, –um   highest

sumō, –ere, sumpsī, sumptum   to take, assume

super   prep. + acc., over, above

superbus, –a, –um   proud, arrogant

supernus, –a, –um   over, above

superō, –āre, –āvī, –ātum   to overcome, conquer

supersum, superesse, superfuī, superfutūrus   to survive, remain

suprā   adv. and prep. + acc., over, above

surgō, –ere, surrexī, surrēctum   to rise

suscipiō, –ere, –cēpī, –ceptum   to undertake, accept

sustineō, –ēre, –tinuī, –tentum   to support, uphold

suus, sua, suum   reflexive possessive pron., his own, her own, etc.

———

taceō, –ēre, –uī, –itum   to be quiet

tālis, –e   such a kind

tam   adv., so, to such a degree

tamen   conj., nevertheless, anyway, yet

tamquam   adv., like, just as

tandem   adv., finally

tangō, –ere, tetigī, tactum   to touch

tantus, –a, –um   so great, so big

tardus, –a, –um   slow, late

tectum, –ī, n.   roof, house

tēcum   with you

tellus, tellūris, f.   the earth

tēlum, –ī, n.   a weapon (especially a pointy one that is thrown)

templum, –ī, n.   sacred area, temple

temptō, –āre, –āvī, –ātum   to try, test

tempus, temporis, n.   time

tendō, –ere, tetendī, tentum or **tensum**   to stretch, try

tenebrae, –ārum, f. pl.   the dark, darkness, gloom

teneō, –ēre, –uī, tentum   to hold, have

tener, tenera, tenerum   tender, soft

tergum, –ī, n.   the back

terra, –ae, f.   land, soil

tertius, –a, –um   third

timeō, –ēre, –uī   to be afraid, fear

timor, –is, m.   fear

tollō, –ere, sustulī, sublātum   to raise, carry away, destroy

torus, –ī, m.   bed, couch; knot, lump

tot   adv., so many

tōtus, –a, –um   whole, entire

trādō, –ere, trādidī, trāditum   to hand over, surrender

trahō, –ere, traxī, tractum   to pull, drag

transeō, –īre, –iī, –itum   to cross

trēs, tria   three

tristis, –e   sad

triumphus, –ī, m.   a triumphal parade, a victory

Trōia, –ae, f.   Troy

tū   pron., you (sing.)

tum   adv., at that time, then

tunc   adv., at that time, then

turba, –ae, f.   crowd, mob

turpis, –e   ugly, shameful

turris, turris, f.   tower

tūtus, –a, –um   safe

tuus, tua, tuum   your (sing.)

———

ubi   conj., where, when

ullus, –a, –um   any

ultimus, –a, –um   last, farthest

ultra   adv. and prep. + acc., on the far side of

umbra, –ae, f.   shadow, shade

umquam   adv., ever

unda, –ae, f.   water, wave

unde   adv., from what place

undique   adv., from all sides

ūniversus, –a, –um   all together

ūnus, –a, –um   one

urbs, urbis, f.   city

usque   adv., all the way, completely

ūsus, –ūs, m.   use, practice, skill

ut (utī)   conj., as, because, when

uterque, utraque, utrumque   each (of two)

ūtilis, –e   useful

ūtor, ūtī, ūsus sum   (with abl.) to use; to benefit oneself (by means of)

uxor, uxōris, f.   wife

—

vacō, –āre, –āvī, –ātum   to be empty

vacuus, –a, –um   empty, hollow

vagus, –a, –um   wandering

valdē   adv., very much, really

valeō, –ēre, valuī, valitum   to be strong

varius, –a, –um   diverse, fickle

vātes, vātis, c.   prophet

–ve   enclitic conj., or

vehō, –ere, vexī, vectum   to carry; (middle voice with abl.), to ride

vel   conj., or (a nonlimiting choice between things)

velut   adv., like, as

veniō, –īre, vēnī, vēntum   to come

ventus, –ī, m.   wind

Venus, Veneris, f.   Venus, charm, beauty

vēr, vēris, n.   spring (the season)

verbum, –ī, n.   word

vērō   adv., indeed, yes

versus, –ūs, m.   a turn, row, line (esp. of poetry)

vertō, –ere, vertī, versum   to turn

vērus, –a, –um   true, real

vester, vestra, vestrum   your (pl.)

vestis, vestis, f.   clothing

vetus, veteris   old

via, –ae, f.   road, way

vīcīnus, –a, –um   neighboring

vicis   change

victor, victōris, m.   winner

victōria, –ae, f.   victory

videō, –ēre, vīdī, vīsum   to see; (passive voice) to seem, be seen

vigilō, –āre, –āvī, –ātum   to be awake, watch

vincō, –ere, vīcī, victum   to conquer

vinculum, –ī, n.   anything that binds, e.g., chain

vīnum, –ī, n.   wine

vir, –ī, m.   man

virgō, virginis, f.   a young woman

virtūs, –tūtis, f.   manliness, courage

vīs, vīs, f., vīrēs, vīrium, f. pl.   force, strength

vīta, –ae, f.   life

vitium, –ī, n.   crime, vice, an imperfection

vīvō, –ere, vīxī, vīctum   to live

vīvus, –a, –um   alive, living

vix   adv., barely, with difficulty

vocō, –āre, –āvī, –ātum   to call, summon

volō, –āre, –āvī, –ātum   to fly

volō, velle, voluī   to be willing, want

volucer, –cris, –cre   flying

voluptās, –tātis, f.   pleasure

vōs   pron., you (pl.)

vōtum, –ī, n.   a vow

vōx, vōcis, f.   voice

vulnus, vulneris, n.   a wound

vultus, –ūs, m.   facial expression

Appendix B

Latin Literature

Before identifying the best examples of Latin literature, a couple of qualifications need to be made. First, only about 10 percent of what the ancient Romans wrote survives, and almost 10 percent of that was written by Cicero. It would be like future generations only having a tenth of what had been written in English, and a tenth being from a cranky, often pompous know-it-all (which is not an entirely unfair description of Cicero). So, in reading through the summaries below, bear in mind that only a fraction of the work written by the various individuals survives. Nonetheless, some of those fragments constituted the bulk of what educated people studied for the better part of 1,800 years. Today, many of these authors are no longer read except in upper-level college courses.

Classical Latin Literature

- **Lucretius** (ca. 98–55 B.C.E.). Lucretius is best known for his lengthy poem, *De Rerum Natura* ("On the Nature of Things"), which is nothing short of an explanation of the whole universe. Though Lucretius's Latin is pretty challenging (even for experienced readers), his views, known as epicureanism, form an important philosophical tradition.
- **Catullus** (84–54 B.C.E.). A lyric poet whose works are in sharp contrast to those of Lucretius. Because of his frank erotic references, many of Catullus's 100 poems

remained censored or untranslated until the twentieth century. Only with the advent of modern writers, such as Henry Miller and Allen Ginsberg, did Catullus seem tame by comparison.

- **Marcus Tullius Cicero** (106–43 B.C.E.). Trained in rhetoric and Roman law, Cicero was an eloquent orator and advocate who championed republican government. His many essays, letters, and speeches (in written form, the latter were often highly polished versions of what Cicero had actually said) set a prose standard that is still emulated. The reason that so much of Cicero's writings survives is because he was among the few "pagan" writers that leaders of the medieval Christian Church did not condemn (his works were therefore preserved by the original photocopiers, monastic scribes).
- **Julius Caesar** (100–44 B.C.E.). Caesar was a famous general. You probably didn't know that he was also a major literary figure who wrote detailed accounts of his many campaigns (*Bellum Gallicum* and *Bellum Civile*). In reading Caesar, you will likely run into more military terms than you ever thought existed, but his prose is straightforward and logically organized. More than one contemporary writer could learn a lesson or two from Caesar's clear writing.
- **Vergil** (70–19 B.C.E.). Vergil is, by most accounts, the greatest poet of ancient Rome.

As with Cicero's writings, medieval prelates exempted the works of Vergil from their bonfires (in Vergil's case, it was due to his supposed foreshadowing of Jesus). Many of Vergil's poems extol the virtues of nature (the *Ecologues*) and farm life (the *Georgics*), though we remember him better for his epic poem, the *Aeneid*. The *Aeneid's* twelve books recount the human and mythological origins of Rome; in Western literature, only the *Iliad* and the *Odyssey* surpass its sweep, imagery, and universal themes. If you can't see yourself reading the entire work, at least read Books I–IV.

- **Horace** (65–8 B.C.E.). A writer of great skill, Horace eventually became poet laureate of Rome. His satires did much to create that genre, while his lyric poetry—though often difficult—illustrates enormous range and versatility. Don't try reading Horace unless you have sufficient time to ponder his choices of vocabulary and grammar.

- **Livy** (59 B.C.E.–17 C.E.). Livy is the best-known and most widely read Roman historian. His mammoth history of Rome ran more than a hundred volumes, but only a small number of them survive. Though not exactly pageturners, Livy's works can give you a sense of the challenges that ancient historians faced. Nevertheless, it helps to know a little about Roman history before plunging into Livy's accounts.

- **Ovid** (43 B.C.E.–17 C.E.). As a poet, Ovid's reputation is second only to that of Vergil's. Readers then and since have found his long poem *The Metamorphoses* compelling. In fifteen books, Ovid supplied a veritable encyclopedia of mythology, much of which was

structured around various transformations or metamorphoses. Pyramus and Thisbe, Narcissus and Echo, Jason and Medea, and Daedalus and Icarus are just a few of the familiar characters that populate Ovid's superbly crafted poem.

- **Seneca** (4 B.C.E.–65 C.E.). A stoic philosopher and the Emperor Nero's tutor, Seneca is the point at which scholars mark the beginning of Silver Age Latin. Seneca wrote widely circulated moral essays and tragedies, as well as a biting satire, "Apocolocyntosis" ("Gourdification"), about the death and deification of Emperor Claudius.

- **Petronius** (?–65 C.E.). Petronius was a courtier whose major work was the *Satyricon,* a satire that, among other things, pokes fun at the newly rich and their pompous attitudes. One of the only large sections of the *Satyricon* that survives (often referred to as the *Cena Trimalchionis* ["Trimalchio's Dinner Party"]) is often read in intermediate-level Latin classes.

- **Quintillian** (35 C.E.–95 C.E.). Frequently considered the first pedagogue (one who studies and teaches how to teach), he covered a broad set of Roman educational concerns in his *Institutio Oratoria*. The advice found in that work still rings true to many contemporary teachers.

- **Martial** (45–104 C.E.). Martial was similar to what we would call a bestselling author. No, he really didn't sell much of what he wrote, but the public did enjoy his epigrams. And with more than 1,500 to his credit, Martial certainly gave ancient Romans a large number of these short, often satirical poems to choose from. As with Catullus, some of

Martial's poems were considered obscene by many later generations.

- **Pliny** (62–113 C.E.). An earnest public servant who lived through a tumultuous period in Roman history, Pliny wrote the *Epistulae* (letters), which offers some of the most revealing first-person accounts that still survive about life in the ancient world. Pliny is often called Pliny the Younger to distinguish him from his uncle, Pliny the Elder. Both the Elder and the Younger witnessed the eruption of Mt. Vesuvius (the one that buried Pompeii) in 79 C.E.; the latter lived to tell about it, the former did not.
- **Tacitus** (c. 55–115? C.E.). Tacitus was a relatively reliable, if sometimes cynical, historian. Only fragments of some of his major works (*Histories* and *Annals*) exist, though his biography of his father-in-law (*Agricola*) and description of Germany (*Germānia*) are mostly complete. Tacitus's writing style is very succinct—he's well named ("taciturn")—but he is among the hardest Roman prose authors you will read.

- **Juvenal** (c. 50–c. 130 C.E.). Perhaps the most gifted satirist who wrote in Latin. His sixteen satires heaped scorn on the vices he perceived in imperial Rome. Regrettably, his gifts for satire were not matched by simplicity in his prose style. In short, save Juvenal for last, as he is among the hardest of all authors to read in the original Latin.

Postclassical Latin Literature

- Augustine's *City of God* (begun in 413 C.E.)
- Bede's *Ecclesiastical History of England* (completed in 731 C.E.)
- Aquinas's *Summa Theologica* (1266–1273)
- Moore's *Utopia* (1516 C.E.)
- Bacon's *Novum Organum* (1620 C.E.)
- Newton's *Principia Mathematica* (1687 C.E.)

Appendix C

Answer Key to Exercises

Chapter 4

Recognizing Conjugations

accipiō	3rd *–iō*
agō	3rd
amō	1st
audiō	4th
capiō	3rd *–iō*
dīcō	3rd
dō	1st
faciō	3rd *–iō*
habeō	2nd
pōnō	3rd
sum	irregular
teneō	2nd
veniō	4th
videō	2nd

Practice Conjugating the Imperfect

1. *pōnō:*

ponēbam	*ponēbāmus*
ponēbās	*ponēbātis*
ponēbat	*ponēbant*

2. *capiō:*

capiēbam	*capiēbāmus*
capiēbās	*capiēbātis*
capiēbat	*capiēbant*

3. *amō:*

amābam	*amābāmus*
amābās	*amābātis*
amābat	*amābant*

4. *habeō:*

habēbam	*habēbāmus*
habēbās	*habēbātis*
habēbat	*habēbant*

5. *audiō:*

audiēbam	*audiēbāmus*
audiēbās	*audiēbātis*
audiēbat	*audiēbant*

Practice Conjugating the Perfect

1. *pōnō:*

posuī	*posuimus*
posuistī	*posuistis*
posuit	*posuērunt*

2. *capiō:*

cēpī	*cēpimus*
cēpistī	*cēpistis*
cēpit	*cēpērunt*

3. *amō:*

amāvī	*amāvimus*
amāvistī	*amāvistis*
amāvit	*amāvērunt*

4. *habeō:*

habuī	*habuimus*
habuistī	*habuistis*
habuit	*habuērunt*

5. *audiō:*

audīvī	*audīvimus*
audīvistī	*audīvistis*
audīvit	*audīvērunt*

Latin-to-English Translations

N.B. (*Nota Bene,* "note well"): Because there are so many possible correct answers for Latin to English translations, all cannot be given in the key. If you are unsure if your variation is possible, review the lesson and consider the thoughts and ideas expressed by the words.

1. *accēpī*—I received
2. *amābās*—you used to love
3. *cēpit*—he took
4. *dabāmus*—we were giving
5. *dīcēbat*—she kept saying
6. *erant*—they were (and maybe still are)
7. *fēcimus*—we have made
8. *fuērunt*—they were (but aren't anymore)
9. *agēbam*—I was doing
10. *habuistis*—you had

English-to-Latin Translations

1. she used to love—*amābat*
2. you (plural) have given—*dedistis*
3. he was (and maybe still is)—*erat*
4. he was (and isn't anymore)—*fuit*
5. I did—*ēgī* or *fēcī*

Chapter 5

Practicing Noun Declensions

canis: 3rd, *canem/canēs*
dea: 1st, *deam/deās*
deus: 2nd, *deum/deōs*
diēs: 5th, *diem/diēs*
dominus: 2nd, *dominum/dominōs*
domus: 4th, *domum/domūs*
homō: 3rd, *hominem/hominēs*
locus: 2nd, *locum/locōs* (or *loca*)
manus: 4th, *manum/manūs*
mulier: 3rd, *mulierem/mulierēs*
nihil: none, *nihil* or *nīl*
pater: 3rd, *patrem/patrēs*
rēs: 5th, *rem/rēs*
rēx: 3rd, *rēgem/rēgēs*
servus: 2nd, *servum/servōs*
tempus: 3rd, *tempus/tempora*
vir: 2nd, *virum/virōs*
vīta: 1st, *vitam/vitās*

Latin-to-English Translations

1. *Servum tenuit.* He held the slave.
2. *Dominī servōs habēbant.* The masters used to have slaves.
3. *Canis mulierem amābat.* The dog loved the woman.
4. *Mulierēs hominēs accēpērunt.* The women welcomed the people.
5. *Dominōs servī nōn amābant.* The slaves did not like their masters.

English-to-Latin Translations

1. They were considering the situation. *Rem habēbant.*
2. People considered the king god. *Hominēs rēgem deum habuērunt.*
3. The woman used to like the house. *Mulier domum amābat.*
4. You had time. *Tempus habuistī* (or *habuistis*).
5. The man loved his dog. *Vir canem amābat.*

Chapter 6

Practice with First and Second Declension Adjectives

1. *vīta longa:* long life (nom. sing.)
2. *deās bonās:* good goddesses (acc. pl.)
3. *rem aliam:* another situation (acc. sing.)
4. *domūs magnās:* big houses (acc. pl.)
5. *hominēs malōs:* evil people (acc. pl.)
6. *manūs meās:* my hands (acc. pl.)
7. *pater suus:* his father (nom. sing.)
8. *servōs altōs:* tall slaves (acc. pl.)
9. *tempus bonum:* good time (nom. or acc. sing.)
10. *tempora bona:* good times (nom. or acc. sing.)

Practice with Third Declension Adjectives

1. *nihil facile:* nothing easy (nom. or acc. sing.)
2. *mulierem tristem:* sad woman (acc. sing.)
3. *vitae brevēs:* short lives (nom. pl.)
4. *dominōs felicēs:* lucky masters (acc. pl.)
5. *vīta fēlix:* happy life (nom. sing.)
6. *rēx senex:* old king (nom. sing.)
7. *mulier senex:* old woman (nom. sing.)
8. *diēs fēlīcēs:* lucky days (nom. or acc. pl.)
9. *mīlitem fortem:* brave soldier (acc. sing.)
10. *rēs gravēs:* serious matters (nom. or acc. pl.)

Practice with Substantives

1. *omnis:* every man/woman
2. *multa:* many things
3. *dulcia:* sweet things
4. *senem:* an old man/woman
5. *tristēs:* sad men/women
6. *difficile:* a difficult thing
7. *brevia:* short things
8. *bonum:* a "good man" (masculine acc. sing.) or

"good thing" (neuter nom. or acc. sing.)
9. *multī*: many men
10. *aliae*: other women

Chapter 7
Forming Comparatives

1. *hominem fortiorem*: a rather brave person
2. *vitās longissimās*: very long lives
3. *canis felicissimus*: an extremely lucky dog
4. *nihil gravius*: nothing too serious
5. *difficillima*: very difficult things; a very difficult woman
6. *deōs fortiorēs*: stronger gods

7. *vir senior*: an older man
8. *rem faciliorem*: a pretty easy affair
9. *diēs brevissima*: a very short day
10. *mulierēs dulcissimae*: the sweetest women

Forming Irregular Comparatives and Superlatives

1. *canēs optimī*: very good dogs
2. *domus minor*: a smaller house
3. *locus extrēmus*: a really faraway place
4. *pessimōs*: incredibly bad men
5. *nihil superius*: nothing higher

6. *rēgēs plurimī*: very many kings
7. *maximum*: the biggest man (masc. acc. sing.) *or* the biggest thing (neut. nom. or acc. sing.)
8. *loca īma*: the lowest places
9. *tempus prius*: an earlier time
10. *dominum meliorem*: a pretty good master

Latin-to-English Translations

1. *Tum mīlitēs Troiānī et deās et deōs offendērunt.* Then the Trojan soldiers offended both the gods and the goddesses.
2. *Iam tempora erant neque gravia neque difficilia.* At this point there were neither serious nor difficult things.
3. *Aliī canēs ācrius quam aliī latrābant.* Some dogs were barking more fiercely than others.
4. *Sīc habuit mulier vitam breviorem sed dulcem.* Thus the woman had a rather short but sweet life.
5. *Quam magnus fuit pater tuus!* How great your father was!

Practicing Adverbs

	Adjective	Adverb	Comparative	Superlative
1.	*fēlix*	*fēlīciter*	*felicius*	*felicissimē*
2.	*longus*	*longē*	*longius*	*longissimē*
3.	*malus*	*male*	peius	*pessimē*
4.	*celer*	*celeriter*	*celerius*	celerrimē
5.	*brevis*	*breviter*	brevius	*brevissimē*
6.	———	diū	*diūtius*	*diūtissimē*
7.	prūdēns	*prūdenter*	*prūdentius*	*prūdentissimē*
8.	magnus	magnopere	*magis*	*maximē*
9.	*bonus*	bene	*melius*	*optimē*
10.	*facilis*	facile	*facilius*	*facillimē*

English-to-Latin Translations

1. The bad master cared for his slaves rather poorly. *Dominus malus servōs suōs peius curābat.*
2. My work used to be easier than your work. *Labor meus erat facilior quam labor tuus.*
3. The king held power for as long a time as he could. *Rēx potestātem quam diūtissimē tenēbat.*
4. The goddess was sad because she saw extremely difficult times. *Dea tristis erat quia tempora difficillima vīdit.*
5. Your dog used to love really big bones. *Canis tuus ossa maxima amābat.*

Chapter 8

Preposition Practice

1. *prō homine:* on behalf of a person
2. *inter bella:* between wars
3. *trans silvam:* across the forest
4. *per oppidum:* through the town
5. *sub arbore:* under the tree (place where)
6. *sub arborem:* under the tree (motion toward)
7. *ab urbe:* from the city
8. *dē monte:* down from the mountain
9. *circum domum:* around the house
10. *propter pecuniam:* on account of money

Forming the Ablative Case

animus:	*animō, animīs*
annus:	*annō, annīs*
bellum:	*bellō, bellīs*
cūra:	*curā, curīs*
equus:	*equō, equīs*
fīlius:	*filiō, filiīs*
hostis:	*hoste, hostibus*
mensis:	*mense, mensibus*
nōmen:	*nomine, nominibus*
nox:	*nocte, noctibus*
oppidum:	*oppidō, oppidīs*
terra:	*terrā, terrīs*
urbs:	*urbe, urbibus*
via:	*viā, viīs*

Latin-to-English Translations

1. *Nuntius noster ad castra Romāna properāvit ubi hostēs vīdit.* Our messenger hurried to the Roman camp when he saw the enemy.
2. *Graecī bellum multōs annōs Troiae gessērunt.* The Greeks waged war at Troy for many years.
3. *Māter, nomine Livia, cum filiīs Veiōs saepius ambulābat.* The mother, named Livia, used to walk rather often to Veii with her children/sons.
4. *Hominēs in illō oppidō vera nōn dicēbant.* The people in that town weren't telling the truth (true things).
5. *Drusus unā diē Veronam equō celerrimō pervēnit.* Drusus made it to Verona in one day on an extremely fast horse.
6. *Homō certus erat et minimē mendax.* He was a dependable man and hardly a liar.
7. *Pater filium suum in terrās extrēmās mīsit.* The father sent his son to very far-away lands.
8. *Castra sub monte mediā nocte magnā cum dīligentiā posuimus.* We pitched camp very carefully at the foot of the mountain in the middle of the night.
9. *Romānī et Gallōs et Germānōs post paucōs annōs vīcērunt.* The Romans conquered both the Gauls and the Germans after a few years.
10. *Plurimī Athenae vīcīnōs in urbem suam propter timorem diū nōn accipiēbant.* Very many people in Athens didn't welcome their neighbors for a long time out of fear.

English-to-Latin Translations

1. We used to go from Capua to Brundisium by means of the Via Appia. *Capuā Brundisium Viā Appiā cedēbāmus.*
2. The Romans were much luckier than the Germans. *Romānī erant multō fēliciōrēs Germānīs.*
3. The father sailed to Greece because he was looking for his son. *Pater ad Graeciam navigāvit quia filium petēbat.*
4. He found his son in Sparta. *Filium Spartae invēnit.*
5. All the people in Rome loved the new emperor named Titus. *Omnēs Romae imperātorem novum nomine Titum amābant.*

Chapter 9

Practice Your Declensions

1. *cor, cordis,* n. (heart)

Case	Singular	Plural
Nominative	cor	corda
Genitive	cordis	cordum
Dative	cordī	cordibus
Accusative	cor	corda
Ablative	corde	cordibus

2. *ignis, ignis,* m. (fire)

Case	Singular	Plural
Nominative	ignis	ignēs
Genitive	ignis	ignium
Dative	ignī	ignibus
Accusative	ignem	ignēs
Ablative	igne	ignibus

3. *vīlla, vīllae,* f. (farmhouse)

Case	Singular	Plural
Nominative	villa	villae
Genitive	villae	villārum
Dative	villae	villīs
Accusative	villam	villās
Ablative	villā	villīs

4. *fidēs, fideī,* f. (trust)

Case	Singular	Plural
Nominative	fidēs	fidēs
Genitive	fideī	fidērum
Dative	fideī	fidēbus
Accusative	fidem	fidēs
Ablative	fidē	fidēbus

5. *squālor, squāloris,* m. (roughness)

Case	Singular	Plural
Nominative	squālor	squālorēs
Genitive	squāloris	squālorum
Dative	squālorī	squāloribus
Accusative	squālorem	squālorēs
Ablative	squālore	squāloribus

6. *nāsus, nāsī,* m. (nose)

Case	Singular	Plural
Nominative	nāsus	nāsī
Genitive	nāsī	nāsōrum
Dative	nāsō	nāsīs
Accusative	nāsum	nāsōs
Ablative	nāsō	nāsīs

7. *iubar, iubaris,* n. (light-beam)

Case	Singular	Plural
Nominative	iubar	iubaria
Genitive	iubaris	iubarium
Dative	iubarī	iubaribus
Accusative	iubar	iubaria
Ablative	iubarī	iubaribus

8. *rītus, rītūs,* m. (ceremony, rite)

Case	Singular	Plural
Nominative	rītus	rītūs
Genitive	rītūs	rītuum
Dative	rītuī	rītibus
Accusative	rītum	rītūs
Ablative	rītū	rītibus

Latin-to-English Translations

1. *Mens virī nōn valēbat.* The man's mind was not strong.
2. *Amor mātris filiō aegrō mē permōvit.* The mother's

love for her sick son moved me deeply.

3. *Deī deaeque hominēs urbium, quī rītūs sanctōs atque sacrōs numquam observābant, saepe relīnquebant.* Gods and goddesses often abandoned the people of cities who never observed sacred and holy rites.

4. *In mediō oppidō stābant et corpus rēgis mortuī omnibus monstrāvit.* They stood in the middle of the town

and he showed everyone the body of the dead king.

5. *Pars civium lacrimābant, cēterī gaudēbant.* Some of the citizens wept, others were glad.

English-to-Latin Translations

1. After a few months they caught the sad man in the country near Cumae. *Post paucōs mensēs tristem rurī prope Cumās cēpērunt.*

2. Cumae was closer to Rome than Brundisium. *Cumae erat propior Romae Brundisiō/quam Brundisium.*

3. They took the man by ship across the sea. *Virum/Hominem trans mare navī duxērunt.*

4. He came home very unwillingly. *Domum invītissimē vēnit.*

5. He stayed in jail for many days with the others. *In carcere multōs diēs cum cēterīs manēbat.*

Chapter 10

Conjugating the Subjunctive

1. *canō, canere, cecinī, cantum*

Person	Imperfect Singular	Imperfect Plural	Pluperfect Singular	Pluperfect Plural
1st	canerem	canerēmus	cecinissem	cecinissēmus
2nd	canerēs	canerētis	cecinissēs	cecinissētis
3rd	caneret	canerent	cecinisset	cecinissent

2. *absum, abesse, āfuī, āfutūrus*

Person	Imperfect Singular	Imperfect Plural	Pluperfect Singular	Pluperfect Plural
1st	abessem	abessēmus	āfuissem	āfuissēmus
2nd	abessēs	abessētis	āfuissēs	āfuissētis
3rd	abesset	abessent	āfuisset	āfuissent

3. *fleō, flēre, flēvī, flētum*

Person	Imperfect Singular	Imperfect Plural	Pluperfect Singular	Pluperfect Plural
1st	*flērem*	*flērēmus*	*flēvissem*	*flēvissēmus*
2nd	*flērēs*	*flērētis*	*flēvissēs*	*flēvissētis*
3rd	*flēret*	*flērent*	*flēvisset*	*flēvissent*

Latin-to-English Translations

1. (purpose) *Puella caelum omnī nocte spectābat ut stellās comātās invenīret.* The girl used to watch the sky every night to find comets.
2. (result) *Cum corde tam gravī filium āmissum exspectābat pater infelix ut mox exspīrāret.* The unlucky father waited for his lost son with such a heavy heart that he soon died.
3. (*cum* clause) *Cum rēx clārus Romam advēnisset, senātorēs epulās maximās posuērunt.* When/Since the famous king had come to Rome, the senators put (on) very large banquets.
4. (result) *Vergilius erat poeta tālis ut nēmō carmina nōn caneret.* Vergil was such a poet that no one wasn't singing his songs (i.e., everyone was).
5. (purpose) *Graecī Troiam multīs navibus advēnēunt ut urbem caperent.* The Greeks came to Troy in many ships in order to capture the city.

English-to-Latin Translations

1. (*cum* clause) Since the slave feared his master, he ran away. *Cum servus dominum suum timuit, fūgit.*
2. (result) The dogs were so fierce that no one would enter the house. *Canēs tam ācrēs erant ut nēmo domum intrāret.*
3. (purpose) The Greeks came to Troy to conquer the Trojans. *Gaecī Troiam advēnērunt ut Trōianōs vincerent.*
4. The women of the town left their houses in the middle of the night. *Mulierēs oppidī mediā nocte domūs suās relīquērunt.*
5. (purpose) They walked for many days so the evil men wouldn't capture them. *Multās diēs ambulābant nē malī eās caperent.*

Chapter 11

Conjugating the Six Tenses

1. *iaciō, iacere, iēcī, iactum* (to throw)

Person	Present	Imperfect	Future	Perfect	Pluperfect	Future Perfect
1st, sing.	*iaciō*	*iaciēbam*	*iaciam*	*iēcī*	*iēceram*	*iēcerō*
2nd, sing.	*iacis*	*iaciēbās*	*iaciēs*	*iēcistī*	*iēcerās*	*iēceris*
3rd, sing.	*iacit*	*iaciēbat*	*iaciet*	*iēcit*	*iēcerat*	*iēcerit*
1st, pl.	*iacimus*	*iaciēbāmus*	*iaciēmus*	*iēcimus*	*iēcerāmus*	*iēcerimus*
2nd, pl.	*iacitis*	*iaciēbātis*	*iaciētis*	*iēcistis*	*iēcerātis*	*iēceritis*
3rd, pl.	*iaciunt*	*iaciēbant*	*iacient*	*iēcērunt*	*iēcerant*	*iēcerint*

2. *iaceō, iacēre, iacuī, iacitum* (to lie, i.e., maintain a horizontal position)

Person	Present	Imperfect	Future	Perfect	Pluperfect	Future Perfect
1st, sing.	*iaceō*	*iacēbam*	*iacēbō*	*iacuī*	*iacueram*	*iacuerō*
2nd, sing.	*iacēs*	*iacēbās*	*iacēbis*	*iacuistī*	*iacuerās*	*iacueris*
3rd, sing.	*iacet*	*iacēbat*	*iacēbit*	*iacuit*	*iacuerat*	*iacuerit*
1st, pl.	*iacemus*	*iacēbāmus*	*iacēbimus*	*iacuimus*	*iacuerāmus*	*iacuerimus*
2nd, pl.	*iacetis*	*iacēbātis*	*iacēbitis*	*iacuistis*	*iacuerātis*	*iacueritis*
3rd, pl.	*iacent*	*iacēbant*	*iacēbunt*	*iacuērunt*	*iacuerant*	*iacuerint*

Latin-to-English Translations

1. *Verba Lātina tam bene discēbat ut omnia sīcut mātrem suam cognōvit.* He was learning Latin words so well that he knew all (of them) like his own mother.

2. *Cum ācria nōn essent, arma servīs reddidimus.* Since they weren't sharp, we gave the weapons back to the slaves.

3. *Puellae plus aquae bibērunt nē sitīrent.* The girls drank more water so that they wouldn't be thirsty.

4. *Canis miser os petet, alius tamen canis os facile invēnerit.* The poor dog will look for his bone, but another dog will have easily found the bone.

5. *Ubi canis quidem fēlix os invēnerit, ōre domum feret.* When the lucky dog does indeed find the bone, he will carry it home in his mouth.

6. *Pecuniam reddit, nam tale praemium nōn meret.* He is giving the money back because he doesn't deserve a prize.

7. *Iter brevissimum capiētis ut Brundisium quam primum perveniātis.* You will take

the shortest route so you will arrive at Brundisium as soon as possible.

8. *Post mortem imperātoris, exercitus urbem vī et igne rapiet.* After the death of the emperor, the army will seize the city by force and by fire.

9. *Cum cīvēs rēgem dīvum nōn habērent, dona tamen sacerrima atque cārissima dābant.* Although the citizens didn't consider the king divine, they gave (him) very holy and expensive gifts anyway.

10. *Cenābis bene apud mē.* You will dine well at my house.

English-to-Latin Translations

1. Finally they will tell the women everything. *Tandem mulieribus omnia dicent.*

2. When the slave had worked for a fairly long time, his master said, "Enough." *Cum servus diūtius labōrāverat, dominus suus "satis" dīxit.*

3. The horses are drinking water out of the stream. *Equī aquam ex rivō bibunt.*

4. You learn things faster than your sister. *Rēs*

celerius quam soror tua (cog)noscis.

5. The soldiers killed the men so they wouldn't tell the truth. *Mīlitēs hominēs occidērunt nē vera dicerent.*

Chapter 12

Latin-to-English Translations

1. *Cum Carthagine rediissent, multa dē urbe narrābant.* When they had returned from Carthage, they told many things about the city.

2. *Parum sapientiae habēre nolō.* I don't want to have too little wisdom.

3. *Tot arma in hostēs intulērunt nostrī ut hostēs statim fūgerent.* Our men brought so many weapons against the enemy that the enemy immediately fled.

4. *Mīlitēs autem in castra redīre nolunt quod fortissimī sunt et minimē ignāvī.* The soldiers, however, don't want to go back to camp because they are very brave and not lazy in the least.

5. *Puerī domum properāre voluērunt nam in ludō totum diem esse nolēbant.* The boys wanted to hurry home because they didn't want to be in school all day.

6. *Cum Graecī urbem Trōiam perdidissent, multī hominēs tamen superfuērunt.* The Greeks destroyed the city of Troy, but many people survived anyway.

7. *Ubi dea miserōs in periculō vīderat, adiuvāre volēbat at nōn poterat.* When the goddess had seen the poor people in danger, she wanted to help but couldn't.

8. *Soror perterrita fuit, cum frāter suus periit.* The sister was very frightened when her brother died.

9. *Omnia multā arte cūrāque conficere poteris.* You will be able to do everything with great skill and care.

10. *Paucī tanta tam facillimē gerere possunt.* Few are able to accomplish such great things with such extreme ease.

Figuring Out Meaning

1. *conveniō:* to come together
2. *perambulō:* to walk through
3. *praeterdūcō:* to lead beyond
4. *superpōnō:* to put over
5. *absum:* to be away
6. *suscipiō:* to undertake
7. *praedīcō:* to say ahead (of time)
8. *suburbānus:* at the foot/edge of a city

9. *perfacile:* very easily
10. *ingerō:* to bring in/upon
11. *transferō:* to carry across
12. *incredibilis:* unbelievable
13. *obsum:* to be in the way (or opposed)
14. *discedō:* to go away
15. *inventor:* a finder
16. *repugnō:* to fight back
17. *ignoscō:* not to know
18. *excipiō:* to take (out of something), to receive
19. *praeparō:* to get something ready ahead of time
20. *remaneō:* to stay back

Chapter 13

Latin-to-English Translations

1. *Accidit ut istud bellum effugere nōn possēmus.* It happened that we weren't able to escape that war.
2. *Hī, quī anteā oppidōs suōs numquam relīquerant, trans mare transiērunt.* These men, who had never left their towns before, went across the sea.
3. *Mors Augustī, quī Romae imperātor prīmus erat, magna tristitiae causa erat.* The death of Augustus, who was the first emperor in Rome, was the cause of great sadness.

4. *Vīs tempestātis tanta erat ut milia nāvium frumentī, vinī, et servōrum plēnārum dēlēvit.* The force of the storm was so great that it destroyed thousands of ships full of grain, wine, and slaves.
5. *Ego mihi mortem servitūdine mālō.* I prefer death to slavery for myself.
6. *Rēx illam, cuius filius eum servāvit, in matrimonium ducet.* The king will marry that woman whose son saved his life.
7. *Filia quīnta eius multō pulchrior quam cēterae est.* His fifth daughter was much more beautiful than the others.
8. *Domus, quae contrā sē dīvīsa est, stāre nōn potest.* A house which is divided against itself cannot stand.
9. *Eō diē hominēs centum in mediō oppidō sē contulērunt.* A hundred people gathered in the middle of the town that day.
10. *Septimā diē post casum Pompēiīs, petere coepimus ullōs quī superfuerant.* On the seventh day after the disaster at Pompeii, we began to look for any who had survived.

English-to-Latin Translations

1. Labiēnus was so skilled in (with respect to) the art of war that Caesar retained him. *Labiēnus tam perītus arte bellī erat ut Caesar eum retinuit.*
2. The senate gave great honors to you alone. *Senātus tibi sōlī magnōs honōrēs dedit.*
3. Those brave men (whom we were just talking about) climbed this mountain in four days. *Eī fortēs quattuor diēbus hunc montem ascendērunt.*
4. We brought the bodies of the men who had fallen back to the camp. *Corpora virōrum quī ceciderant in castra retulimus.*
5. There were few who survived. *Paucī erant quī superfuērunt.*

Chapter 14

Latin-to-English Translations

1. *Cum gens Iuliī Caesaris pauper esset, ille tamen nōtus dīvesque factus est.* Although Julius Caesar's family was poor, he became famous and wealthy.

2. *Familia propria cuique cara esse debet.* One's own family ought to be dear to each person.
3. *Omnia quae mihi monstrābās mīrābar nam tibi nōn credidī.* I marveled at everything you were showing me because I didn't believe you.
4. *Tam irātus est ut tōtum exercitum oppidum orīrī iubēret.* He was so angered that he ordered the entire army to attack the town.
5. *Deinde nova quae tam diū exspectābantur Athēnīs lāta sunt et gāvīsī sunt.* Then the news that was awaited for such a long time was brought from Athens and they rejoiced.

English-to-Latin Translations

1. If you (plural) follow us, you (plural) will be safe. *Sī nōs sequēminī, tūtī eritis.*
2. You (singular) will always be loved by me with all my heart. *Pectore/Corde tōtō ā mē semper amāberis.*
3. We were amazed at the carnage of the first day. *Caedem prīmī diēī mīrātī sumus.*

4. Your brother used my advice. *Frāter tuus consiliō meō ūsus est.*
5. The old men of this town dared to speak with great enthusiasm in the senate at Rome. *Veterēs/Senēs huius oppidī magnō cum studiō in Cūria Rōmae loquī ausī sunt.*

Chapter 15

Latin-to-English Translations

1. *Dulce et decorum est prō patriā morī.* It is sweet and proper to die for one's country.
2. *Aliī ad theatrum vīsum veniēbant, aliī ut vīsī essent.* Some came to the theater to see, others to be seen.
3. *Librō scriptō, gāvīsī sunt.* After the book was written, they rejoiced.
4. *Nōbis Rōmā profectūrīs, pluere coepit.* When we were about to depart from Rome, it started to rain.
5. *Hospitibus ad ianuam pervenientibus, canēs latrābant.* The dogs kept barking as guests were arriving at the door.
6. *Caesar inquit, "Alea iacienda est."* Caesar said, "The die must be cast."

7. *Mīlitēs mortuōs ē campō tractōs diē sequentī sepelīvērunt.* On the following day they buried the dead soldiers who had been dragged from the field.
8. *Agrīs colentibus, aurum invēnit agricola.* The farmer found gold as the fields were being tended to.
9. *Vīta beāta fautīs ā Fortunā reperitur.* For the favored, a blessed life is found by Fortune.
10. *Vīta beāta ā Fortunā fautīs reperitur.* For those favored by Fortune, a blessed life is found.

English-to-Latin Translations

1. The boy saw his father dying. *Puer patrem morientem vīdit.*
2. The boy saw his father dead. *Puer patrem mortuum vīdit.*
3. The boy saw his father on the verge of dying. *Puer patrem moritūrum vīdit.*
4. I intended to send that letter to you tomorrow. *Illās litterās ad tē cras missūrus fuī.*

5. If Fortune stays nearby (not far off), we will be saved. *Sī Fortūna haud procul manēbit, servābimur.*

Chapter 16

Latin-to-English Translations

1. *Quare tālia mala Quintum, virum tantō ingeniō, contingunt?* Why do such evils happen to Quintus, a man of such great talent?

2. *Nisi senatorēs in Forō sēdissent, barbarīs Rōmam invadentibus, tam saevē interfectī nōn essent.* If the senators hadn't sat in the Forum while the barbarians were invading Rome, they wouldn't have been so savagely killed.

3. *Signō datō, incipientne ludī?* Will the games begin once the signal has been given?

4. *Unde venit ille sonus?* Where is that sound coming from?

5. *Sī id bellum iustum esset, spēs fieret libertātī.* If that war were just, there would be hope for freedom.

6. *Sī captivōs hodie permittet, statim in aciēs hostium redībunt.* If he lets the prisoners go today, they will return immediately to the battle line of the enemy.

7. *Librōs iam semel lectōs amicīs dare solēmus.* We usually give books that have already been read once to friends.

8. *Etsi librōs nōn cupiunt, libenter eōs accipiunt.* Even if they don't want the books, they gladly take them.

9. *Quis, velut Cicerō vel Dēmosthenēs, in oratiōne sīc praestat ut cunctīs persuadēre potest?* Who, like Cicero or Demosthenes, excels in oratory such that he can persuade everybody?

10. *Sī illa arbor ingens cadat, domus vestra quidem deleātur.* If that huge tree should fall, your house would certainly be destroyed.

English-to-Latin Translations

1. If the army has attacked the Germans twice, why have they not been conquered? *Sī exercitus Germānōs bis aggressī est, cur victī nōn sunt?*

2. You will help me, won't you? *Nōnne mē iuvābis?*

3. You won't help me, will you? *Num mē iuvabis?*

4. Will you help me? *Mēne iuvabis?*

5. If anyone approaches the door, should he be allowed in? *Sī quis ad ianuam accēdat, permittatur?*

Chapter 17

Latin-to-English Translations

1. *Troiā relictā, Aenēas ā Venere, deā mātreque suā, Hesperiam petere coactus est.* Once he had abandoned Troy, Aeneas was compelled by Venus, a goddess and his mother, to head for Hesperia.

2. *Titus Livius scripsit Hersiliam uxōrem Rōmulī esse.* Titus Livius (Livy) wrote that Hersilia was the wife of Romulus.

3. *Dīcitur cor istius virī foedum fuisse et minimē mundum.* It is said that the heart of that man was foul and not in the least clean.

4. *Negāvit iterum iterumque sē ubi aurum celātum esset scīre.* He denied over and over that he knew where the gold had been hidden.

5. *Mulierēs intersē colloquentēs nondum nesciēbant sē spectārī.* The women who were talking among themselves did not yet know that they were being watched.

English-to-Latin Translations

1. We felt that we would be safer at home. *Sensimus nōs domī tūtiōrēs fore (futūrōs esse).*
2. They kept asking whether we had seen the god himself. *Rogābant/Quaerēbant num deum ipsum vīdissēmus.*
3. The senator said that Caesar was sending a messenger to Rome. *Senātor dixit Caesarem nuntium Rōmam mittere.*
4. The senator said that Caesar would send a messenger to Rome. *Senātor dixit Caesarem nuntium Rōmam missūrum (esse).*
5. The senator said that Caesar had sent a messenger to Rome. *Senātor dixit Caesarem nuntium Rōmam mīsisse.*

Chapter 18

Latin-to-English Translations

1. *Latrōnem capite, canēs, nē effugiat!* Catch the robber, dogs! Don't let him get away! (*or . . .* so that he doesn't get away!)
2. *Canibus imperāvī ipse ut latrōnem capiant nē effugiat.* I myself ordered the dogs to catch the robber so he wouldn't get away.
3. *Latrōnem capiant canēs. Ita nōn effugiat.* Let the dogs catch the robber. That way he won't get away.
4. *Metuō nē latrō effugiat.* I'm afraid the robber will get away.
5. *Vereor ut canēs latrōnem capiant.* I fear that the dogs won't catch the robber.
6. *Utinam canēs latrōnem capiant!* I hope the dogs catch the robber!
7. *Nisi canēs latrōnem cēpissent, effūgisset.* If the dogs hadn't caught the robber, he would have gotten away.
8. *Nesciō utrum canēs latrōnem capiant an effugiat.* I don't know whether the dogs will catch the robber or he'll get away.
9. *Canibus veteribus, nesciō quīn effugiat latrō.* Since the dogs are old, I don't know why the robber shouldn't get away.
10. *Cum canēs latrōnem cēpissent, ille tamen effūgit.* Even though the dogs had caught the robber, he got away anyway.

Index

A

-*a*, 66
A, 86–87, 98
Ab, 86–87
Ablative absolute, 203
Ablative case
    for adjectives, 66–69
    for nouns, 48–51
    and passive voice, 189
    for prepositions, 88–94, 97–99
Ablative of agent, 189
Ablative of description, 109
Ac, 114
Accents, 16
Accipio (to take, receive), 35, 154
Accusative case
    for adjectives, 61, 66–70
    for nouns, 48–51, 57
    and objects, 54
    for prepositions, 88–89
Acer, 67–68, 74
Active voice
    endings for, 33–34, 181
    explanation of, 22, 179–81
Ad, 97
Adjectives
    agreement of, 60–61, 64, 67
    declensions of, 63–70, 80, 174–75
    demonstrative adjectives, 161–65
    examples of, 7
    explanation of, 59
    forming comparatives, 74–77
    forming irregular comparatives, 79
    forming superlatives, 79
    gender of, 63–70, 161–66

indefinite adjectives, 218
intensive adjectives, 168–70
interrogative adjectives, 218
irregular comparatives, 78–79
for making comparisons, 73
numbers, 175–76
parts of, 63
superlative degree, 76–77, 79
terminations, 67–70
verbal adjectives, 185–86, 196, 200
Advenit, 40
Adverbs
    examples of, 7
    forming, 79–80
    irregular adverbs, 80, 82
    for making comparisons, 73, 81–82
    practicing, 82
-*ae*, 52
Aeneid, 258
Ago (to do), 35, 182–87, 196
Agr-, 48
Agreement
    of adjectives and nouns, 60–61, 64, 67
    of nouns and verbs, 56
Albus, 13
Aliquis, 218
Alphabet, 14–15
Altus, 74, 76
Amicus, 71
Amo (to love, like), 35, 36, 120–21, 182–84, 196, 219
Ancient Rome
    culture of, 12
    invasions of, 10–11
    story of, *xi–xii*, 263

Anglo-Saxons, 11
Answer key, 286–98
Antepenult, 17
Aorist aspect, 24–25, 38, 132
Arbor, 45
-*are*, 51, 130
-*are* verbs, 28
Atque, 114
Audeo (to dare), 191
Audio (to hear), 35, 182–84, 219

B

-*ba*-, 33, 36
Beef, 11
Benefits of Latin, 259–65
Bible, 264
Boeuf, 11
Bonas, 61, 71
Boni, 61
Bonus, 60, 61, 63–65
Britain, 10–12
Byzantine Empire, 264

C

Caedo, 153
Caelum, 52
Caeruleus, 13
Caesar, Julius, *xi*, 10, 14, 257, 258
Candeo (to shine), 156
Candidus, 13
Canes latrabant, 34
Canis, 3, 10, 45
Capio (to take, catch, grab), 35, 36, 154, 155, 182–84, 242

Capto, 155
Carpe diem, 10
Carrus, 45
Case system, 46–54
Castra, 11
Catalan, 47
Catholic Church, 14, 264
Celerius, 82
Celtic languages, 11
Christian Church, 264
Church Latin, 14, 264
Cicero, 258
Cities, 99, 100
Civis, 45
Classical Latin, 14, 89
Classical Latin literature, 257, 258,
    264–65, 283–85
Claudius, 10
Colors, 13
Commands, giving, 241–44
Commentaries on the Gallic War, 257
Communis, 10
Comparative endings, 74
Comparatives, 74–84
Comparisons, 73–84
Complementary infinitive, 152, 228
Completed aspect, 24–26, 132
Conditions, 221–22
Conjugation exercises
    imperfect tenses, 37
    perfect tenses, 40
    subjunctives, 121
    tenses, 136
Conjugations
    example of, 34
    explanation of, 28–29
    perfect tense, 135
    pluperfect tense, 135
    present tense, 130–31
    recognizing, 35
Conjunctions, 7, 246
Consonant combinations, 17
Consonants, 16
Continuous aspect, 24–26, 132
Cow, 11

Cucurr-, 25
Cucurreat, 24
Cucurrerit, 24
Cucurrit, 24
Culture, 12, 17
Cum clauses, 92–93, 124–26, 161
Cur, 215
Curr-, 25
Currebat, 24
Currit, 24, 134

D
-dam, 218
Dare, 27, 34, 35, 39
Dative case
    for adjectives, 66–69, 113
    declensions of, 110–11
    explanation of, 103, 110
    and gerunds, 208
    with intransitive verbs, 113–14
    for nouns, 48–51
    for possession, 112–13
    uses of, 111–13
Dative of agent, 208
Datum, 27, 34, 35, 39
De, 98
De Amicitia, 258
De Senectute, 258
Declensions
    of adjectives, 63–70, 80, 174–75
    of comparatives, 75–76
    of dative case, 110–11
    of genitive case, 52, 54, 105–6
    of nouns, 47–54
    practicing, 53, 70
Dedi, 27, 34, 35, 39
Deliberative subjunctive, 248
Demonstrative adjectives, 161–65
Demonstrative pronouns, 165–66
Denominative verbs, 156
Dental stop, 199
Deponent verbs, 190–91, 196
Derivatives, 10, 12
Deus, 52, 54
Dice-, 32

Dicebantur, 32, 33
Dicere, 32
Dico (to say, tell), 32, 35, 242
Dictionaries, 7, 8, 13, 27
Dictum, 32
Dies, 51
Diphthongs, 16, 17
Direct object, 201
Direct question, 235–36
Direct statement, 233
Dix-, 32
Dixi, 32
Do (to give), 26, 34, 35, 39
Doceo, 196
Domus, 50, 87, 99
Double negatives, 261
Dual, 21
Duco, 36, 219, 242
Duo, 175

E
-e, 66
E, 86–87, 98
Editio Vulgata, 254
Egyptians, 14
-ei, 52
Enclitic, 114, 214
Endings
    for active voice, 33–34, 181
    of adjectives, 74
    comparative endings, 74
    for nouns, 44
    for passive voice, 33, 181
    for perfect tense, 39
    personal endings, 33–34, 39, 227
    for verbs, 33–34, 227
    of words, 4–6, 9
England, 10–12
English declensions, 47
English language
    classes of, 11
    deeper understanding of, 261–62
    and Latin, 2–6, 10
    Old English, *xi*

English-to-Latin translations, 13–14, 42, 58, 84, 101–2, 116, 128, 142, 178, 194, 212, 225, 238
Eo (to go), 147–48
-er, 49, 76
Eram, 145
-ere, 28, 51, 130
-erunt, 121
Esam, 145
Esse (to be), 41, 56, 144–45, 206, 220
Et, 114
Et alia (and others), *xii*
Et cetera (and others), *xii*
Etruscans, 14
Europe, 10–12
Ex, 86–87
Exclamatory words, 7, 240–41
Exempli gratia (for sake of example), *xii*
Exercitus, 52, 54

F

Facio (to make, do), 35, 193, 196, 242
Felis, 10
Fero (to bring), 148–49, 184, 198, 200, 220–21, 242
Fides, 45, 52
Fifth declension, 51
Fio, 193
First declension, 48, 52, 63–65
First Oration Against Catiline, 258
First person, 21
First person pronouns, 160–61
Flash cards, 8
Fortis, 74, 76
Fourth declension, 50–52
France, 12
French, *xii*, 11, 47, 260
Frequentative verbs, 155
Fui (to be), 41, 144–45, 206
Future active participles, 199–200
Future indicative, 129, 132–34, 222
Future participles, 196
Future passive, 184
Future perfect indicative, 129, 135–38

Future perfect tense, 21, 24
Future tense, 21, 23, 24
Futurus (to be), 41, 144–45, 206

G

Gender, 44–45, 63–70
Genitive case
    for adjectives, 66–70
    declensions of, 52, 54, 105–6
    descriptions, 109
    explanation of, 103
    for nouns, 46, 48–51, 104
    objective case, 108–9
    partitive case, 108
    plural forms, 105–6
    possessive case, 107
    for pronouns, 104, 160–61
    singular forms, 105–6
    subjective case, 108–9
    uses of, 107–9
Germanic languages, 10
Germany, 12
Gerundives, 206–8
Gerunds, 205–8
Grammatical moods, 117–28. *See also* Moods
Grammatical voice, 179–94. *See also* Voice
Greek, 12, 23, 262, 264
Greeks, 14

H

Habeas corpus, 10
Habebant, 55
Habeo (to have, hold, consider), 35, 36, 120–21, 182–84, 219, 234
Habiturum esse, 234
Habuerunt, 61
Hic, 162, 166
History, 263
Homines, 17
Hominesque, 17
Homo, 50
Hora, 96–97
Hortatory subjunctives, 245–46

Hortor (to urge), 245
Humus, 45, 99
Hypotaxis, 256, 257

I

-i, 32, 38, 39, 52, 66, 110, 120–21
I-stem nouns, 105–6
-ia, 66
Iacio (to recline, lie), 219
Id est (that is), *xii*
Idem, 169–70
-ie-, 36
-ii-, 147
Ille, 164, 166
-ime, 81
Imperative active, 242
Imperative mood, 22, 32, 118–19, 241–43
Imperative passive, 243
Imperfect indicative, 222
Imperfect passive, 183
Imperfect subjunctive mood, 119–20, 222
Imperfect subjunctive passive, 184, 187
Imperfect tense
    conjugating, 29, 37
    examples of, 24
    explanation of, 21, 23, 31
    forming, 36
    using, 36–37
Impersonal verbs, 229–31
-imus, 76, 121
In, 86–87, 97
Inceptive verbs, 156
Indefinite adjectives, 218
Indefinite pronouns, 218
Index cards, 8
Indicative mood
    conditions for, 221–22, 241
    and *cum* clauses, 125
    explanation of, 21–23, 118–19
    tenses of, 32–33, 129–38
Indirect commands, 243–44
Indirect discourse, 232–36
Indirect object, 112
Indirect question, 235–36
Indirect statement, 232–34

Indo-Europeans, 10, 21
Infinitives, 227–38
    conjugating, 28
    explanation of, 119, 152
    forms of, 228–29
    indirect question, 235–36
    indirect statement, 232–34
    objective infinitives, 231–32
    splitting, 261
    subjective infinitives, 229–31
    tenses, 228–29, 234–36
    and voice, 188, 228
Inflection, 3, 4–5, 253
Ingens, 69–70
Instrumental ablative case, 91–93
Instrumental case, 88, 89, 91
Intensive adjectives, 168–70
Intensive pronouns, 168–70
Interjections, 7, 240–41
Interrogative adjectives, 218
Interrogative pronouns, 216–17
Interrogative sentences, 213–25
Intransitive verbs, 57, 113–14, 180
Invenio (to find), 12, 243
-*io*, 26, 27, 28, 35, 36, 130
Ipse, 168–69
-*ire* verbs, 28, 130, 147
Irregular adverbs, 80, 82
Irregular comparatives, 78–79
Irregular verbs, 28, 41, 143, 150, 152, 193
-*is*, 52
Is, 164–65, 166
Islands, 99, 100
-*isse*-, 120–21
-*issime*, 81
-*issimus*, 76–77
Iste, 162–63, 166
-*isti*, 121
-*istis*, 121
-*it*, 121
Italian, *xi*, 10, 260
Italian Modern Latin, 47
Italy, 12
Iter, 50
Itum, 147

Iubeo (to order), 246
-*ium*, 66, 105–6
-*ius*, 81

J
Jerome, 254
Jussive subjunctives, 245–46

L
Latin
    benefits of knowing, 259–65
    and English, 2–6, 10
    reading, 251–58
    reasons for learning, *x*
    understanding, 1–8
    as universal language, 11–12
    vocabulary derived from, *xii*, 261–62
    word order in, 2–3, 54–55
Latin dictionaries, 7, 8, 13, 27
Latin-English vocabulary, 268–82. *See also* Vocabulary lists
Latin literature, 257, 258, 264–65, 283–85
Latin poetry, 258
Latin textbook, 265
Latin-to-English translations, 13–14, 42, 58, 84, 101–2, 116, 128, 141, 156–57, 177–78, 194, 211, 224–25, 238, 250
Latrabant, 34, 40
Latum (to bring), 148, 198, 200, 220–21
Lavo, 190
Law and Latin, 262
Learning tips, 8, 13
Legal terminology, 262
Literature, 257, 258, 264–65, 283–85
Locative case, 88, 89
Longus, 74, 76
Lord's Prayer, *xi*

M
-*m*, 131
Macron, 16
Magnus, 82
Malo (to be more willing), 150–51, 220
Manus, 50

Mater, 50
Medical terminology, 262–63
Mediterranean, 260, 264
Memorization, 7, 9
Mensa, 45
Meus, 107
Middle voice, 22, 180, 189–91
Mille, 176
-*mini*, 243
Mitteris, 16
Mitto (to send, release, throw), 120–21, 199
Modern English, 11
Modern Latin, *xi–xii*
Modern world, 12–13
Modifiers. *See* Adjectives
Modus operandi (way of operating), 2
Monosyllabic *i*-stems, 106
Months, 176
Moods, 21–23, 32, 117–28
Morior (to die), 191, 243
Multum, 82
Multus, 108

N
Nauta, 48
-*ne*, 214
Ne, 123, 124, 244, 246, 247
Neuter *i*-stems, 106
New Testament, 264
Nihil, 108
Nolo (to be unwilling), 150, 220, 242
Nominative case
    for adjectives, 61, 66–70
    for nouns, 48–51
    for subjects, 54–56
Nomino (to name), 156
Non, 246, 247
Nonne, 214
Norman French, *xii*, 11
Normandy, 11
Noster, 107
Nouns
    agreement of, 56, 60–61
    case uses, 46–47, 61

classes of, 47–54
elements of, 44–46
endings for, 44
examples of, 6
genders, 44–45
plural forms, 46
principal parts of, 51–53
singular forms, 46
verbal nouns, 205, 206, 208
-ns, 196
-ntis, 196
-ntur, 33
Num, 215
Numbers, 175–76

O

-o, 131
Objective genitive case, 108–9
Objective infinitives, 231–32
Objects, 54–55, 57, 112, 201, 207–8, 233
Old English, *xi*
Old Italian, *xi*
Old Testament, 264
Omnis, 68–69, 71
"On Friendship," 258
"On Old Age," 258
Optative mood, 118–19, 247
Os, 104
Ossis, 104

P

Paradigm, 183
Parallel structure, 256
Parasyllabic *i*-stems, 106
Parataxis, 256, 257
Pareo, 113
Participial phrases, 200–204
Participles, 195–212
    explanation of, 26, 185–86
    future active participles, 199–200
    future participles, 196
    participial phrases, 200–204
    past participles, 26
    perfect participles, 196
    perfect passive participles, 198–99

present active participles, 196–98
present participles, 26, 196
understanding, 196
Partitive genitive case, 108
Parts of speech, 6–7
Passage in Latin, 254–55
Passive periphrastic, 208
Passive voice
    and ablative of agent, 189
    endings for, 33, 181
    explanation of, 22–23, 180–81
    in perfect system, 185–87
    in present infinitive, 188
    in present system, 181–84
    understanding, 181–88
Past participles, 26
Past tense
    explanation of, 21, 23
    and verbs, 26
Penult, 17
Perfect indicative mood, 121, 222
Perfect participles, 196
Perfect passive, 186
Perfect passive participles, 198–99
Perfect subjunctive, 220–21
Perfect subjunctive active, 220
Perfect subjunctive passive, 221
Perfect system tenses, 24–25, 29
Perfect tense
    conjugating, 40
    endings for, 39
    examples of, 24
    explanation of, 21, 25, 31
    forming, 39
    stems of, 38–39
    using, 40
Personal endings, 33–34, 39, 227
Personal pronouns, 160–61
Phoenicians, 14
Phonetics, 14, 17
Places, 97–100
Pluperfect indicative, 129, 135–38
Pluperfect passive, 187
Pluperfect subjunctive mood, 120–21
Pluperfect subjunctive passive, 187, 222

Pluperfect tense
    examples of, 24
    explanation of, 21
Plural nouns, 46, 48–51
Plural verbs, 21, 23
Plus, 108
Poetry, 258
Pono (to put, place), 35
Porto (to carry, bring), 242–43
Portuguese, *xii*, 47, 260
Posse (to be able), 145, 220
Possessive dative case, 112–13
Possessive genitive case, 107
Possum (to be able), 145, 152, 220
Potential subjunctive, 247
Potis, 146
Potui (to be able), 145
Predicate, 56, 201
Predicate nominative, 56
Prefixes, 152–54
Premo (to press, push), 242
Prepositional phrases, 86–88
Prepositions, 85–102
    ablative case, 88–94, 97–99
    accusative case, 88–89
    case forms, 90
    examples of, 7, 86–88, 90, 100
    explanation of, 85
    list of, 86, 88
    practicing, 90
Present active participles, 196–98
Present indicative, 129–32, 222
Present infinitive active, 188, 228
Present infinitive passive, 188, 228
Present participles, 26, 196
Present passive, 182
Present subjunctive, 219–20, 222
Present subjunctive active, 219
Present system tenses
    conjugating, 29
    explanation of, 24–25, 27
Present tense
    examples of, 24
    explanation of, 21, 23, 25
    and verbs, 26

Primary sequence, 236
Proficiency, maintaining, 264–65
Pronouns, 159–78
    demonstrative pronouns, 165–66
    examples of, 6
    indefinite pronouns, 218
    intensive pronouns, 168–70
    interrogative pronouns, 216–17
    personal pronouns, 160–61
    reflexive pronouns, 166–68
    relative pronouns, 170–74
Pronunciations, 14
Proto-Indo-European roots, 23, 46, 88, 89, 91, 97, 99, 144
Provençal, 47
Puer, 48
Purpose clause, 122–23

Q

Qualis, 216
Quam, 75, 151
Quando, 216
Quanti, 216
Quantus, 216
Quare, 215
-que, 114, 214, 218
Question mark, 215
Questions, asking, 213–25
Qui, 170–71, 216, 218
Quid, 216–17
Quis, 216–18
Quo, 216
Quod, 216
Quom, 126
Quomodo, 215
Quot, 215
Quotiens, 216
Quotus, 216

R

-re, 32, 36, 38, 131, 242, 243
Reading Latin, 251–58
Reagan, Ronald, 180
Receite, 11
Recepta, 11

Reduplication, 39
Reflexive pronouns, 166–68
Relative clauses, 171–73
Relative clauses of purpose, 173–74
Relative pronouns, 170–74
Religion, 264
Res, 51
Respect group, 91, 93–94
Result clause, 123–24
Rex, 52
-ris, 243
Roman alphabet, 14–15
Roman authors, 257, 258, 264–65, 283–85. *See also* Caesar, Julius
Roman Catholic Church, 14, 264
Roman Republic, 163
Romance languages, 47, 260
Romanian, 47, 260
Rome
    culture of, 12
    invasions of, 10–12
    story of, *xi–xii*, 263
    of today, 11–12
Rus, 99

S

Second declension, 48–49, 52, 63–65
Second person, 21
Second person pronouns, 160–61
Secondary sequence, 236
Semideponent verbs, 191
Sentio (to perceive, experience, realize), 196
Sequor (to follow), 243
Servus, 48
Si, 214
Sic, 214
Sine, 98
Singular nouns, 46, 48–51
Singular verbs, 21
Spain, 12
Spanish, *xii*, 47, 260
Special places, 98–100
Splitting infinitives, 261
Steno pads, 8

Stewart, Potter, 85
Study tips, 8, 13
Sub, 86–87, 97
Subjective genitive case, 108–9
Subjective infinitives, 229–31
Subjects, 54–56, 201, 233
Subjunctive mood
    conditions for, 221–22, 241
    conjugating, 121
    and *cum* clauses, 124–26
    explanation of, 22, 118–19
    independent subjunctives, 245–48
    showing purpose, 122–23
    showing results, 123–24
    tenses of, 32, 120–21, 219–22, 235–36
Subordinate clauses, 125, 236, 256
Subordinating conjunctions, 122–25, 245, 246
Substantives, 71–72, 161, 198, 203
Suffixes, 152, 154–56
-sum, 198
Sum (to be), 35, 41, 56, 144–46, 186–87, 198, 200, 206, 208, 220
Sundials, 96
Superlative degree, 76–77, 79
Supines, 27, 198, 208–9
-sus, 198
Suus, 107
Syllabic augment, 38
Syllables, 17
Syntax, *xii*, 2–3, 6, 253

T

Tamen, 125–26, 203
Taxis, 256
-te, 242
Tele-, 12
Templum, 49
Temporal sense, 38, 202–3
Tempus, 45, 52, 54, 125
Teneo (to hold, grasp), 35, 199
Tense indicators, 32–33, 36
Tenses, 21–27, 61, 136. *See also specific tenses*
Terminations, 67–70

Terra, 52

Third declension, 49–50, 52, 66–70

Third person, 21, 23

Third person reflexive pronoun, 167–68

Time issues, 96–97, 129–42, 202–3

Timeo, 198, 200

"To be," 144–47

"To be more willing," 150–51

"To be unwilling," 150

"To be willing," 149

"To bring," 148–49

"To go," 147–48

"To prefer," 150–51

"To want," 149

"To want more," 150–51

"To wish," 149

Totus, 174–75

Towns, 99, 100

Transitive verbs, 57, 180

Translations, 13–14, 42, 58, 84, 101–2, 116, 128, 141–42, 156–57, 177–78, 194, 211–12, 224–25, 238, 250

Tres, 176

Tuli (to bring), 148, 198, 200, 220–21

-*tum*, 198

-*tus*, 198

Tuus, 107

U

Ubi, 96, 215

Ultima, 17

-*um*, 49, 66, 105–6

Unde, 216

Understanding Latin, 1–8

Unus, 175

-*urus*, 198

-*us*, 52

Ut, 122–23, 244, 246

Utinam, 247

V

Vacuum, 16

Vado, 148

Vale, 17

Velle (to be willing), 149, 220

Venerunt, 40

Veniebant, 37

Veniebat, 55

Venio (to come), 35, 36, 37, 120–21, 242

Venire, 37

Ventum, 37

Verb stems, 32

Verbal adjectives, 185–86, 196, 200

Verbal aspect
aorist aspect, 24–25, 28, 132, 134
completed aspect, 24–26, 132, 134
continuous aspect, 24–26, 132, 134
and participles, 26

Verbal nouns, 205, 206, 208

Verbs
agreement of, 56
conjugations, 28–29
denominative verbs, 156
deponent verbs, 190–91, 196
elements of, 20–23, 33, 227
endings, 33–34, 227
examples of, 7
of fearing, 246
frequentative verbs, 155
impersonal verbs, 229–31
importance of, 19–29
inceptive verbs, 156
infinitives, 28, 119, 152, 188, 227–38
intransitive verbs, 57, 113–14, 180
irregular verbs, 28, 41, 143, 150, 152, 193
making, 155–56
moods, 21–23, 32, 117–25
parts of, 26–29
person, 21, 23, 33–34
plural forms, 21, 23
principal parts of, 26–28
sections of, 32–35
semideponent verbs, 191
singular forms, 21
stems of, 32
studying, 20
tense indicators, 32–33, 36
tenses, 21, 23–24, 26–27

transitive verbs, 57, 180
voice, 21–23, 33

Vergil, 258

Vester, 107

Video (to see), 35, 198, 199, 200, 242–43

Vigiliae, 96

Villae, 11

Vinum, 11

Viri, 61

-vision, 12

Vitas, 61

Vocabantur, 22

Vocabulary
building, 143–58
derived from Latin, *xii*, 261–62
learning strategies, 6–8

Vocabulary lists, 53, 61–62, 83, 95, 114–15, 126–27, 139–40, 176–77, 192, 209–10, 223–24, 236–37, 248–49, 268–82

Vocative case, 240–41

Voco (to call), 240

Voice, 21–23, 33–34, 179–94, 228

Volo (to be willing), 149, 220

Vowel combinations, 16

Vowel weakening, 154

Vowels, 16, 17

W

William the Conqueror, 11

Word endings, 4–6, 9

Word order, 2–3, 54–55

THE EVERYTHING SERIES!

BUSINESS & PERSONAL FINANCE

Everything® Accounting Book
Everything® Budgeting Book, 2nd Ed.
Everything® Business Planning Book
Everything® Coaching and Mentoring Book, 2nd Ed.
Everything® Fundraising Book
Everything® Get Out of Debt Book
Everything® Grant Writing Book, 2nd Ed.
Everything® Guide to Buying Foreclosures
Everything® Guide to Fundraising, $15.95
Everything® Guide to Mortgages
Everything® Guide to Personal Finance for Single Mothers
Everything® Home-Based Business Book, 2nd Ed.
Everything® Homebuying Book, 3rd Ed., $15.95
Everything® Homeselling Book, 2nd Ed.
Everything® Human Resource Management Book
Everything® Improve Your Credit Book
Everything® Investing Book, 2nd Ed.
Everything® Landlording Book
Everything® Leadership Book, 2nd Ed.
Everything® Managing People Book, 2nd Ed.
Everything® Negotiating Book
Everything® Online Auctions Book
Everything® Online Business Book
Everything® Personal Finance Book
Everything® Personal Finance in Your 20s & 30s Book, 2nd Ed.
Everything® Personal Finance in Your 40s & 50s Book, $15.95
Everything® Project Management Book, 2nd Ed.
Everything® Real Estate Investing Book
Everything® Retirement Planning Book
Everything® Robert's Rules Book, $7.95
Everything® Selling Book
Everything® Start Your Own Business Book, 2nd Ed.
Everything® Wills & Estate Planning Book

COOKING

Everything® Barbecue Cookbook
Everything® Bartender's Book, 2nd Ed., $9.95
Everything® Calorie Counting Cookbook
Everything® Cheese Book
Everything® Chinese Cookbook
Everything® Classic Recipes Book
Everything® Cocktail Parties & Drinks Book
Everything® College Cookbook
Everything® Cooking for Baby and Toddler Book
Everything® Diabetes Cookbook
Everything® Easy Gourmet Cookbook
Everything® Fondue Cookbook
Everything® Food Allergy Cookbook, $15.95
Everything® Fondue Party Book
Everything® Gluten-Free Cookbook
Everything® Glycemic Index Cookbook
Everything® Grilling Cookbook
Everything® Healthy Cooking for Parties Book, $15.95
Everything® Holiday Cookbook
Everything® Indian Cookbook
Everything® Lactose-Free Cookbook
Everything® Low-Cholesterol Cookbook

Everything® Low-Fat High-Flavor Cookbook, 2nd Ed., $15.95
Everything® Low-Salt Cookbook
Everything® Meals for a Month Cookbook
Everything® Meals on a Budget Cookbook
Everything® Mediterranean Cookbook
Everything® Mexican Cookbook
Everything® No Trans Fat Cookbook
Everything® One-Pot Cookbook, 2nd Ed., $15.95
Everything® Organic Cooking for Baby & Toddler Book, $15.95
Everything® Pizza Cookbook
Everything® Quick Meals Cookbook, 2nd Ed., $15.95
Everything® Slow Cooker Cookbook
Everything® Slow Cooking for a Crowd Cookbook
Everything® Soup Cookbook
Everything® Stir-Fry Cookbook
Everything® Sugar-Free Cookbook
Everything® Tapas and Small Plates Cookbook
Everything® Tex-Mex Cookbook
Everything® Thai Cookbook
Everything® Vegetarian Cookbook
Everything® Whole-Grain, High-Fiber Cookbook
Everything® Wild Game Cookbook
Everything® Wine Book, 2nd Ed.

GAMES

Everything® 15-Minute Sudoku Book, $9.95
Everything® 30-Minute Sudoku Book, $9.95
Everything® Bible Crosswords Book, $9.95
Everything® Blackjack Strategy Book
Everything® Brain Strain Book, $9.95
Everything® Bridge Book
Everything® Card Games Book
Everything® Card Tricks Book, $9.95
Everything® Casino Gambling Book, 2nd Ed.
Everything® Chess Basics Book
Everything® Christmas Crosswords Book, $9.95
Everything® Craps Strategy Book
Everything® Crossword and Puzzle Book
Everything® Crosswords and Puzzles for Quote Lovers Book, $9.95
Everything® Crossword Challenge Book
Everything® Crosswords for the Beach Book, $9.95
Everything® Cryptic Crosswords Book, $9.95
Everything® Cryptograms Book, $9.95
Everything® Easy Crosswords Book
Everything® Easy Kakuro Book, $9.95
Everything® Easy Large-Print Crosswords Book
Everything® Games Book, 2nd Ed.
Everything® Giant Book of Crosswords
Everything® Giant Sudoku Book, $9.95
Everything® Giant Word Search Book
Everything® Kakuro Challenge Book, $9.95
Everything® Large-Print Crossword Challenge Book
Everything® Large-Print Crosswords Book
Everything® Large-Print Travel Crosswords Book
Everything® Lateral Thinking Puzzles Book, $9.95
Everything® Literary Crosswords Book, $9.95
Everything® Mazes Book
Everything® Memory Booster Puzzles Book, $9.95

Everything® Movie Crosswords Book, $9.95
Everything® Music Crosswords Book, $9.95
Everything® Online Poker Book
Everything® Pencil Puzzles Book, $9.95
Everything® Poker Strategy Book
Everything® Pool & Billiards Book
Everything® Puzzles for Commuters Book, $9.95
Everything® Puzzles for Dog Lovers Book, $9.95
Everything® Sports Crosswords Book, $9.95
Everything® Test Your IQ Book, $9.95
Everything® Texas Hold 'Em Book, $9.95
Everything® Travel Crosswords Book, $9.95
Everything® Travel Mazes Book, $9.95
Everything® Travel Word Search Book, $9.95
Everything® TV Crosswords Book, $9.95
Everything® Word Games Challenge Book
Everything® Word Scramble Book
Everything® Word Search Book

HEALTH

Everything® Alzheimer's Book
Everything® Diabetes Book
Everything® First Aid Book, $9.95
Everything® Green Living Book
Everything® Health Guide to Addiction and Recovery
Everything® Health Guide to Adult Bipolar Disorder
Everything® Health Guide to Arthritis
Everything® Health Guide to Controlling Anxiety
Everything® Health Guide to Depression
Everything® Health Guide to Diabetes, 2nd Ed.
Everything® Health Guide to Fibromyalgia
Everything® Health Guide to Menopause, 2nd Ed.
Everything® Health Guide to Migraines
Everything® Health Guide to Multiple Sclerosis
Everything® Health Guide to OCD
Everything® Health Guide to PMS
Everything® Health Guide to Postpartum Care
Everything® Health Guide to Thyroid Disease
Everything® Hypnosis Book
Everything® Low Cholesterol Book
Everything® Menopause Book
Everything® Nutrition Book
Everything® Reflexology Book
Everything® Stress Management Book
Everything® Superfoods Book, $15.95

HISTORY

Everything® American Government Book
Everything® American History Book, 2nd Ed.
Everything® American Revolution Book, $15.95
Everything® Civil War Book
Everything® Freemasons Book
Everything® Irish History & Heritage Book
Everything® World War II Book, 2nd Ed.

HOBBIES

Everything® Candlemaking Book
Everything® Cartooning Book
Everything® Coin Collecting Book
Everything® Digital Photography Book, 2nd Ed.

Everything® Drawing Book
Everything® Family Tree Book, 2nd Ed.
Everything® Guide to Online Genealogy, $15.95
Everything® Knitting Book
Everything® Knots Book
Everything® Photography Book
Everything® Quilting Book
Everything® Sewing Book
Everything® Soapmaking Book, 2nd Ed.
Everything® Woodworking Book

HOME IMPROVEMENT

Everything® Feng Shui Book
Everything® Feng Shui Decluttering Book, $9.95
Everything® Fix-It Book
Everything® Green Living Book
Everything® Home Decorating Book
Everything® Home Storage Solutions Book
Everything® Homebuilding Book
Everything® Organize Your Home Book, 2nd Ed.

KIDS' BOOKS

All titles are $7.95
Everything® Fairy Tales Book, $14.95
Everything® Kids' Animal Puzzle & Activity Book
Everything® Kids' Astronomy Book
Everything® Kids' Baseball Book, 5th Ed.
Everything® Kids' Bible Trivia Book
Everything® Kids' Bugs Book
Everything® Kids' Cars and Trucks Puzzle and Activity Book
Everything® Kids' Christmas Puzzle & Activity Book
Everything® Kids' Connect the Dots
    Puzzle and Activity Book
Everything® Kids' Cookbook, 2nd Ed.
Everything® Kids' Crazy Puzzles Book
Everything® Kids' Dinosaurs Book
Everything® Kids' Dragons Puzzle and Activity Book
Everything® Kids' Environment Book $7.95
Everything® Kids' Fairies Puzzle and Activity Book
Everything® Kids' First Spanish Puzzle and Activity Book
Everything® Kids' Football Book
Everything® Kids' Geography Book
Everything® Kids' Gross Cookbook
Everything® Kids' Gross Hidden Pictures Book
Everything® Kids' Gross Jokes Book
Everything® Kids' Gross Mazes Book
Everything® Kids' Gross Puzzle & Activity Book
Everything® Kids' Hanukkah Puzzle and Activity Book
Everything® Kids' Hidden Pictures Book
Everything® Kids' Horses Book
Everything® Kids' Joke Book
Everything® Kids' Knock Knock Book
Everything® Kids' Learning French Book
Everything® Kids' Learning Spanish Book
Everything® Kids' Magical Science Experiments Book
Everything® Kids' Math Puzzles Book
Everything® Kids' Mazes Book
Everything® Kids' Money Book, 2nd Ed.
Everything® Kids' Mummies, Pharaoh's, and Pyramids
    Puzzle and Activity Book
Everything® Kids' Nature Book
Everything® Kids' Pirates Puzzle and Activity Book
Everything® Kids' Presidents Book
Everything® Kids' Princess Puzzle and Activity Book
Everything® Kids' Puzzle Book

Everything® Kids' Racecars Puzzle and Activity Book
Everything® Kids' Riddles & Brain Teasers Book
Everything® Kids' Science Experiments Book
Everything® Kids' Sharks Book
Everything® Kids' Soccer Book
Everything® Kids' Spelling Book
Everything® Kids' Spies Puzzle and Activity Book
Everything® Kids' States Book
Everything® Kids' Travel Activity Book
Everything® Kids' Word Search Puzzle and Activity Book

LANGUAGE

Everything® Conversational Japanese Book with CD, $19.95
Everything® French Grammar Book
Everything® French Phrase Book, $9.95
Everything® French Verb Book, $9.95
Everything® German Phrase Book, $9.95
Everything® German Practice Book with CD, $19.95
Everything® Inglés Book
Everything® Intermediate Spanish Book with CD, $19.95
Everything® Italian Phrase Book, $9.95
Everything® Italian Practice Book with CD, $19.95
Everything® Learning Brazilian Portuguese Book with CD, $19.95
Everything® Learning French Book with CD, 2nd Ed., $19.95
Everything® Learning German Book
Everything® Learning Italian Book
Everything® Learning Latin Book
Everything® Learning Russian Book with CD, $19.95
Everything® Learning Spanish Book
Everything® Learning Spanish Book with CD, 2nd Ed., $19.95
Everything® Russian Practice Book with CD, $19.95
Everything® Sign Language Book, $15.95
Everything® Spanish Grammar Book
Everything® Spanish Phrase Book, $9.95
Everything® Spanish Practice Book with CD, $19.95
Everything® Spanish Verb Book, $9.95
Everything® Speaking Mandarin Chinese Book with CD, $19.95

MUSIC

Everything® Bass Guitar Book with CD, $19.95
Everything® Drums Book with CD, $19.95
Everything® Guitar Book with CD, 2nd Ed., $19.95
Everything® Guitar Chords Book with CD, $19.95
Everything® Guitar Scales Book with CD, $19.95
Everything® Harmonica Book with CD, $15.95
Everything® Home Recording Book
Everything® Music Theory Book with CD, $19.95
Everything® Reading Music Book with CD, $19.95
Everything® Rock & Blues Guitar Book with CD, $19.95
Everything® Rock & Blues Piano Book with CD, $19.95
Everything® Rock Drums Book with CD, $19.95
Everything® Singing Book with CD, $19.95
Everything® Songwriting Book

NEW AGE

Everything® Astrology Book, 2nd Ed.
Everything® Birthday Personology Book
Everything® Celtic Wisdom Book, $15.95
Everything® Dreams Book, 2nd Ed.
Everything® Law of Attraction Book, $15.95
Everything® Love Signs Book, $9.95
Everything® Love Spells Book, $9.95
Everything® Palmistry Book
Everything® Psychic Book
Everything® Reiki Book

Everything® Sex Signs Book, $9.95
Everything® Spells & Charms Book, 2nd Ed.
Everything® Tarot Book, 2nd Ed.
Everything® Toltec Wisdom Book
Everything® Wicca & Witchcraft Book, 2nd Ed.

PARENTING

Everything® Baby Names Book, 2nd Ed.
Everything® Baby Shower Book, 2nd Ed.
Everything® Baby Sign Language Book with DVD
Everything® Baby's First Year Book
Everything® Birthing Book
Everything® Breastfeeding Book
Everything® Father-to-Be Book
Everything® Father's First Year Book
Everything® Get Ready for Baby Book, 2nd Ed.
Everything® Get Your Baby to Sleep Book, $9.95
Everything® Getting Pregnant Book
Everything® Guide to Pregnancy Over 35
Everything® Guide to Raising a One-Year-Old
Everything® Guide to Raising a Two-Year-Old
Everything® Guide to Raising Adolescent Boys
Everything® Guide to Raising Adolescent Girls
Everything® Mother's First Year Book
Everything® Parent's Guide to Childhood Illnesses
Everything® Parent's Guide to Children and Divorce
Everything® Parent's Guide to Children with ADD/ADHD
Everything® Parent's Guide to Children with Asperger's
    Syndrome
Everything® Parent's Guide to Children with Anxiety
Everything® Parent's Guide to Children with Asthma
Everything® Parent's Guide to Children with Autism
Everything® Parent's Guide to Children with Bipolar Disorder
Everything® Parent's Guide to Children with Depression
Everything® Parent's Guide to Children with Dyslexia
Everything® Parent's Guide to Children with Juvenile Diabetes
Everything® Parent's Guide to Children with OCD
Everything® Parent's Guide to Positive Discipline
Everything® Parent's Guide to Raising Boys
Everything® Parent's Guide to Raising Girls
Everything® Parent's Guide to Raising Siblings
Everything® Parent's Guide to Raising Your
    Adopted Child
Everything® Parent's Guide to Sensory Integration Disorder
Everything® Parent's Guide to Tantrums
Everything® Parent's Guide to the Strong-Willed Child
Everything® Parenting a Teenager Book
Everything® Potty Training Book, $9.95
Everything® Pregnancy Book, 3rd Ed.
Everything® Pregnancy Fitness Book
Everything® Pregnancy Nutrition Book
Everything® Pregnancy Organizer, 2nd Ed., $16.95
Everything® Toddler Activities Book
Everything® Toddler Book
Everything® Tween Book
Everything® Twins, Triplets, and More Book

PETS

Everything® Aquarium Book
Everything® Boxer Book
Everything® Cat Book, 2nd Ed.
Everything® Chihuahua Book
Everything® Cooking for Dogs Book
Everything® Dachshund Book
Everything® Dog Book, 2nd Ed.
Everything® Dog Grooming Book

Everything® Dog Obedience Book
Everything® Dog Owner's Organizer, $16.95
Everything® Dog Training and Tricks Book
Everything® German Shepherd Book
Everything® Golden Retriever Book
Everything® Horse Book, 2nd Ed., $15.95
Everything® Horse Care Book
Everything® Horseback Riding Book
Everything® Labrador Retriever Book
Everything® Poodle Book
Everything® Pug Book
Everything® Puppy Book
Everything® Small Dogs Book
Everything® Tropical Fish Book
Everything® Yorkshire Terrier Book

REFERENCE

Everything® American Presidents Book
Everything® Blogging Book
Everything® Build Your Vocabulary Book, $9.95
Everything® Car Care Book
Everything® Classical Mythology Book
Everything® Da Vinci Book
Everything® Einstein Book
Everything® Enneagram Book
Everything® Etiquette Book, 2nd Ed.
Everything® Family Christmas Book, $15.95
Everything® Guide to C. S. Lewis & Narnia
Everything® Guide to Divorce, 2nd Ed., $15.95
Everything® Guide to Edgar Allan Poe
Everything® Guide to Understanding Philosophy
Everything® Inventions and Patents Book
Everything® Jacqueline Kennedy Onassis Book
Everything® John F. Kennedy Book
Everything® Mafia Book
Everything® Martin Luther King Jr. Book
Everything® Pirates Book
Everything® Private Investigation Book
Everything® Psychology Book
Everything® Public Speaking Book, $9.95
Everything® Shakespeare Book, 2nd Ed.

RELIGION

Everything® Angels Book
Everything® Bible Book
Everything® Bible Study Book with CD, $19.95
Everything® Buddhism Book
Everything® Catholicism Book
Everything® Christianity Book
Everything® Gnostic Gospels Book
Everything® Hinduism Book, $15.95
Everything® History of the Bible Book
Everything® Jesus Book
Everything® Jewish History & Heritage Book
Everything® Judaism Book
Everything® Kabbalah Book
Everything® Koran Book
Everything® Mary Book
Everything® Mary Magdalene Book
Everything® Prayer Book

Everything® Saints Book, 2nd Ed.
Everything® Torah Book
Everything® Understanding Islam Book
Everything® Women of the Bible Book
Everything® World's Religions Book

SCHOOL & CAREERS

Everything® Career Tests Book
Everything® College Major Test Book
Everything® College Survival Book, 2nd Ed.
Everything® Cover Letter Book, 2nd Ed.
Everything® Filmmaking Book
Everything® Get-a-Job Book, 2nd Ed.
Everything® Guide to Being a Paralegal
Everything® Guide to Being a Personal Trainer
Everything® Guide to Being a Real Estate Agent
Everything® Guide to Being a Sales Rep
Everything® Guide to Being an Event Planner
Everything® Guide to Careers in Health Care
Everything® Guide to Careers in Law Enforcement
Everything® Guide to Government Jobs
Everything® Guide to Starting and Running a Catering
    Business
Everything® Guide to Starting and Running a Restaurant
**Everything® Guide to Starting and Running
    a Retail Store**
Everything® Job Interview Book, 2nd Ed.
Everything® New Nurse Book
Everything® New Teacher Book
Everything® Paying for College Book
Everything® Practice Interview Book
Everything® Resume Book, 3rd Ed.
Everything® Study Book

SELF-HELP

Everything® Body Language Book
Everything® Dating Book, 2nd Ed.
Everything® Great Sex Book
**Everything® Guide to Caring for Aging Parents,
    $15.95**
Everything® Self-Esteem Book
Everything® Self-Hypnosis Book, $9.95
Everything® Tantric Sex Book

SPORTS & FITNESS

Everything® Easy Fitness Book
Everything® Fishing Book
Everything® Guide to Weight Training, $15.95
Everything® Krav Maga for Fitness Book
Everything® Running Book, 2nd Ed.
Everything® Triathlon Training Book, $15.95

TRAVEL

Everything® Family Guide to Coastal Florida
Everything® Family Guide to Cruise Vacations
Everything® Family Guide to Hawaii
Everything® Family Guide to Las Vegas, 2nd Ed.
Everything® Family Guide to Mexico
Everything® Family Guide to New England, 2nd Ed.

Everything® Family Guide to New York City, 3rd Ed.
**Everything® Family Guide to Northern California
    and Lake Tahoe**
Everything® Family Guide to RV Travel & Campgrounds
Everything® Family Guide to the Caribbean
Everything® Family Guide to the Disneyland® Resort, California
    Adventure®, Universal Studios®, and the Anaheim
    Area, 2nd Ed.
Everything® Family Guide to the Walt Disney World Resort®,
    Universal Studios®, and Greater Orlando, 5th Ed.
Everything® Family Guide to Timeshares
Everything® Family Guide to Washington D.C., 2nd Ed.

WEDDINGS

Everything® Bachelorette Party Book, $9.95
Everything® Bridesmaid Book, $9.95
Everything® Destination Wedding Book
Everything® Father of the Bride Book, $9.95
Everything® Green Wedding Book, $15.95
Everything® Groom Book, $9.95
Everything® Jewish Wedding Book, 2nd Ed., $15.95
Everything® Mother of the Bride Book, $9.95
Everything® Outdoor Wedding Book
Everything® Wedding Book, 3rd Ed.
Everything® Wedding Checklist, $9.95
Everything® Wedding Etiquette Book, $9.95
Everything® Wedding Organizer, 2nd Ed., $16.95
Everything® Wedding Shower Book, $9.95
Everything® Wedding Vows Book,3rd Ed., $9.95
Everything® Wedding Workout Book
Everything® Weddings on a Budget Book, 2nd Ed., $9.95

WRITING

Everything® Creative Writing Book
Everything® Get Published Book, 2nd Ed.
Everything® Grammar and Style Book, 2nd Ed.
Everything® Guide to Magazine Writing
Everything® Guide to Writing a Book Proposal
Everything® Guide to Writing a Novel
Everything® Guide to Writing Children's Books
Everything® Guide to Writing Copy
Everything® Guide to Writing Graphic Novels
Everything® Guide to Writing Research Papers
Everything® Guide to Writing a Romance Novel, $15.95
Everything® Improve Your Writing Book, 2nd Ed.
Everything® Writing Poetry Book